For Hunger-proof Cities

For Hunger-proof Cities

Sustainable Urban Food Systems

Edited by
**Mustafa Koc,
Rod MacRae,
Luc J.A. Mougeot,**
and
Jennifer Welsh

INTERNATIONAL DEVELOPMENT RESEARCH CENTRE
Ottawa • Cairo • Dakar • Johannesburg • Montevideo • Nairobi • New Delhi • Singapore

Published by the
International Development Research Centre
PO Box 8500, Ottawa, ON, Canada K1G 3H9

in association with the
Centre for Studies in Food Security, Ryerson Polytechnic University
Toronto, ON, Canada M5B 2K3

© International Development Research Centre 1999

Canadian Cataloguing in Publication Data

Main entry under title :

For hunger-proof cities : sustainable urban food systems

Includes bibliographical references.
"Most of the papers in this volume were presented at the International Conference on Sustainable
Urban Food Systems, ... at Ryerson Polytechnic University, Toronto..."— p.4.

ISBN 0-88936-882-1

1. Food supply — Congresses.
2. Food supply — Developing countries — Congresses.
3. Nutrition policy — Congresses.
4. Sustainable agriculture — Congresses.
5. Urban health — Congresses.
I. Koc, Mustafa, 1955-   .
II. International Development Research Centre (Canada)

HD9000.9A1H86 1999   641.3   C99-980227-5

IDRC Books endeavours to produce environmentally friendly publications. All paper used is recycled as
well as recyclable. All inks and coatings are vegetable-based products.

Contents

Part 5. Ecological and Health Concerns

Part 6. Engendering the Food System

Part 7. The Politics of Food and Food Policy

Part 8. Toward Food Democracy

...🕭 🕭 🕭...

Acknowledgments

This book is dedicated to Dan Leckie (1950–1998), whose work and dedication helped make Toronto one of the world's most liveable cities. Among many other commitments, Dan helped establish the Toronto Food Policy Council in 1990. At the time of his sudden death from a brain aneurism, he was working for the International Council on Local Environmental Initiatives. We were consolidating this manuscript when he died, and this tragic loss made us recognize that his life's work embodied both the social goals that were core to our project and the means of achieving them.

A number of individuals and collectivities should also be acknowledged for their contributions. We want to thank the program committee of the International Conference on Sustainable Food Systems and our cosponsors, FoodShare Metro Toronto, Oxfam Canada, and the Toronto Food Policy Council. Special appreciation is extended to the editorial committee (advisory) and referees: Patricia Allen (Center for Agroecology and Sustainable Food Systems, University of California), Deborah Barndt (Environmental Studies, York University), Hélène Delisle (Nutrition, Université de Montréal), Christine Furedy (Urban Studies, York University), Ken Dahlberg (Department of Political Science, Western Michigan University), Karen Krug (Environmental Policy Institute, Brock University), Tim Lang (Centre for Food Policy, Thames Valley University), Graham Riches (Social Work, University of Northern British Columbia), and Valerie Tarasuk (Department of Nutritional Sciences, University of Toronto). In addition to their contribution to this volume, these people assisted in the preparation of the conference. We are also grateful to Martha McCarney for painstakingly copyediting the final version of these papers.

Financial support was generously provided by the International Development Research Centre (IDRC), the Social Sciences and Humanities Research Council, and Ryerson Polytechnic University. We greatly appreciate their generosity and encouragement. IDRC has been a leading proponent of research on Urban Agriculture through its highly innovative Cities Feeding People program. IDRC support has facilitated the participation of youth delegates from around the world. We chose IDRC Books as the publisher of this volume to make the book available to the widest readership. We are grateful to Bill Carman and the very competent editorial team of IDRC Books for their assistance and patient work. We also want to thank Luc Mougeot and Brenda Lee Wilson of the Cities Feeding People program of IDRC for their leadership and enthusiastic support.

The Toronto Food Policy Council and FoodShare Toronto have been important collaborators in our reflection and action on sustainable urban food systems. Ryerson's Centre for Studies in Food Security is committed to generating research and innovative practices responsive to societal needs, sharing information and resources across all sectors, and contributing to the food-security knowledge base. Several other case studies on urban food systems presented at the conference are planned for publication as part of our Working Papers Series at the Centre for Studies in Food Security.

We hope the questions raised here will be discussed in other communities and in other cities and that the dialogue generated will lead to global cooperation for lasting solutions.

Mustafa Koc

Introduction: Food Security Is a Global Concern

Mustafa Koc, Rod MacRae, Luc J.A. Mougeot, and Jennifer Welsh

In recent decades, demographic and economic growth have challenged the limits of economic, social, and ecological sustainability, giving rise to questions about food security at the global level. Despite technological advances that have modernized the conditions of production and distribution of food, hunger and malnutrition still threaten the health and well-being of millions of people around the world.

Access to food is still perceived by many as a privilege, rather than a basic human right, and it is estimated that about 35 000 people around the world die each day from hunger. An even larger number of people (mainly women, children, and the elderly) suffer from malnutrition. Far from disappearing, hunger and malnutrition are on the increase, even in advanced industrialized countries like Canada, where each year an estimated 2.5 million people depend on food banks. About 30 million people in the United States are reported to be unable to buy enough food to maintain good health. The continuing reality of hunger and the unsustainability of current practices, both locally and globally, make food security an essential concern.

According to the United Nations Food and Agriculture Organization's (FAO's) widely accepted definition,

> *"Food security" means that food is available at all times; that all persons have means of access to it; that it is nutritionally adequate in terms of quantity, quality and variety; and that it is acceptable within the given culture. Only when all these conditions are in place can a population be considered "food secure."*

To achieve lasting self-reliance at the national and household levels, initiatives must be founded on the principles of economic feasibility, equity, broad participation, and the sustainable use of natural resources.

In recent years, most of the research initiatives for food security have focused on four key components of the FAO's definition:

- *Availability* — Providing a sufficient supply of food for all people at all times has historically been a major challenge. Although technical and scientific innovations have made important contributions focused on quantity and economies of scale, little attention has been paid to the sustainability of such practices.

- *Accessibility* — The equality of access to food is a dimension of food security. Within and between societies, inequities have resulted in serious entitlement problems, reflecting class, gender, ethnic, racial, and age differentials, as well as national and regional gaps in development. Most measures to provide emergency food aid have attempted to help the disadvantaged but have had limited success in overcoming the structural conditions that perpetuate such inequities.

1

- *Acceptability* — As essential ingredients in human health and well-being, food and food practices reflect the social and cultural diversity of humanity. Efforts to provide food without paying attention to the symbolic role of food in people's lives have failed to solve food-security problems. This dimension of food security is also important in determining whether information and food-system innovations will be accepted in a country, given the social and ecological concerns of its citizens.

- *Adequacy* — Food security also requires that adequate measures are in place at all levels of the food system to guarantee the sustainability of production, distribution, consumption, and waste management. A sustainable food system should help to satisfy basic human needs, without compromising the ability of future generations to meet their needs. It must therefore maintain ecological integrity and integrate conservation and development.

Unfortunately, a number of global economic and ecological problems continue to limit the prospect of global food security. World per capita cereal production (62% of least-developed countries' [LDCs'] food consumption), for example, has been increasing only marginally in recent years. In fact, it has even been on the decline in sub-Saharan Africa and in Latin America and the Caribbean, particularly in low-income countries struck by economic reforms, natural and other disasters, and other factors. The LDCs' dependence on net food imports has been growing and is set to continue to grow; currently, 104 of 132 LDCs are net importers, although imports have brought little relief overall (Singer 1997). In sub-Saharan Africa, the number of chronically undernourished people more than doubled in 1970–91, notwithstanding that this region depended on food aid for half its total food imports. The population of this region is expected to more than double by 2020 (de Haen and Lindland 1997).

Regional and global economic crises and chronic problems of underdevelopment make the situation particularly bad in the developing world. The overall mean per capita income of so-called Black Africa, for example, is, at its best, no higher than it was in 1960, and the region has less weight in the global economy today than it did in the 1960s (Brandt 1997). Economic informalization clearly accompanies an economy's disintegration. Real prices in domestic food markets have increased over the last few years and are set to increase further. To improve food security and global food supplies, policy scenarios of the 2020 Vision Initiative require increased exports of staple foods from industrialized countries to the LDCs (von Braun 1997). But insufficient purchasing power among the world's poorest 800 million people remains a primary obstacle to such strategies.

Multilateral agreements in trade and investment further threaten the availability and accessibility of food for large segments of the world's population. Many experts agree that the reduction in world surpluses and the increase in international prices encouraged by the Uruguay Round of the General Agreement on Tariffs and Trade pose an immediate threat to regions already suffering severe food insecurity. The duration of this threat is unknown.

Global prospects for improving food security are further threatened by environmental limitations on production increases, even in Green Revolution countries, and by growing poverty. In Asia, a large share of the population will soon be without access to adequate food supplies (Zarges 1997). So, despite the technical modernization of food production and distribution, hunger and malnutrition still undermine the health and well-being of millions of people and actually seem to be worsening, particularly among low-income urban residents. This led Dr Uwe Werblow (1997) of the European Commission in Brussels to recommend favouring production of more traditional food crops in rural areas and developing non-land-using production in peri-urban and urban areas.

Food security and urban populations

Although the consequences can be visible, the causes and the scope of food-security problems for urban populations may not be apparent. From production to consumption, the food system comprises complex interrelated and interdependent parts: social and economic elements, agencies, processes, and structures. Their interdependent relationship requires a structural and systemic analysis focusing on global as well as local linkages. The rural–urban and local–global interrelationships make it impossible to study urban food-security issues in isolation. Yet, it is also clear that the extraordinary urban growth in the 20th century and increasing threats to food security for millions of urban dwellers merits particular attention. The scope and urgency of the problems require analyses of food-security questions for urban areas and new policies and practices to encourage the adoption of sustainable urban food systems.

Food security has become an increasing concern of urban populations. We identify four major challenges to focus our analysis. First, urban centres have expanded enormously, in population and in size. In the 20th century, urban growth has reached unprecedented levels in most parts of the world. In three recent decades alone, the urban population in developed countries doubled, from 448 million in 1950 to 875 million in 1990. In the same period the urban population in developing countries more than quintupled, from 280 million to 1.6 billion. In 1990, 33% of the world's urban population was living in cities with 1 million or more inhabitants. By the end of this century, six of the largest cities will be found in the developing world. Having urban settlements approaching 30 million people will likely strain already overburdened services in countries with limited resources and extreme income inequalities. Urban expansion has converted a significant portion of green space and good-quality, often scarce, agricultural land. It has already increased water and air pollution and created serious waste-disposal problems. Also, zoning bylaws, speculative land markets, and soil and water contamination have created obstacles to effective local food systems and urban agriculture.

A second challenge has been the unevenness of access to food. Historically, poverty has been predominantly a rural phenomenon. Yet, as the majority of the world's population moves to urban areas, we are seeing a reversal in the regional distribution of poverty. World Bank (1990) figures indicated that in 1988 about 25% of the poorest segments of the developing world were living in urban areas. The World Bank also estimated that by 2000 this will reach 50% (World Bank 1990). In developing countries, the ranks of the urban poor have swelled as a result of such factors as the continuous migration of the rural poor into the cities, the limited ability of the urban informal sector to absorb the unemployed, the limited employment opportunities in formal labour markets, negative impacts of the global economic crisis, and the austerity measures adopted to deal with foreign debt. In Eastern Europe and the industrialized West the situation is not much better. A decline in full-time, secure, well-paid employment (the result of economic downsizing), the dismantling of the welfare state and social pro-grams, and the feminization of poverty have turned urban poverty into a truly global phenomenon. Most observers agree that the increase in poverty has been the biggest threat to food security. Unfortunately, most of the solutions have been limited to patch-work remedies, such as food banks, food aid, and similar emergency responses.

The third challenge is overcoming the inability of the existing market and ser-vice agencies to respond to the highly diverse social and cultural mosaic of the urban population. The complexity of cities — the diversity of their class, gender, ethnic, and demographic characteristics and their corresponding needs and access problems — creates new challenges in the attempt to ensure urban food security. Although the mar-kets and traditional service agencies target certain "consumers," thousands of others are marginalized. Food retail chains often ignore poor neighbourhoods in the North and South alike, and the location of bulk-produce stores in suburbs limits the access of smaller families, elderly people, people with disabilities, and those who depend on pub-lic transit. The diversity of food practices arising from most cities' complex ethnic com-position also creates distinct access problems. Unfortunately, most retailers, food banks, and public-service agencies fail to respond to the unique traditions of cultural minorities and thereby pressure people into making significant dietary changes to con-form to what the dominant food system provides.

The fourth challenge is the growing commodification and globalization of the agrifood system. The majority of people in urban populations have very little under-standing of how their food is produced, transported, processed, or distributed. The dominant structures of production, distribution, and marketing of food often ignore local solutions for efficient and accessible production and distribution. Although the global food system claims to offer more choice at an affordable cost for the individual consumer, it has actually created obstacles for more sustainable local food systems. In many places, even in-season, locally grown foods tend to be more expensive or more difficult to find than those shipped in from thousands of miles away (Bonanno et al. 1994; McMichael 1994; Goodman and Watts 1997). Often food grown locally is exported while thousands of local residents may be suffering hunger and malnutrition. Questions can be raised about the long-term economic, ecological, and political sustainability of the so-called success of the current food system, with its global division of labour, com-modified food economy, increasing regional specialization, industrialized agriculture, and transcontinental networks of distribution.

About this book

Most of the papers in this volume were presented at the International Conference on Sustainable Urban Food Systems, organized by the Centre for Studies in Food Security, at Ryerson Polytechnic University, Toronto, with the cooperation of the International Development Research Centre, FoodShare Toronto, Oxfam Canada, and the Toronto Food Policy Council. The conference was hosted by the university in May 1997, and the aim was to include research papers, opinion pieces, and visionary papers to create a forum to stimulate further discussion and generate new ideas in this field. This volume reflects the original intention of the conference by bringing together the contributions of a group of academics, community organizers, policymakers, practitioners, and youth representatives. The authors are concerned about food-security issues and have been involved in research and applied projects in the field. These projects, grounded in the practices of everyday life, involve the work of street vendors, antihunger advocates, environmentally conscious chefs, and urban gardeners. However trivial they may be, they have generated a sense of hope in others involved in similar small-scale projects all over the world.

This book aims to develop a conceptual and practical framework for sustainable urban food systems. Several papers propose ways to improve the availability and accessibility of food for urban residents and the feasibility of various forms of more self-reliant local food systems. For instance, the book contains insights on how existing structures for marketing and distribution can improve accessibility, why and how different forms of urban food production and distribution are emerging, and how these structures can become part of local food systems that better respond to food-security needs, especially those of urban dwellers.

To reflect the global nature of the dominant food system, the conference participants were drawn from both the North and the South to share their concerns about food security and their experiences of local and global initiatives for sustainable food systems worldwide. The book covers a range of issues, such as urban food systems, local food systems, urban and community agriculture, gender roles in food-security strategies, hunger and income insecurities, and health and ecological concerns, and points out the linkages among these. The reader can learn from the rich sample of case studies.

This volume, like the conference, is more of an open invitation to scholars, practitioners, and policymakers to focus their attention on urban food-security concerns. Food is an essential part of life. Therefore, food-security concerns require public awareness. Changes in the food system require public regulation and cannot be left to the vagaries of the marketplace. Although the achievements of the dominant food system are worth acknowledging, its fairness, sustainability, and feasibility are highly questionable. Given the rising populations of megacities, the food-security needs of urban populations will require governments to develop comprehensive and participatory interventions to avoid future catastrophes. The surest ways to avoid disaster are to be prepared and to understand the nature of the problems, as well as the available opportunities. Most of the papers included in this volume identify a number of common concerns and solutions:

- Local food systems offer long-term sustainable solutions, both for the environment and for local and regional economic development. By linking the productive activities in the surrounding bioregion to the consumers in metropolitan centres, local food systems can reduce greenhouse gases and other pollutants caused by long-distance transportation and storage. They can reduce the vulnerability of food-supply systems to the impacts of weather and market-related supply problems of distant producers, offer greater choice through regional variations in biodiversity, provide fresher and more nutritious products in season, allow for more effective regional control of quality and chemical inputs, and create the potential for local development and employment opportunities. A regional or national network of local food systems does not necessarily diminish the possible advantages of the global food system for food security; rather, it would enhance these advantages.

- Cities need to encourage urban and peri-urban agriculture, aquaculture, food forestry, and animal husbandry, as well as safe waste recycling, as elements of more self-reliant local food-system initiatives. Food and nonfood production can tap idle resources and, through income and savings, improve food security, local employment, and urban resource management. From a food-democracy viewpoint, one's right to be fed needs to embrace one's right to feed oneself. Future plans for the flexible, creative, and combined use of urban space and form need to include permanent and temporary food production within metropolitan regions and to create land reserves for productive green space.

- Cities and metropolitan regions need to give priority to the availability and accessibility of food and develop their own food-security plans as part of their social and economic planning. Food-policy councils should be formed to advise local governments and planners.

- Food banks and other community assistance programs should only be relied on as emergency measures, rather than being institutionalized as permanent mechanisms for food access. Food banks often serve two goals: to assist low-income consumers and to distribute surplus food. To reduce poverty and inequities in access, structural measures need to be undertaken to provide long-term food security. At the same time, mechanisms for distribution of surplus food can be developed to respond to specific community needs, without stigmatizing the poor.

- No single solution will solve the problem of food insecurity. What is needed is a list of choices and a commitment to the principles of food security (listed above). The best recipe we can offer is to establish globally interlinked local food systems that use diverse technical, social, and economic resources to improve the availability and accessibility of sustainably produced and distributed, culturally acceptable food. Reaching this goal requires unique local solutions, as well as global cooperation to solve common problems.

- Finally, the concept of food democracy was the central theme of the conference's keynote speaker, Tim Lang. Moving beyond the notion that consumers act as rational beings who focus on their individual interests, the concept of food democracy (or food citizenship) recognizes that consumers can identify the interests of others (food workers, other consumers, future generations, and other species). As citizens, we can participate in shaping the food system and the ways consumption of food in our communities expresses the values of family and culture.

Given the complexity of the food chain and the limitations of a conference setting, it is practically impossible to include or even claim to do justice to all dimensions of urban food-security questions. Our goal was to create a forum by inviting people who share similar concerns and a similar desire to achieve a sustainable food system. We accept and respect the diversity of opinions on this issue, and we do not claim to offer all the answers. While focusing on urban food systems we recognize that cities have evolved as hubs of economic and cultural life — their success in terms of dense populations is also the source of their vulnerability — and that their survival depends on the ways they relate to their local, regional, national, and global contexts.

References

Bonanno, A.; et al., ed. 1994. From Columbus to ConAgra: the globalization of agriculture and food. University Press of Kansas, Lawrence, KS, USA.

Brandt, H. 1997. Development policy in sub-Saharan Africa after 15 years of structural adjustment. Agriculture and Rural Development, 4(2), 22–24.

de Haen, H.; Lindland, J. 1997. World cereal utilization, production and trade in year 2020. Agriculture and Rural Development, 4(2), 10–13.

Goodman, D.; Watts, M., ed. 1997. Globalising food: agrarian questions and global restructuring. Routledge, London, UK; New York, NY, USA.

McMichael, P., ed. 1994. The global restructuring of agro-food systems. Cornell University Press, Ithaca, NY, USA.

Singer, H.W. 1997. A global view of food security. Agriculture and Rural Development, 4(2), 3–6.

von Braun, J. 1997. Food security for all by the year 2020? Agriculture and Rural Development, 4(2), 14–17.

Werblow, U. 1997. A radically changing world: globalisation and food security up to the year 2020. Agriculture and Rural Development, 4(2), 7–9.

World Bank. 1990. Structural adjustment and sustainable growth: the urban agenda for the 1990s. World Bank, Washington, DC, USA.

Zarges, W. 1997. Food security for all by the year 2020? Who will meet increased import demand from developing countries? Agriculture and Rural Development, 4(2), 18–19.

PART 1

THE CONCEPT OF URBAN FOOD SECURITY

...❧ ❧ ❧...

For Self-reliant Cities: Urban Food Production in a Globalizing South

Luc J.A. Mougeot

Introduction

Globalization over the last 30 years has been pressing national economies to become more interdependent.[1] However, a view emerging from major sectors of the development community and from this book, in particular, is that the reinstatement of a proper measure of food self-reliance is urgently needed. Today, most developing countries are net food importers, and their dependence on imports is growing. Combined with persistent constraints, from fiscal to physical, this dependence results in food insecurity for large sectors of the population, particularly the urban poor (Singer 1997).

A growing number of countries have seen a resurgence of urban food production, and this has made urban food suppliers more self-reliant and urban households less food insecure. This reality is now recognized by more governments and development agencies. As a consequence, urban food production is likely to be promoted and managed in a better way over the next decades. However, recent international studies point to information gaps that must be addressed so that urban food production for consumption and for trade can be more timely and suitably phased into comprehensive urban and agricultural policies for the 21st century. This paper reviews these studies and identifies issues for development research and training support.

Globalization and urbanization

"Capitalism ... thrives on the construction of difference" (AlSayyad 1997, p. 211). Perhaps as never before, the struggle between advocates of interdependent specialization and advocates of self-reliant diversity has grown intense, even volatile. After decades of rapid advances in national welfare, more states and people now see their assets and prospects for social equity, economic resilience, and environmental integrity either threatened or eroded. Global interventions in national finances and international trade can help to trigger corrections needed in specific cases, but forms of targeting and processes that are insensitive to local settings have done little to improve the conditions for human development, if they have not made them worse (see, for example, the review of structural-adjustment programs [SAPs] in sub-Saharan Africa by Brandt

---

[1] Simai (1994, p. 283) defines *globalization* as "the entirety of such universal processes as technological transformation; interdependence caused by mass communications; trade and capital flows; homogenization and standardization of production and consumption; the predominance of the world market in trade, investment and other corporate transactions; special and institutional integration of markets; and growing identity or similarity of economic regulations, institutions, and policies."

[1997] and the more general review by Picciotto and Weaving [1997]). Healthy national accounts and poor people could give way to "global wealth and national poverty" (Emmerij 1997, p. 100).

It is becoming more difficult for countries to retain meaningful sovereignty that includes the ability to define and rank their own challenges, let alone to choose and control the resources needed to address them (Simai 1997). Fiscal and trade reforms are driving countries into a global game with little if any margin for safe retreat in case of failure. This is a game in which the stakes grow higher and competition grows fiercer with each additional player. It is one in which the weak nations have to impose often medieval-style social contracts on their people to be allowed to keep playing. This is particularly evident in major Southern cities. The proliferation of city-authority forums, colloquiums, and associations and their number and prominent role at Habitat II speak to the need for greater national and international attention to the daunting challenges.

Advocates of globalization stress the need for the simultaneous specialization and interdependence of systems to curb planetary degradation and reduce inequities among peoples. Opponents of globalization reply that such degradation and inequities have been largely and consciously instigated by the same planetary expansion of predatory markets for production and consumption. They stress that diversity and self-reliance are essential to locally dependable and globally robust strategies. What may ultimately be at stake is neither interdependence nor self-reliance — one to the exclusion of the other — but a balance that promotes the welfare of deprived people.

Basic differences between Northern and Southern countries or cities suggest the need to emphasize self-reliance in the South. First, both the scale and the growth rate of sectoral insufficiencies or deficiencies make problems in the South qualitatively distinct from those in the North. Second, practicable solutions to these distinct problems are themselves qualitatively distinct. The capacities and constraints of prevailing sociopolitical systems in Southern societies differ among themselves and differ sharply from those in the North. The forces of globalization may disregard distinct sociocultural contexts and solutions. Foreign experts walk in and out, often oblivious to people's relentless and creative quest for a livable relationship with available resources (Ranis and Stewart 1997). The apparent chaos is actually surprisingly orderly, and Northern governments and Southern elites alike often belittle the seeds of upscaling and upgrading: incremental and multipurpose housing, utility sharing, short-distance employment, local recycling of local waste, diverse food procurement, multiple skills for multiple incomes, dense informal-assistance networking, local reinvestment of local savings, and resident-run neighbourhood surveillance. At a street level, these are facets of how Southern cities work, day in and day out. A globalization process that ignores the cultural "placefulness," or specificity, of problems and solutions may do little for human development in places where it is most needed. Many think that globalization is currently fueling an urban paradox: not only has economic growth slowed down globally in recent decades but disparities have continued to worsen between the haves and the have-nots at all scales (Emmerij 1997).

Urban food systems of the South

Globalization and urbanization are affecting the food supply of cities in the North and in the South. The North has developed a highly integrated and energy-intensive food-supply system. This system and the formal market essentially coincide. The formal market has specialized seed-to-recycling operations, competitive import–export out-reach, relentless value-adding activities, and aggressive marketing. The market exter-nalizes several social and environmental costs (Kneen 1997); it reduces, or relocates abroad, a growing share of jobs and investment formerly based in Northern economies, not only through control of processing and marketing but increasingly through production abroad. Northern countries have been exporting surpluses of less nutritious food, often through dumping, and importing more nutritious items that are often unaffordable to the people who live where these items are produced. In this way, the market has effectively stabilized or lowered the cost of Northern labour. At the same time, food purchases also represent smaller and declining shares of Northern con-sumers' incomes. Although poverty and food insecurity are on the rise in the North, as a result of unemployment and much reduced public assistance, they remain more lim-ited there than in the South. Poor people in the North benefit from greater public assis-tance and, increasingly, the programs of nongovernmental organizations (NGOs). However, market "improvements" of the formal food sector (policy lobbies for cost internalization, corporate transfers of retail outlets from inner cities to suburbia, dis-counted large-format retailing, middle-class-driven market niches for organically grown food) further worsen the urban poor's food security in Northern societies.[2]

In the South, the market — particularly the formal component — still has a more limited role in the urban food-supply system. According to Drakakis-Smith (1990), the urban food system has the following components: food-producing areas (domestic rural and urban and foreign), marketing networks, and urban consumption centres. Urbanization quantitatively and qualitatively affects all system components. The mar-keting network's response to urbanization (growth, spatial concentration, and changes in food demand) also affects the relative mix of acquisition methods (exchange, pro-duction, transfer) among different income groups, as well as the system's use of supply areas (domestic rural and urban and foreign).

Over the last 30 years (and for decades to come), several factors have worked together to undermine the ability of formal Southern food markets to cater to the needs of swelling numbers of city dwellers. On the supply side, export-oriented and hard-currency-earning agricultural policies have increasingly dictated crop choices, credit programs and incentives, technical extension and research, and distribution networks. The frequency and adverse effects of civil and natural disasters are growing in devel-oping countries and are bound to more and more disrupt rural food production and supply lines to cities. The migration of rural youth to cities has been intense and will continue to be for decades in sub-Saharan Africa and in many Asian countries. This affects rural food production, which is still largely small scale and labour intensive. Subsidies to decrease food prices in cities are less frequent today, and this exacerbates price variability. High transaction costs may discourage rural producers from supplying critical markets, and markets may lack the institutional framework they need to oper-ate effectively (Jones 1996). Where high-quality food is produced, larger quantities of a wider range of products are diverted to export markets for longer periods of the year. As a result, surpluses sold domestically may become smaller, less diverse, or only tem-porarily available and may be sold at export prices to a local elite. Some developing countries actually import staple surpluses from the North that are lower-quality sources

---

[2] *Food security* is defined as access by all people at all times to the food required for a healthy life; at the household level, at issue is the household's ability to secure enough food to ensure adequate dietary intake for all of its members (Von Braun et al. 1993).

of calories and proteins and are foreign to local diets and know-how. Because of the latest round of the General Agreement on Tariffs and Trade, more of those imports will have to be bought at higher prices. Given that 104 out of 132 developing countries are already net food importers and their dependence is set to worsen, and given the experience with social emergency funds in the 1990s (Raffer 1997), the overall effectiveness of proposed compensatory and targeting mechanisms, such as a food-import facility, must be questioned.

On the demand side, the capacity of the urban poor and middle class to purchase the good-quality food they need is undermined by a number of factors: currency devaluations; reduced purchasing power; salary reductions; formal-job retrenchment and the informalization of employment; elimination of subsidies for needs such as food, housing, transportation, and health care; and the very uneven access of different income groups to retail food within cities. In 1990, households in nearly half of the largest metropolitan centres in lower-income countries were already spending 50–80% of their income on food (PCC 1990). This figure was higher for low-income households. The cost of food has notably increased in dollarized Latin American economies and in currency-devalued West African countries. It is likely to grow in recession-struck East Asian economies. Already, the cash spent by the urban poor in many places is insufficient to meet daily requirements.

No matter how efficient urban food-supply markets may be, rapid urbanization and growing urban poverty will complicate the demand side of the equation for decades to come. Poverty is increasingly an urban phenomenon: more of the rural poor are migrating to the cities, more of those born in cities are of poor families, and more urban middle-class residents fall under the poverty line. If in 1988 at least 25% of the developing world's absolute poor were living in urban areas, by 2000 they are expected to constitute 56% of the world's poor households (UNICEF 1993; WRI et al. 1996). This trend has been evident in Latin America and the Caribbean for some time: by 1986, more poor were already living in cities than in rural areas, and by 2000 they could make up as much as 47% of the region's urban population (Izquierdo 1997). Urban poverty will affect women more than men and children more than adults and more households overall as more households come to be headed by a woman.

As urban populations become poorer, more of the food insecure will be found in cities. Food security is the most vital of all basic needs. Food insecurity undermines people's ability to learn, work, and make progress on other fronts. Malnutrition is a result of pronounced food insecurity. People in large cities may suffer from as much malnutrition as those in rural areas. In fact, the rate of malnutrition is often higher in urban slums than in typical rural areas. United Nations Children's Fund (UNICEF) studies showed that increased food insecurity was associated with increases in urban poverty during the 1980s (Immink 1994).

Supply and demand constraints to the conversion of Southern urban food systems to formal urban food markets have led to informal sources of supply. In higher income countries, distinct networks have evolved in various types of production, ranging from petty and small-scale to capitalized and large-scale production. Yet, in a forthcoming article, Ratta and Nasr (1999) contend that in the developing world the traditional supply structure often overlaps with the new structure. Such a development accommodates, for instance, the resurgence of urban food production, big and small, in the African urban food-supply system. According to Ratta and Nasr, several macrotrends will sustain urban food production's growing role during the next 30 years or so, particularly in sub-Saharan Africa. The fastest urban growth will occur in the countries that are least equipped to feed the people in their cities. Within less than a generation, African cities will contain as many people as the whole continent holds today. This will take place despite lagging economic growth and slow development of marketing networks. A gap is widening between population growth and growth in staple-cereal production. This is exacerbated by limited foreign exchange for imports to make up for deficits. Urban poverty and food insecurity will expand considerably for several reasons, including demographic and fiscal ones.

Urban food production in more self-reliant urban food systems

An integral part of urban food-supply systems since ancient times (Mougeot 1994), urban food production has expanded enormously since the 1970s in major cities of Africa and Latin America. This has been a response to insufficient, inadequate, unreliable, and unaffordable food supplies from rural and foreign sources. Growth in urban food production depends on poverty level, household size, city layout, access to land and water, official attitudes, and climate. In a country such as Zimbabwe, which has been affected by an SAP and droughts for years, the capital, Harare, has abundant open space for area-dependent grain crops. In Harare, open-space cultivation — excluding fallows, homestead cultivation, and crop fields extending beyond official city limits — doubled its acreage between 1990 and 1994 to some 16% of the city's area (ENDA–ZW 1994). Similarly, in Cairo, the largest city of Africa and the Middle East, with population densities averaging 32 000 people per km^2, 16% of households (30% in slums) keep small animals, mainly poultry (Gertel 1997).

Until recently, such phenomena were dismissed as a temporary adjustment inspired by recent arrivals to cities. Now many recognize that these phenomena are buttressed by an enduring web of factors. In any given urban food system, the mix of acquisition methods and supply areas is mediated by several constraints and opportunities. Central to urban food production's role in the urban food system are the ways in which marketing networks adapt to urbanization under different conditions. Because demand is ruled more by affordability than by availability, different income groups resort predictably to different mixes of acquisition modalities, jointly determining the relative contributions of production areas (urban, rural, foreign) and marketing channels (formal, informal).

Lourenço-Lindell (1995, 1999) studied urban-poor households, with special reference to food consumption and involvement in food production and distribution. She used a broadened concept of entitlement (beyond possession-based entitlement) that encompasses behaviours rooted in social and cultural codes, such as charity and safety networks, institutional conditions, and illegal practices. This approach enabled her to document the direct contribution of urban agriculture to provision strategies.[3]

---

[3] *Urban agriculture* has been defined as "an industry that produces, processes and markets food and fuel, largely in response to the daily demand of consumers within a town, city or metropolis, on land and water dispersed throughout the urban and peri-urban area, applying intensive production methods, using and reusing natural resources and urban wastes, to yield a diversity of crops and livestock" (Smit et al. 1996, p. 3). This article focuses on food production, including that which is nonmarket-demand driven, but nonfood production also improves household food security by generating income that can be spent on food and other food-related needs.

Her study indicated how central urban agricultural production can be to such strategies through the many ways producers may be influenced (mutual help among producers, community welfare, and burial groups) and may in turn participate in formal and informal channels of acquisition in the urban food-supply system. Urban farmers generate employment and earn additional, often seasonal, income or savings for other basic needs (processed food), link up with the food trade, produce foodstuff otherwise unavailable or unaffordable, reduce dependence on purchased food, enhance their own exchange entitlement, and provide gifts of food and meal sharing. Also, they unintentionally help to reduce food insecurity inasmuch as other people rob them of their crops, animals, and assets. This last effect is far from insignificant, according to several surveys (for example, Lee-Smith et al. 1987). The literature on urban food supply in the South seems to have disregarded other possibly significant strategies for people to provide for their own needs: gleaning, gathering, and gifts from rural kin.

Urban food production on the development agenda

Urban food production has shifted from being a scientific curiosity to being an urban policy issue and development tool in the same way as did squatter housing and informal employment in the 1960s and 1970s. Urban agriculture, specifically urban food production, is not unlike those appropriate solutions to qualitatively distinct urban challenges of the South. It is simply a new coping strategy, changing the way people in cities feed themselves. This transition in urban food production is outlined as follows.

Step 1: Object of scientific study

Pioneering surveys on urban food production date back to at least the late 1950s, to the work of French geographers in West Africa. Since then researchers supported by Coopération française (French cooperation), the International Development Research Centre (IDRC), the University of the United Nations, and others have documented the diversity of urban farming systems worldwide, the diversity of practitioners, and the scale of their operations. They have surveyed and estimated the importance of food production as a land use and as a source of employment and food. Covering at least 90 cities in 31 countries of East and South Asia, the Middle East, Europe, sub-Saharan Africa, South and Central America, the Caribbean, and North America, these studies formed the basis for a book by The Urban Agriculture Network, commissioned by the United Nations Development Programme (UNDP) (Smit, Ratta, and Bernstein 1996).

The studies revealed the following:

- Urban agriculture, including food production, is typically practiced over smaller and more dispersed areas than rural agriculture, uses land and water more sparingly and efficiently, integrates systems more effectively, and produces much higher yields and more specialty crops and livestock.

- More than 40 production systems and subsystems have been observed in city cores, wedges, and peripheries. These diverse urban sites, including home spaces, rights of way, road and stream sides, land reserves, flood plains and hillsides, water bodies, and wetlands, are used in both the short and the longer terms.

- As with other land uses, urban agriculture adapts to city development, with the less space-dependent forms surviving in central areas and the more land-demanding forms migrating to less coveted locations.

- Most urban farmers are low-income men and women who grow food largely for their own consumption on small plots that they do not own, with little if any support or protection.

- Producers tend not to be recent arrivals and in many cases were born in the city where they live.

- Agricultural production for the producers' own use provides much if not most of poor households' supply of nutritious food, which would otherwise be out of their reach.

- Urban agriculture benefits the long-term nutritional health of children in poor farming households and has made food aid redundant in places where it is practiced extensively.

- Savings from the producers' consumption of their own produce represent up to several months of annual income, and income from sales may be spent on other basic needs or invested in other businesses.

- Urban producers cope with greater competition over resources, environmental stress, tenure and crop insecurity, and inadequate or nonexistent legal, financial, and technical support. These problems result in hazardous practices; loss of resources or products; foregone gains in employment, productivity, yields, and profits; idle and wasted resources; and loss of dependable and affordable supplies of fresh and nutritious food.

- In francophone Africa, urban agriculture does not compete with, but complements, rural agriculture because it reduces seasonal price fluctuations and diversifies the food supplied to cities.

The UNDP-commissioned study estimated that 800 million people are now engaged in urban agriculture worldwide; of these, 200 million would be producing for the market and 150 million would be employed full time. These estimates were derived from extrapolations, academic surveys, and official statistics. Still, even if such estimates were halved, nearly 0.5 billion urban producers would indicate that an important change is under way in our cities, particularly in the South. In several cities, urban food production is already a major employer, land user, and supplier of food; and specific crops and livestock are estimated to reach multimillion-dollar market values (Mougeot 1994). Multiplier effects of activities in this sector have been observed up- and downstream, but they are still unquantified.

Step 2: Management issues for domestic policy

Local public interventions for effective promotion and management of low-income urban food production have been growing in the South since the late 1970s. So far, there is scant evidence in the literature of any opposition to this kind of urban agriculture, but the debate is likely to heat up as production grows in scale and begins to affect interests in more tangible ways. However, in places where people have overtly opposed this type of agricultural production, the opposition tends to be strong initially and to weaken with time, with reactions shifting from repression to tolerance to selective support, at which point the focus is on issue management. Urban agricultural practices occurring on public open space are frequently an issue, and more so when they occur on private residential space. Animal husbandry on both public and private land raises more concern than plant cultivation does. Opposition in developing countries has tended to come from technocrats rather than politicians; people in urban-planning, public-health, and environmental circles tend to object more than those in the employment, community-service, and agricultural spheres. Generally, official intolerance or repression has been giving way to cautiously receptive attitudes and official practices. The general picture has improved considerably over the last 30 years.

Long before international agencies recognized urban food production, Southern governments, particularly city authorities, were its main promoters. Policy and planning reviews have followed from official recognition. These in turn have led to selective endorsement of ongoing activities, incorporation of new ones into planning, and their regulation. Examples include the following:

- Presidential and local official declarations have pressed citizens into becoming more self-reliant in both rural and urban areas (Cuba, Philippines, Tanzania). In newly independent countries, elections have made politicians more accountable than before and thus more responsive to the ways their constituencies cope with food insecurity. More countries are supporting communal gardening and production cooperatives.

- New capital cities have been designed to accommodate urban food production, and more authorities are supporting it, even providing subsidies (Côte d'Ivoire, Tanzania). This support occurs initially in secondary cities and then in principal urban centres (Kenya, Tanzania). Master plans of existing cities have been revised to set the framework for practical initiatives (Tanzania, Zaire).

- More city planners acknowledge that some colonial regulations and standards are unrealistically demanding or remain largely unenforceable. On humanitarian and political grounds, repression of technically illegal food production is becoming less defensible (Zimbabwe).

- More cities are reviewing and adapting technical planning norms to facilitate urban food production. Cities are creating permanent institutional programs and agencies to exploit flexible zoning modalities; allocate open spaces to communal agriculture through purpose-specific leaseholds; and legalize organized activities, entitling farmers to credit and technical assistance (Argentina, Costa Rica, Cuba, Guinea Bissau, Peru).

- More cities are using multistakeholder consultation to resolve conflicts and set courses of action regarding urban agricultural issues (Ghana, Tanzania, Zimbabwe).

- More recently, national governments have been developing more policy instruments (Ghana, Kazakhstan) and institutional facilities for urban food production. Public utilities have leased land, entered into partnerships with producers, or become producers themselves (Mexico, Senegal, South Africa, Tunisia).

Step 3: Sustainable-development tool for international cooperation

In the official international-development community, bilateral agencies seem to have initially taken the lead in interventions in urban agriculture. By the late 1990s, multilateral agencies were making it possible to include urban agriculture on the formal agendas of international summits and forums. Both bilateral and multilateral agencies are creating intersectoral working groups to incorporate urban agricultural concerns into their structures and programs (Food and Agriculture Organization of the United Nations [FAO], Gesellschaft für Technische Zusammenarbeit [GTZ, agency for technical cooperation]), and they are now formalizing new delivery mechanisms (IDRC, Natural Resources International [NRI], World Bank). They are also collaborating more on specific projects.

Among bilaterals, IDRC has since the early 1990s been supporting research that informs policy and technology interventions in three areas: non-space-dependent production technology affordable to low-income urban producers (for example, Peru), community-based waste-reuse and environmentally appropriate practices (northeast Brazil, Cambodia, and Senegal), and urban policies receptive to urban agriculture (Uganda, Zimbabwe). This research is often supported jointly with other agencies to create enhanced impact (see examples below).

More bilaterals are active in the field: the Canadian International Development Agency (CIDA) and GTZ have been supporting urban food production in metropolitan green belts (La Habana, Maputo). CIDA, with IDRC, is supporting the development by the Cooperative for American Relief Everywhere (CARE) of space-confined production systems for income generation in low-income districts (for example, Port-au-Prince). Swedeplan has helped local governments to incorporate intraurban food production into social-housing projects (Maseru, in Lesotho [Greenhow 1994]). The Department for International Development (United Kingdom) has supported NRI studies on urban waste–peri-urban food production interactions in Nigeria. Dutch Cooperation promotes the incorporation of urban agriculture into city zoning for poverty alleviation (peri-urban zoning for high-density residential areas with productive open spaces in Addis Ababa, Ouagadougou, and with IDRC, in Cochabamba and Harare). GTZ is assisting the development of peri-urban vegetable-production systems and recently reviewed the state of the art in urban animal husbandry. The Danish International Development Agency has financed urban fuelwood plantations (Ethiopia) and has channeled funds through banks to assist cooperatives of female urban farmers (Tanzania). The Fonds national suisse de la recherche scientifique (Swiss national fund for scientific research) has funded studies on the sanitary impact of wastewater use in small urban agriculture projects in West Africa. Institut français de recherche scientifique pour le développement en coopération (French institute for scientific research to promote development and cooperation) has supported agronomic and socioeconomic research on market horticulture in Togo (Schilter 1991). More recently, French Cooperation and the European Union have charged the Centre de coopération internationale en recherche agronomique pour le développement (CIRAD, Centre for international cooperation on agronomic research for development) with feasibility surveys for the development of peri-urban horticulture in capital cities of several West and Central African countries (David and Moustier 1993; Moustier 1996). The Ford Foundation has assisted market-oriented horticulture in Nairobi (Undugu Society). The Rockefeller Foundation, the World Health Organization, the International Food Policy Research Institute, and IDRC have recently funded the Noguchi Memorial Institute for Medical Research to conduct an assessment of urban agriculture for Ghana's national action plan on food and nutrition.

Among multilaterals, UNDP is advising local governments on how urban agriculture can make the development of their cities more sustainable. UNDP and FAO have been providing technical training and feasibility studies for several production systems within (hydroponics) and at the edge (vegetable gardening) of cities (Chile, Colombia, Dominican Republic, and Nicaragua). The United Nations Centre for Human Settlements has been supporting, with IDRC, a multistakeholder approach to urban-management action plans that formally addresses urban food production. UNICEF and related international NGOs, such as CARE and Oxford Committee for Famine Relief, have implemented urban food-production projects. The World Bank, UNDP, IDRC, and the European Union have been supporting work on the treatment and reuse of solid waste from cities in peri-urban agriculture in metropolitan districts of Brazil, Cambodia, Chile, and Peru.

The World Bank–UNDP Water Sanitation Program has issued project-design guidelines for municipal waste-water reuse in agriculture (Khouri et al. 1994). The World Bank recently funded projects recommending the inclusion of agriculture as a land use in new-city master plans (First Uganda Urban project). It commissioned an assessment that came out in favour of comprehensive World Bank support to urban agriculture in sub-Saharan Africa (Smit, Ratta, and Nasr 1996). Regional banks (Development Bank of Southern Africa, Inter-American Development Bank) and the multi-donor-supported Urban Management Program have also supported urban agriculture projects. Many of these multi- and bilateral organizations, plus other institutions, were initially convened by UNDP in 1992, in New York, and organized into the Support Group on Urban Agriculture (SGUA) at their Ottawa meeting in 1996. The SGUA agreed to create a global support facility, defined workplan priorities, and took charge of specific tasks to improve information and coordination among agencies for communication, research, policy, technical assistance, and credit and investment in urban agriculture (SGUA 1996).

The emerging development arena for urban agriculture

The emergence of a development arena for urban agriculture is informed by trends influencing the growth of the industry, the range of actors and the information they need to properly promote and manage such growth, and specific key areas in need of research and training to provide more enlightened and strategic interventions.

Development trends influencing future food production

An assessment to the year 2005 (Smit 1996) suggests that worldwide urban food production will continue to expand. Between 1993 and 2005, urban agriculture may increase its share of world food production from 15% to 25–33%, its share of vegetable, meat, fish, and dairy products consumed in cities from 33% to 50%; and the number of urban farmers from 200 million to 400 million. Smit's (1996) background paper, commissioned by IDRC for the Third Meeting of the SGUA, indicates that several current trends in urban agriculture are likely to expand and to transform the way it is done well into the next century:

- Lower-density urban expansion will increase land available for interim or permanent urban farming;

- Urban food production will continue to compete and outrun rural production in certain crops as urban production techniques improve;

- Following promotional programs and projects in the 1970s and 1980s, more national and local governments and specific public sectors will support urban food production in the South, for its food-security, job, and environmental benefits, and in the North, for its provision of a healthier product;

- Urban food production will be accepted and implemented more systematically as an intervention in food and social-security programs (environmental agencies and programs will also increasingly include urban agriculture);

- Urban waste will be more commonly used as a production input because home and community-based treatment of waste will outperform massive and nonselective sewerage and landfill systems;

- Information and communication technologies will enable small producers and processors to access and share prompt and reliable technical and market information, have access to credit, and organize themselves in virtual corporations;

- Community and civic organizations will increasingly support urban food production, and women will continue to dominate the industry in production, processing, and marketing (urban agriculture will grow with women's inexorable achievement of greater legal and financial rights);

- Public–private partnerships are accelerating, and national and local urban agricultural organizations appear destined to come together in regional networks;

- Food markets in many of the world's low-, medium-, and high-income countries will carry an increasing share of products grown and raised in urban areas (informal food markets will behave more like today's formal ones, and formal and informal markets will be better interrelated); and

- Urban planning will more widely incorporate agriculture as another land use or urban-space economy.

To accelerate these trends will require expertise and information well beyond what is currently available. The SGUA's current perception is that new research needs to be more prescriptive and operational, catering to the needs of local, national, and international actors for concrete interventions in urban agriculture.

Recent international conferences have raised information issues for the promotion and improvement of specific food-production systems in urban and peri-urban areas. For instance, in late 1994, Germany's Foundation for International Development and its Council for Tropical and Subtropical Agricultural Research sponsored an international workshop, organized by the Food and Agriculture Development Centre, on "Vegetable Production in Peri-urban Areas in the Tropics and Subtropics" (Richter et al. 1995). Areas of development-research needs for urban and peri-urban horticulture were identified. France's CIRAD carried out an international networking seminar in early 1998, which stressed the need for more prescriptive research on complementarities between production and consumption systems particularly suited to urban and peri-urban needs, as well as on synergies between compatible agricultural and nonagricultural urban land uses. Urban forestry has attracted considerable attention in recent meetings of the World Forestry Congress. The FAO's forestry journal, *Unasylva*, has dedicated at least two issues to the subject, and its Forest Resources Division commissioned a concept paper on the potential for urban forestry in developing countries, followed by a series of case studies (Carter 1995; Murray 1997).

In 1995, the FAO, the World Association for Animal Production, and the Korean Society of Animal Science held an International Symposium on Supply of Livestock Products to Rapidly Expanding Urban Populations. This represented a major effort in using subsectoral analyses to address supply challenges. The joint FAO–International Institute for Land Reclamation and Improvement roundtable stressed the growth of the urban and peri-urban components of the livestock subsector and the need to pay greater attention to both the large and the small livestock components of urban agriculture (FAO et al. 1995; Wilson 1995). Since then the FAO's focus has shifted away from supply issues to production-related animal- and human-health risks (Phelan, personal communication, 1998[4]). In 1997, an international workshop on hydroponics, organized by Peru's Universidad Nacional Agraria La Molina (national university of agriculture), highlighted the still neglected potential of space-confined technologies to resolve urban poverty, technological advances for input-cost reduction, and the need for socioeconomic evaluations to fine-tune training, financing, and marketing (Mougeot 1997).

Taken from these and other sources, the following is a list of areas in which research and training are particularly urgent if enlightened development interventions are to occur in food production in and around cities over the next few decades (IDRC 1997):

- *Operational terminology* — Methodologies, baseline surveys and census-taking, best-practice dissemination;
- *Urban food security* — Comprehensive food assistance and self-reliant food supply;
- *Public health and nutrition* — Risk assessment, regulations and enforcement, micronutrient production for the producers' own use, and nutritional benefits to households;
- *Urban land management* — Productive landscapes, institutional frameworks, flexible and evolving zoning of farming systems, creative private–public tenure and usufruct to expand access to nonbuilt space and use of built-up space, multiple land-use synergies, food production in social housing, and financing of resources;
- *Urban waste management* — Separation at source of compostable waste and decentralized community-scale systems for treatment and reuse, acceptance, and demand for variously composted waste, as well as cost recovery of treated inputs used in urban agriculture;
- *Service provision* — Validation for credit, investment, risk assessment, microfinancing, marketing, extension, and communications;

[4] Joe Phelan, FAO, personal communication, April 1998.

- *Need for production of specific commodities* — The following:

  - *Vegetable horticulture* — Policy, agronomic and crop production, chemicals in peri-urban systems, and affordability and feasibility of space-confined systems,

  - *Fuel and food forestry* — Inclusion in city planning, participation of the urban poor, technical bases, and legal protection,

  - *Animal husbandry* — Baseline data on supply and demand, ecosystem health, zero-grazing intensification, and decentralized processing,

  - *Waste-water aquaculture* — Cultural, public-health, and socioeconomic issues, with rural–urban comparative advantages of the aforementioned systems; and

- *Gender analysis* — Women are often the majority, have added burdens of household subsistence (general food provisioning and child nutrition), may concentrate on home-based or space-confined production of specific crops, or be discriminated against in their access to off-plot natural resources, technical extension, or financial support (Hovorka 1998).

Conclusions

Greater interdependence should not undermine developing countries' abilities to meet their people's basic needs. However, globalization forces are strengthening some urban food systems while making others more vulnerable to international trade. Dr Uwe Werblow (1997), head of the European Commission Department of Agriculture and Rural Development in East and Southern Africa, thinks developing countries must pursue two self-reliance strategies to address their food-security crisis well into the next century: favour a broader product base with more traditional cereals and root crops; and produce in peri-urban and urban areas. In an increasingly urban world, more of the food that people consume will doubtless be grown closer to where they live. Urban agriculture brings about other nonfood self-reliance benefits that have not been discussed here, not the least of which are employment and the use of waste and open spaces. Local authorities have for some time and international agencies have more recently become more responsive to this unfolding reality. In early 1998, the FAO initiated an internal policy-review process, for its forthcoming program of work and budget, that for the first time in its history explicitly addressed urban and peri-urban agriculture. This may have an enormous impact on how Southern national governments develop geographically more comprehensive agricultural and urban strategies in the next century. The already large role of urban food production in many Southern urban food-supply systems, for the producers' own consumption and for the market, is increasingly read as being part of the way the South characteristically appropriates the globalization process, rather than resisting it. Because of the removal of subsidies for export production and because of burgeoning low-income consumer urban markets in the South, food production in and around cities is more attractive than ever. A challenge for governments and agencies alike will be to ensure that their interventions balance requirements for local self-reliance (for basic-needs satisfaction) with trade potentials (for income generation) and make cities healthier and more livable.

References

AlSayyad, N. 1997. From vernacularism to globalism. *In* Kirdar, U., ed., Cities fit for people. United Nations, New York, NY, USA. pp. 205–214.

Brandt, H. 1997. Development policy in sub-Saharan Africa after 15 years of structural adjustment. Agriculture and Rural Development, 4(2), 22–24.

Carter, E.J. 1995. The potential of urban forestry in developing countries: a concept paper. Forestry Department, Food and Agriculture Organization of the United Nations, Rome, Italy.

David, O.; Moustier, P. 1993. Systèmes maraîchers approvisionnant Bissau. Centre de coopération internationale en recherche agronomique pour le développement, Montpellier, France. Unité de recherche économie des filières n° 7.

Emmerij, L. 1997. In the midst of paradoxes: an urban renaissance? *In* Kirdar, U., ed., Cities fit for people. United Nations, New York, NY, USA. pp. 100–108.

ENDA–ZW (Environment and Development Activities – Zimbabwe). 1994. Urban agriculture in Harare. Final report. ENDA-ZW, Harare, Zimbabwe. IDRC 93-0024. 47 pp.

FAO; WAAP; KSAS (Food and Agriculture Organization of the United Nations; World Association of Animal Producers; Korean Society of Animal Science). 1995. Executive summary: proceedings of the FAO/WAAP/KSAS International Symposium on Supply of Livestock Products to Rapidly Expanding Urban Populations. *In* Wilson, R.T., ed., Supply of livestock products to rapidly expanding urban populations. Food and Agriculture Organization of the United Nations, Rome, Italy. pp. vii–xxx.

Gertel, J. 1997. Animal husbandry, urban spaces and subsistence production in Cairo. Agriculture and Rural Development, 4(2), 49–51.

Greenhow, T. 1994. Urban agriculture: can planners make a difference? International Development Research Centre, Ottawa, ON, Canada. Cities Feeding People Report 12.

Hovorka, A. 1998. Gender resources for urban agriculture research: methodology, directory, and annotated bibliography. Cities Feeding People Program, International Development Research Centre, Ottawa, ON, Canada. CFP Report 26.

IDRC (International Development Research Centre). 1997. Development research in urban agriculture: an international awards program. IDRC, Ottawa, ON, Canada. Mimeo.

Immink, M. 1994. The urban poor and household food security. United Nations Children's Fund, New York, NY, USA. Urban Examples, No. 19.

Izquierdo, F.J. 1997. La hidroponia popular y su potencial en procesos de superacion de la pobreza: rol de la FAO. *In* Delfin, A.R., ed., Hidroponia: una esperanza para Latinoamérica. Universidad Nacional Agraria La Molina, Lima, Peru. pp. 251–276.

Jones, S. 1996. Food markets in developing countries: what do we know? International Development Centre, University of Oxford, Oxford, UK. Food Studies Group Working Paper 8.

Khouri, N.; Kalbermatten, J.M.; Bartone, C.R. 1994. Reuse of wastewater in agriculture: a guide for planners. United Nations Development Programme – World Bank Water and Sanitation Program. World Bank, Washington, DC, USA. Water and Sanitation Report 6.

Kneen, B. 1997. Trading fruit: promoting sustainable alternatives to Canadian fruit choices. International Conference on Sustainable Urban Food Systems, May 1997, Ryerson Polytechnic University, Toronto, ON, Canada. Mimeo.

Lee-Smith, D.; Manundu, M.; Lamba, D.; Kuria Gathuru, P. 1987. Urban food production and the cooking fuel situation in urban Kenya — national report: results of a 1985 national survey. Mazingira Institute, Nairobi, Kenya.

Lourenço-Lindell, I. 1995. The informal food economy in a peripheral urban district: the case of Bandim District, Bissau. Habitat International, 19(2), 195–208.

——— 1999. How do the urban poor stay alive? Food provision in a squatter settlement of Bissau. African Urban Quarterly. (In press.)

Mougeot, L.J.A. 1994. Urban food production: evolution, official support and significance. International Development Research Centre, Ottawa, ON, Canada. Cities Feeding People Report 8.

——— 1997. Introduccion IDRC. *In* Delfin, A.R., ed., Hidroponia: una esperanza para Latinoamérica. Universidad Nacional Agraria La Molina, Lima, Peru. pp. 6–7.

Moustier, P. 1996. Organization in the Brazzavillian vegetable market. Wye College, University of London, London, UK. PhD thesis.

Murray, S. 1997. Urban and peri-urban forestry in Quito, Ecuador: a case study. Forestry Department, Food and Agriculture Organization of the United Nations, Rome, Italy.

PCC (Population Crisis Committee). 1990. Cities: life in the world's 100 largest metropolitan areas. PCC, Washington, DC, USA.

Picciotto, R.; Weaving, R. 1997. Structural adjustment programs — an assessment. Agriculture and Rural Development, 4(2), 25–28.

Raffer, K. 1997. Helping Southern net food importers after the Uruguay Round: a proposal. World Development, 25(11), 1901–1907.

Ranis, G.; Stewart, F. 1997. The urban informal sector within a global economy. In Kirdar, U., ed., Cities fit for people. United Nations, New York, NY, USA. pp. 246–259.

Ratta, A.; Nasr, J. 1999. Urban agriculture and the African urban food supply system. African Urban Quarterly, 11(2–3). (In press.)

Richter, J.; Schnitzler, W.H.; Gura, S., ed. 1995. Vegetable production in periurban areas in the tropics and subtropics — food, income and quality of life. German Foundation for International Development; Food and Agriculture Development Centre, Feldafing, Germany.

Schilter, C. 1991. L'agriculture urbaine à Lomé : approches agronomiques et socio-économiques. Karthala, Paris, France.

SGUA (Support Group on Urban Agriculture), ed. 1996. Third Meeting of the Support Group on Urban Agriculture. Proceedings, 18–19 Mar 1996. International Development Research Centre, Ottawa, ON, Canada. Cities Feeding People Report 17.

Simai, M. 1997. A globalizing world. In Kirdar, U., ed., Cities fit for people. United Nations, New York, NY, USA. pp. 50–70.

Singer, H.W. 1997. A global view of food security. Agriculture and Rural Development, 4(2), 3–6.

Smit, J. 1996. Urban agriculture, progress and prospect: 1997–2005. International Development Research Centre, Ottawa, ON, Canada. Cities Feeding People Report 18.

Smit, J.; Ratta, A.; Bernstein, J. 1996. Urban agriculture: an opportunity for environmentally sustainable development in sub-Saharan Africa. Environmentally Sustainable Division, African Technical Department, World Bank, Washington, DC, USA. Post-UNCED Series, Building Blocks for Africa 2025, Paper No. 11.

Smit, J.; Ratta, A.; Nasr, J. 1996. Urban agriculture: food, jobs, and sustainable cities. United Nations Development Programme, New York, NY, USA. Publication Series for Habitat II, Vol. 1.

UNICEF (United Nations Children's Fund). 1993. UNICEF rapport annuel 1993. UNICEF, New York, NY, USA.

Von Braun, J.; McComb, J.; Fred-Mensah, B.K.; Pandya-Lorch, R. 1993. Urban food insecurity and malnutrition in developing countries. International Food Policy Research Institute, Washington, DC, USA. 47 pp.

Werblow, U. 1997. A radically changing world: globalisation and food security up to year 2020. Agriculture and Rural Development, 4(2), 7–9.

Wilson, R.T. 1995. Summary of the Joint FAO/ILRI Roundtable on Livestock Development Strategies for Low-income Countries. In Wilson, R.T., ed., Supply of livestock products to rapidly expanding urban populations. Food and Agriculture Organization of the United Nations, Rome, Italy. pp. 9–24.

WRI; UNEP; UNDP; WB (World Resources Institute; United Nations Environment Programme; United Nations Development Programme; World Bank). 1996. World resources 1996–97. Oxford University Press, New York, NY, USA.

...🔥 🔥 🔥...

Urban Food Security in Sub-Saharan Africa

Daniel Maxwell

Introduction

In a recent overview of the urban food situation, Atkinson (1995, p. 152) suggested that given current trends, the question of urban food security may become the "greatest humanitarian challenge of the next century." Yet, this paper argues that food insecurity in African cities is relatively invisible to policymakers and is scarcely recognized in contemporary political debate. This paper very briefly reviews the contemporary urban situation in Africa, discusses the "disappearance" of the urban food problem, and suggests some research questions of policy relevance.

The problems faced by African cities are many. Rates of urban-population growth, which had slowed during the 1980s, are again on the increase (United Nations 1995). The infrastructural and tax bases of cities cannot catch up with the services demanded by their expanding urban populations, and this leads to increased crowding and a deteriorating urban environment (Farvacque and McAuslan 1992; Stren et al. 1992; Becker et al. 1994). Urban economies in sub-Saharan Africa declined markedly during the 1970s and 1980s, and policy reforms initiated under structural-adjustment programs (SAPs) in the 1980s cut many services and certainly cut public-sector employment. In theory, the movement toward more democratic forms of government in contemporary Africa strengthens local and municipal governments. But it also puts increased demands on their already strained capacities, and questions remain about the access of the urban poor to local political processes.

Although poverty is still primarily a rural problem, the rapidly increasing level of urban poverty requires much greater policy attention (Naylor and Falcon 1995). Urban poverty is increasing over much of the continent, and urban analysts believe the extent of urban poverty may be underestimated (Satterthwaite 1995). The urban poor spend a large portion of their income on food (von Braun et al. 1993), which largely means that the poverty problem appears as a food-security problem. Contemporary African urban food economies comprise both a global supermarket for the well to do and a set of very localized coping strategies for the vulnerable (Drakakis-Smith 1991).

Development theory has been ambivalent about African urbanization, which was once equated with modernization and growth but has since been branded as a "parasitic process" and a cause of underdevelopment (Baker and Pedersen 1992, p. 12). Many of the reasons for the change in view have stemmed from "urban-bias" theory (Lipton 1977; Bates 1981), which suggests that because of the greater political clout of urban populations, they are favoured at the expense of rural populations. Urban-bias theory became one of the intellectual cornerstones of SAPs in Africa. During the 1980s and 1990s, policy emphasis was on "getting the prices right," or permitting market forces, rather than (urban-biased) bureaucracies, to set prices, with urban consumers bearing much of the cost of this adjustment (von Braun et al. 1993). Urban-bias theory is still very influential in the views of planners and policymakers in the 1990s, although perhaps not as much as in the past. Fortunately, researchers are reexamining cities and urban poverty, in terms of both research and policy (Amis 1995; Moser 1995; de Haan 1997). However, urban food-security issues have virtually disappeared from the political debate.

Food security and African cities

Definitions of food security used in African policy debates revolve around that of the World Bank (1986): "access by all people at all times to sufficient food for an active healthy life." Other definitions of food security include different elements but emphasize overall food availability, food access, and food use. Recent work on food security also emphasizes the risks to food access and people's ability to cope with such risks (Davies 1996). Most of this conceptual and empirical work has been done in rural areas.

In the 1980s, two major strands of analysis characterized the debate on urban food security in Africa. One centred around the serious matter of "feeding the cities," that is, maintaining the overall supply of food to African cities (World Bank 1981; Eicher 1982; Guyer 1987). The other concerned SAPs (Cornia et al. 1987; Walton and Seddon 1994). These were serious political problems because both food shortages and sudden increases in food prices could — and did — lead to political protests that ultimately toppled governments. Political protests were linked to more than just the availability and price of food; rather, access to food and other basic urban necessities was at their root. Protests occurred in Africa through the 1980s and early 1990s. Not surprisingly, these political disturbances were the strongest in the most urbanized of African countries, most notably Côte d'Ivoire and Zambia (Riley and Parfitt 1994). And, contrary to popular belief, the protestors were not necessarily the poorest people but those who perceived most markedly the changed economic and political circumstances that led to impoverishment and loss of entitlement.

In the short term, the market reforms of the SAPs brought about price shocks that led to political protests. But in the longer term, these reforms appear to have reduced problems in overall supply of food to cities. Certainly, "feeding the cities" is no longer the political issue it was in the 1980s. But removing the major supply constraints has tended to close the political debate, even at a time when differences in access to food at the household or individual level are becoming more acute. Thus, even as food insecurity is becoming a more serious problem for the urban poor it has dropped out of political visibility.

Food insecurity has become politically invisible in contemporary African cities for several reasons. First, to urban managers, urban food insecurity is obscured by more urgent urban problems — unemployment, the burgeoning of the informal sector, overcrowding, decaying infrastructure, and declining services — although food insecurity is directly linked to these other problems. Second, national policymakers have tended to focus less on urban food insecurity than on food insecurity in rural areas, where it is typically a more seasonal and community-wide phenomenon. Third, both urban managers and national policymakers fail to recognize urban food insecurity because, in the 1990s, unless major supply problems or sudden price spikes negatively and simultaneously affect a large number of urban residents, food insecurity must be dealt with at the household or individual level. It rarely becomes a political issue. So long as food insecurity is a household-level problem and does not translate into a political problem, it does not attract policy attention.

To sum up, urban populations and urban poverty in Africa are growing rapidly, and inequality is increasing. The major urban food problems of the 1970s and 1980s — food shortages and price shocks — have apparently been largely resolved, at least in the short to medium term. Because of this, urban food security — having long been defined as the issue of feeding the cities (aggregate food supply and price considerations) — has dropped off the political agenda of urban planners and urban managers; indeed, specifically urban food-security problems receive relatively little attention from national food or nutrition policy planners. Thus, even though the indications are that food insecurity in African cities in the 1990s is on the increase, it is relatively invisible, partly because it tends not to be linked to seasonal or community-wide processes and partly because of a long-held belief that urban populations are better off, or even favoured. But urban food insecurity is directly linked to urban poverty and inequality, and for this reason, research on urban food security in the 1990s must focus on the question of access — access not only to food but also to political processes.

Empirical questions for an analysis of urban food and livelihood security

Several questions must be investigated simultaneously if one is to understand the issues of urban food and livelihood security and make relevant policy recommendations:

1. Have problems of aggregate food supply been resolved?

2. What has happened to real urban food prices and real incomes over time?

3. What has happened to formal safety nets intended to protect the poor?

4. How have people responded to drops in real income? What happened to livelihoods, household organization, and the labour of women?

5. What has been the response of national and local governments to changes at the household level? What happens when the livelihood and survival activities of the urban poor run into direct conflict with actions and policies developed by urban managers and national policymakers to improve infrastructure, attract investment, and lay the foundation for sustainable economic growth, at city and national economic levels?

6. Can examples be found of "constructive reciprocities" between state–local government and civil society? Are there models of collaboration among national and municipal governments, local organizations, and local communities to protect the most vulnerable?

No general answers can be given to these questions. They have to be answered on a case-by-case basis. But answers to these questions are crucial to understanding food insecurity in contemporary urban Africa. In a resource-constrained era, when money for formal safety nets is unlikely to be broadly available, the crucial challenge will be to incorporate the answers to these questions into the policy-formulation process.

References

Amis, P. 1995. Making sense of urban poverty. Environment and Urbanization, 7(1), 145–157.

Atkinson, S. 1995. Approaches and actors in urban food security in developing countries. Habitat International, 19(2), 151–163.

Baker, J.; Pedersen, P.O. 1992. The rural–urban interface in Africa. Scandinavian Institute of African Studies, Uppsala, Sweden.

Bates, R. 1981. Markets and states in tropical Africa. University of California Press, Berkeley, CA, USA. 178 pp.

Becker, C.; Jamer, A.; Morrison, A. 1994. Beyond urban bias in Africa. Heinemann, Portsmouth, NH, USA. 294 pp.

Cornia, G.; Jolly, R.; Stewart, F. 1987. Adjustment with a human face. Clarendon Press, Oxford, UK.

Davies, S. 1996. Adaptable livelihoods. St Martins Press, New York, NY, USA. 335 pp.

de Haan, A. 1997. Urban poverty and its alleviation. IDS Bulletin, 28(2), 1–8.

Drakakis-Smith, D. 1991. Urban food distribution in Africa and Asia. Geographical Journal, 157, 51–61.

Eicher, C. 1982. Facing up to Africa's food crisis. Foreign Affairs, 61(3), 151–174.

Farvacque, C.; McAuslan, P. 1992. Reforming urban land policies and institutions in developing countries. World Bank, Washington, DC, USA. Urban Management Program Paper No. 5. 114 pp.

Guyer, J. 1987. Feeding African cities. Indiana University Press, Bloomington, IN, USA. 249 pp.

Lipton, M. 1977. Why poor people stay poor. Harvard University Press, Cambridge, MA, USA. 467 pp.

Moser, C. 1995. Urban social policy and poverty reduction. Environment and Urbanization, (7)1, 159–171.

Naylor, R.; Falcon, W. 1995. Is the locus of poverty changing? Food Policy, 20(6), 501–518.

Riley, S.; Parfitt, T. 1994. Economic adjustment and democratization in Africa. In Walton, J.; Seddon, D., ed., Free markets and food riots: the politics of global adjustment. Blackwell, Oxford, UK.

Satterthwaite, D. 1995. The under-estimation and misrepresentation of urban poverty. Environment and Urbanization, (7)1, 3–10.

Stren, R.; White, R.; Whitney, J. 1992. Sustainable cities: urbanization and the environment in international perspective. Westview, Boulder, CO, USA. 365 pp.

United Nations. 1995. World urbanization prospects: the 1994 revision, estimates and projections of urban and rural populations and of urban agglomerations. Department of Economic and Social Information and Policy Analysis, United Nations, New York, NY, USA. ST/ESA/SER.A/136.

von Braun, J.; McComb, J.; Fred-Mensah, B.; Pandya-Lorch, R. 1993. Urban food insecurity and malnutrition in developing countries: trends, policies, and research implications. International Food Policy Research Institute, Washington, DC, USA. 47 pp.

Walton, J.; Seddon, D. 1994. Free markets and food riots: the politics of global adjustment. Blackwell, Oxford, UK. 387 pp.

World Bank. 1981. Accelerated development in sub-Saharan Africa. World Bank, Washington, DC, USA. 198 pp.

————— 1986. Poverty and hunger: issues and options for food security in developing countries. World Bank, Washington, DC, USA.

...❦ ❦ ❦...

Combining Social Justice and Sustainability for Food Security

Elaine M. Power

Introduction

In Canada, two broad approaches are taken to promoting domestic food security: one of these seeks to establish a sustainable food system; and the other aims to eliminate poverty. These two approaches correspond to the two main dimensions of food security: the production and supply of an adequate quality and quantity of food; and the ability of individuals to reliably access food (Campbell et al. 1988; Beaudry 1991). Both of these dimensions of food security are threatened in Canada.

In this paper, I explore the roots of these two approaches to food security and the recent attempt to unite the issues of poverty and sustainability in a community-development approach to food security. I am concerned that the impact of the current community-development approach may contribute to "victim blaming" and in the longer term may not benefit either the antipoverty or the sustainability movement. This short overview contains many simplifications and generalizations, which I hope will not detract from the purpose of the paper, which is to promote discussion of these important issues.

The antipoverty approach to food security

The antipoverty, or social-justice, approach to promoting food security starts from the premise that Canada has an adequate food supply and that food insecurity in this country results from people's lack of access to food. Because Canada is an industrialized country, with a market economy, where most citizens buy almost all their food, antipoverty activists assume that food insecurity results from poor people's lack of money to buy food. From this perspective, the opposite of food security is hunger, "the inability to obtain sufficient, nutritious, personally acceptable food through normal food channels or the uncertainty that one will be able to do so" (Davis and Tarasuk 1994, p. 51).

No evidence can be found of hunger on any large scale in Canada between the end of the Great Depression of the 1930s and the beginning of the 1980s (Davis and Tarasuk 1994). The Canadian social-security system grew out of the experiences of the Great Depression and a recognition that the structural forces responsible for poverty require macroeconomic state intervention. The social-security system was designed to give Canadians income security, thus alleviating poverty and hunger, and it reflected several commonly shared values: equity of income security, equality of access to

Canadian institutions, concern for the well-being of every individual, collective social responsibility of all citizens, security in the face of economic uncertainty, social integration and cohesion, work as an integral part of a person's self, economic and social opportunity, self-sufficiency, and faith in democracy (CCSD 1993).

The first indication that the Canadian social safety net was failing, leaving people hungry, was in 1981, when the first food bank was established since the Great Depression (Riches 1986). Food banks became the predominant response to hunger throughout the 1980s and 1990s, spreading to communities all across the country (Davis and Tarasuk 1994). By November 1997, the number of communities with food banks had risen to 501, almost triple the number in 1989 (Canadian Association of Food Banks [CAFB], personal communication, Nov 1997[1]). In 1996, it is estimated that more than 3 million Canadians used food banks.

The antipoverty approach to food security is inseparable from macroeconomic and social-policy analysis, for example, high rates of unemployment, the polarization of the job market into "good" and "bad" jobs, minimum wages well below the poverty line, inadequate welfare benefits, high costs of housing, regressive taxation policies, off-loading of social programs to communities, and the unequal distribution of wealth (Laxer 1996; Riches 1997a, b). The welfare state of the past was not perfect: critics argue that it maintained inequality, institutionalized the feminization of poverty, created work disincentives, and failed to promote participation in society (CCSD 1993; Tarasuk and Davis 1996; MacGregor 1997; Torjman 1997a). But the antipoverty approach to food security rejects the destruction of the welfare state and the neoconservative values of individualism, competition, and inequality and proposes instead to restore values such as equality, fellowship, democracy, and humanitarianism to the foundation of social policy.

The antipoverty approach is concerned with income security, rather than food and food security per se. Community development within this approach focuses on raising awareness of poverty, advocacy with and for poor people, and community economic development. In the words of one antipoverty activist (Debbie Ellison, quoted in Hobbs et al. 1993),

> We challenge people who aren't poor to listen to people who are poor ... to join with us in rejecting American style social programs where food and housing are provided for the poor at the whim of the rich ... to work with us to change our system to end poverty ... to demand that our politicians work for a just society, where people are more equal and where the poor don't have to depend on leftovers from the rich to subsist.

The sustainable-food-systems approach to food security

The sustainable-food-systems approach to food security has roots both in the political-economy critique of the contemporary food system and in the environmental movement. The political-economic critique of the food system analyzes the dramatic changes in the food system over the past 60 years, including the following (Goodman and Redclift 1991; Winson 1993):

- The marginalization of small-scale primary producers and processors;

[1] CAFB, personal communication, November 1997.

- Loss of rural ways of life;

- Horizontal and vertical integration, consolidation, and monopolization in the food industry and agriculture;

- Manipulation of food and its packaging to increase profit; and

- Alienation of food consumers from food producers and from the food that they eat, including "de-skilling," or the loss of people's abilities to grow and prepare food.

Thus, "food has changed from an integrated material and symbolic basis of life — breaking bread, in Western culture — into an array of edible products of complex, often global production chains" (Freidmann 1993, p. 216). As a result, "much of the work connected with food (like other work) has turned into 'jobs'" (Goodman and Redclift 1991, p. 5). These dramatic changes in the food system have been central "to the widening and deepening of capitalist relations within the world economy" (Freidmann 1982, p. 256). From this perspective, corporate control of the food system and the commodification of food are the predominant threats to food security.

Environmentalists have strengthened the food-system critique by showing that environmental degradation poses imminent threats to human living standards and well-being (Buttel 1993). According to the environmental perspective, the capitalistic food system completely disregards its environmental and human costs and is thus unsustainable. The advent of agricultural biotechnology has raised a host of new concerns for critics of the capitalistic food system, such as corporate control over patents for genetic material, new ways of exploiting indigenous people's knowledge, new environmental fears, and new food-safety issues. This analysis provides further evidence of the bankruptcy of the capitalistic food system.

Until recently, the sustainable-food-systems approach to food security has focused on the production side of the food system and has called for sustainable agricultural production. Some scholars have recognized the limitations of this approach and recommended a food-system approach that encompasses food production, distribution, preparation, preservation, consumption, recycling and disposal of waste, and support systems. As Dahlberg (1993) noted, sustainable agriculture can only be successful to the extent that other parts of the food system and the rest of society also become more sustainable. The food-systems approach is appealing because it addresses domestic hunger and is meaningful to a wider audience, including urban dwellers of all classes.

Clancy (1993) and Allen and Sachs (1993) are among those who, in their explications of sustainable food systems, have expressed the need for social justice for the poor (as well as for those marginalized in the agricultural system) and, in Allen's words, the need to reaffirm that "the goal of agriculture is first and ultimately sustaining human life" (Allen 1993, p. 1). Clancy (1994) outlined a number of reasons for people concerned about sustainable agriculture to take an interest in social justice; for example, both agriculture unsustainability and poverty are based in the larger, capitalistic economic system; food is a basic human right; the poor represent a huge new domestic market for farmers; and the interests of small farmers and the urban poor have a "common ideological situation as occupants of marginal positions in the highly capitalized food system" (Clancy 1994, p. 82).

The sustainable-food-systems approach has been applied to food projects for the poor in both Canada and the United States (TFPC 1994; Fisher and Gottlieb 1995; Torjman 1997b). Such projects are of two major types: first, the creation of alternative food-distribution and marketing projects, such as farmers' markets and community-supported agriculture; and, second, "self-provisioning" activities, including people's growing, preserving, and preparing their own food, often in collaboration with others working in community gardens and kitchens. These ways of feeding the hungry are seen as affording the poor more dignity than does charitable food distribution. The self-provisioning activities promote self-reliance and skills development, and alternative distribution and marketing projects foster direct relationships between urban dwellers and farmers. Community-development food projects appeal to community workers because they produce tangible results — good wholesome food — for participants.

All of these types of project emphasize making the food system local and fostering the development of community. As Morris (1996, p. 438) put it, "small is the scale of efficient, dynamic, democratic, and environmentally benign societies." In Canada, the sustainable-food-systems approach is often labeled "community development." In the United States, it is called "community food security." This approach is compatible with communitarianism, as described by Frazer and Lacey (1993, pp. 1–2):

> the thesis that the community, rather than the individual, the state, the nation, or any other system is and should be at the centre of our analysis and our value system. ... Communitarians can be understood to be conducting a straightforward prescriptive argument: human life will go better if communitarian, collective, and public values guide and construct our lives.

Frazer and Lacey noted that the appeal of communitarian ideas is rooted in widespread alienation, our ideals of community — solidarity, reciprocity, love, and support — and contemporary fear that society as we know it is disintegrating. Frazer and Lacey (1993, p. 136) believe that "the fear of the loss of community, and with it identity, lies deep in some cultural vein." Participation in sustainable-food-systems programs is especially appealing because it offers people an opportunity to identify with a defined community, an opportunity to connect with nature, and "the liberating potential of the escape from capitalist relations of production, the release from the alienation of work, and the individualistic search for creative alternatives" (Gerry and Connolly, cited in Redclift and Mingione 1985, p. 4).

Appraising contemporary Canadian food projects

Community-development food projects for the poor are often only one piece of a larger agenda for addressing social and economic inequities (TFPC 1994; OPHAFSWG 1995), but the food projects are currently receiving the most attention as alternatives to food banks and their indignities. Community-development food projects have been isolated from larger agendas of structural change. The rhetoric of "community" has played a large role in the agendas of neoconservative governments, which have combined the ideologies of deregulation and downsizing of government with appeals to the value of communities taking responsibility for many of the functions of the welfare state. Neo-conservative governments "evoke a [romanticized] past era in which stable, integrative, identity-generating communities were a dominant feature of social organization"

(Frazer and Lacey 1993, p. 136). Such communities no longer exist for the majority of the poor, who live in urban centres. But even if they did, the rhetoric ignores the oppressiveness of communities for those who "don't belong," for whatever reason. The rhetoric of community also fails to address issues of power — who gets to join, to speak, to act, to be heard.

Off-loading the functions of the welfare state onto communities, whether through charitable food distribution or community-development food projects, strips away the relative anonymity and universality on which the Canadian welfare system used to be based. Food programs aimed at the poor tend to reinforce the individualistic ideology of neoconservative policies in that they suggest that the victim is to blame, rather than blaming socioeconomic policies that leave the poor without resources. Jolly (1997) described "the corporatization of public policy and the privatization of poverty," in which urban agriculture becomes essential for the poor, but only as a "defensive option" in a two-tiered food system: a market-based system for those who can afford it; and a subsistence, self-sufficiency-based system for those who cannot.

The impact of food programs aimed at the poor is limited by other factors, most importantly by the sheer number of hungry Canadians, the amount of investment that is required to set up and maintain the programs, and the limited amounts of food they can provide. This is true of both charitable food distribution and community-development food projects. Although community-development strategies usually offer more dignity and provide better quality food than food banks, they present other problems. Self-provisioning activities and alternative distribution programs often exclude the most vulnerable because basic levels of resources, which provide stability and an ability to imagine the future (that is, hope), are usually prerequisites for participation.

Community-development food programs may place increased burdens on women, who tend to be primarily responsible for the family's food. Mingione (1985) classified the activities of people to provide for themselves as "extraordinary work for self-consumption" in industrialized countries. He distinguishes these activities from "normal domestic work" and noted that the distinction between normal and extraordinary work for self-consumption changes with time, culture, and place. Self-provisioning activities add to the domestic work time and tend "to be distributed in a discriminative and inequitable manner" (Mingione 1985, p. 32). They also tend to have a low economic return, given the number of hours needed for production. Accordingly, self-provisioning activities tend to be most effective for those with large, multigenerational family structures, in which the household work is shared (Mingione 1985).

More generally, I am uncertain how well the sustainable-food-systems analysis considers class issues in trying to take account of the poor. The mainly privileged proponents of sustainability are most concerned about collective or public goods, such as food quality, health, and the environment (Buttel 1993). For poor people, the issue is more immediate and more personal — how to put food on the table for the next meal. As Bourdieu and Wacquant (1992) pointed out, privileged activists and academics who struggle for an alternative, progressive vision of the future often feel marginalized and misunderstood in their own spheres, and they easily identify with those marginalized in other ways. However, the basis for their identification with the poor is limited. What is significant for middle-class activists may be of no consequence to poor people (and vice versa).

Most poor people — who are economically as well as politically marginalized — want to be full participants in society, including its consumerism. Steedman

(1986, p. 8) explained that for some, poverty promotes an incalculable longing for the things denied, "a subterranean culture of longing for that which one can never have." The symbol of success for a food cooperative I visited, which was run by poor people, was its bank of freezers filled with convenience food, such as individually wrapped chicken *cordon bleu*. People in the dominant middle and upper classes set the standards for what is desirable in our society. For now, these are not the standards promoted through the sustainable-food-systems approach. To promote sustainability — and to promote social justice — we will have to change the dominant culture. We will have to create a society with the preeminent values of respecting the planet and meeting the basic needs of all people, including those in future generations.

Conclusions

Food solutions will not solve the problem of poverty. Without social justice for the poor in the larger society (that is, a guarantee of an adequate and dignified level of material resources to allow every citizen the stability and security to participate fully in society), programs aimed at improving the food problems of the poor will only reinforce individualistic solutions to structural problems, no matter what the intentions of the programers.

In this brief overview, I have tried to show that food security encompasses a diversity of approaches to a variety of problems. The all-inclusiveness of the term *food security* can obscure the nature of the problem. This is important to understand, because the way we frame a problem determines the ways we try to solve it (Tesh 1988). I have also called for reflexivity on the part of academics and activists, because our positions in society affect the ways we understand and frame problems.

The task of bringing together the antipoverty and sustainable-food-systems approaches is neither simple nor self-evident. It involves multiple contradictions and conflicting interests that will remain unresolved unless we acknowledge and elucidate them and then think clearly and carefully about how to overcome them. Democracy cannot thrive without social justice. The planet cannot thrive without sustainability. The future looks bleak unless we find ways to achieve both.

References

Allen, P. 1993. Connecting the social and the ecological in sustainable agriculture. *In* Allen, P., ed., Food for the future: conditions and contradictions of sustainability. Wiley & Sons, Inc., New York, NY, USA.

Allen, P.; Sachs, C. 1993. Sustainable agriculture in the United States: engagements, silences, and possibilities for transformation. *In* Allen, P., ed., Food for the future: conditions and contradictions of sustainability. Wiley & Sons, Inc., New York, NY, USA.

Beaudry, M. 1991. World hunger: let's dare to work towards a solution. Journal of the Canadian Dietetic Association, 52, 151–156.

Bourdieu, P.; Wacquant, L. 1992. The purpose of reflexive sociology (The Chicago Workshop). *In* Bourdieu, P.; Wacquant, L., ed., An invitation to reflexive sociology. University of Chicago Press, Chicago, IL, USA.

Buttel, F. 1993. The production of agricultural sustainability: observations from the sociology of science and technology. *In* Allen, P., ed., Food for the future: conditions and contradictions of sustainability. Wiley & Sons, Inc., New York, NY, USA.

Campbell, C.; Katamay, S.; Connolly, C. 1988. The role of the nutrition professional in the hunger debate. Journal of the Canadian Dietetic Association, 49, 230–235.

CCSD (Canadian Council on Social Development). 1993. An overview of Canadian social policy. CCSD, Ottawa, ON, Canada.

Clancy, K. 1993. Sustainable agriculture and domestic hunger: rethinking a link between production and consumption. *In* Allen, P., ed., Food for the future: conditions and contradictions of sustainability. Wiley & Sons, Inc., New York, NY, USA.

———— 1994. Social justice and sustainable agriculture: moving beyond theory [commentary]. Agriculture and Human Values, 11(4), 77–83.

Dahlberg, K. 1993. Regenerative food systems: broadening the scope and agenda of sustainability. *In* Allen, P., ed., Food for the future: conditions and contradictions of sustainability. Wiley & Sons, Inc., New York, NY, USA.

Davis, B.; Tarasuk, V. 1994. Hunger in Canada. Agriculture and Human Values, 11(4), 50–57.

Fisher, A,; Gottlieb, R. 1995. Community food security: policies for a more sustainable food system in the context of the 1995 Farm Bill and beyond. The Lewis Center for Regional Policy Studies, University of California, Los Angeles, CA, USA. Working Paper No. 5.

Frazer, E.; Lacey, N. 1993. The politics of community: a feminist critique of the liberal–communitarian debate. University of Toronto Press, Toronto, ON, Canada. 268 pp.

Freidmann, H. 1982. The political economy of food: the rise and fall of the postwar international food order. American Journal of Sociology, 88, 246–86.

———— 1993. After Midas' feast: alternative food regimes for the future. *In* Allen, P., ed., Food for the future: conditions and contradictions of sustainability. Wiley & Sons, Inc., New York, NY, USA.

Goodman, D.; Redclift, M. 1991. Refashioning nature: food, ecology, and culture. Routledge, London, UK. 279 pp.

Hobbs, K.; MacEachern, W.; McIvor, A.; Turner, S. 1993. Waste of a nation: poor people speak out about charity. Canadian Review of Social Policy, 31, 94–104.

Jolly, D. 1997. The dialectics of urban agriculture in the context of hunger and food access constraints. Paper presented at the International Conference on Sustainable Urban Food Systems, 22–25 May 1997, Ryerson Polytechnic University, Toronto, ON, Canada.

Laxer, J. 1996. In search of a new left: Canadian politics after the neo-conservative assault. Viking, Toronto, ON, Canada. 232 pp.

MacGregor, S. 1997. Feeding families in Harris' Ontario: women, the Tsubouchi diet, and the politics of restructuring. Atlantis, 21(2), 93–110.

Mingione, E. 1985. Social reproduction of the surplus labour force: the case of southern Italy. *In* Redclift, N.; Mingione, E., ed., Beyond employment: household, gender and subsistence. Basil Blackwell, New York, NY, USA.

Morris, D. 1996. Communities: building authority, responsibility, and capacity. *In* Mander, J.; Goldsmith, E., ed., The case against the global economy and for a turn toward the local. Sierra Club Books, San Francisco, CA, USA.

OPHAFSWG (Ontario Public Health Association Food Security Working Group). 1995. Food for now and the future: a food and nutrition strategy for Ontario. OPHAFSWG, Toronto, ON, Canada.

Redclift, N.; Mingione, E. 1985. Introduction. *In* Redclift, N.; Mingione, E., ed., Beyond employment: household, gender and subsistence. Basil Blackwell, New York, NY, USA.

Riches, G. 1986. Food banks and the welfare crisis. Canadian Council on Social Development, Ottawa, ON, Canada. 171 pp.

———— 1997a. Hunger and the welfare state: comparative perspectives. *In* Riches, G., ed., First World hunger: food security and welfare politics. Macmillan Press Ltd, London, UK.

———— 1997b. Hunger in Canada: abandoning the right to food. *In* Riches, G., ed., First World hunger: food security and welfare politics. Macmillan Press Ltd, London, UK.

Steedman, C. 1986. Landscape for a good woman: a story of two lives. Virago, London, UK. 168 pp.

Tarasuk, V.; Davis, B. 1996. Responses to food insecurity in the changing Canadian welfare state. Journal of Nutrition Education, 28, 71–75.

Tesh, S.N. 1988. Hidden arguments: political ideology and disease prevention policy. Rutgers University Press, New Brunswick, NJ, USA. 215 pp.

TFPC (Toronto Food Policy Council). 1994. Reducing urban hunger in Ontario: policy responses to support the transition from food charity to local food security. TFPC, Toronto, ON, Canada. Discussion Paper No. 1.

Torjman, S. 1997a. Civil society: reclaiming our humanity. Caledon Institute of Social Policy, Ottawa, ON, Canada.

——— 1997b. Cash poor, community rich. Caledon Institute of Social Policy, Ottawa, ON, Canada.

Winson, A. 1993. The intimate commodity: food and the development of the agro-industrial complex in Canada. Garamond Press, Toronto, ON, Canada. 243 pp.

PART 2

LOCAL FOOD SYSTEMS

...❦ ❦ ❦...

Promoting Sustainable Local Food Systems in the United States

Kenneth A. Dahlberg

Introduction

This discussion paper draws on experience with the Local Food Systems Project (LFSP), a three-year project funded by the W.K. Kellogg Foundation and administered by the Minnesota Food Association of Minneapolis, Minnesota.[1]

The LFSP chose six sites to receive technical assistance for developing or strengthening food-policy structures (policy councils, task forces, networks, etc.) within a larger framework of encouraging community and economic development.[2] Two technical-assistance workshops were held, in May 1995 and June 1996. The LFSP also developed resource materials to support these and other local efforts (MFA 1997). In 1998, we hope to publish the lessons learned from the project.

Although only one effort among many, the LFSP combined several important elements. First, it assumed a broad food-systems view.[3] Second, its general theoretical approach embraced political economy, community development, and structural issues (Dahlberg 1996). Third, the project team had had a variety of practical experience. We are convinced that the LFSP's focus — on planning, organizing, and policy development — would be central to the long-term success of both local food systems and community food-security work.

Local food systems in strategic perspective

A variety of groups seeking alternative approaches to food insecurity have shown an increasing and enthusiastic interest in local food-systems work. This approach is even gaining some recognition among more traditional groups (for example, conventional

---

[1] The project team included Kate Clancy, founding member of the Onondaga Food System Council (New York), who is now with the Wallace Institute for Alternative Agriculture; Kenneth Dahlberg, LFSP Director and a professor of political science at Western Michigan University; Jan O'Donnell, Executive Director of the Minnesota Food Association; and Robert Wilson, a chief architect of the Knoxville, Tennessee, Food Policy Council.

[2] The six sites were Los Angeles, CA; Berkshire County, MA; a nine-county planning region around Rochester, NY; Pittsburgh, PA; Austin, TX; and Moyers, WV.

[3] Basically, this means analyzing the interrelationships between levels of food system — household, neighbourhood, municipal, regional, etc. — in terms of their economic, social, health, power, access, equity, and symbolic dimensions, as well as in terms of food cycles: production (agriculture, farmland preservation, farmers' markets, household and community gardens, and small livestock), processing, distribution (transportation, warehousing), access (physical and economic barriers to food, availability of food stores, cafes, street food, and feeding programs), food use (health, nutrition, cooking, food preservation, food safety, and food handling), food recycling (gleaning, food banks, food pantries, and soup kitchens), and the waste stream (composting, garbage fed to animals, etc.).

agricultural groups; antihunger groups; and people in various academic disciplines). This raises the question whether these new local-food groups are becoming a movement. Although some (Gottlieb and Fisher 1996) think this (on the basis of the reform agendas of the groups involved), the project team has concluded (on the basis of the modest social and political support such groups enjoy) that they are not yet a movement.

This suggests that the many groups interested in food issues and food policy need to find common goals and harmonize their approaches. It is difficult to know how to develop and orchestrate a larger community effort, given the demands of modern organizational life. Yet, without a joint effort to build the theoretical, organizational, and political foundations of food-systems work, we risk being either co-opted by more traditional sectors or marginalized. The following is a broad outline of the requirements for such a larger cooperative effort.

Developing a vision

At the local level, it would be useful to conduct a visioning exercise among potential stakeholders to explore and clarify values and goals (see Hancock 1993) while getting them to think in systems terms about their local food system and its sustainability. It would also be useful to bring together representatives of the groups active in food-systems work around the country for similar visioning and goal-setting workshops. Any such workshop should be based on a federated, bottom-up vision that gives priority to local goals and needs as long as they are consistent with the requirements of sustainability at other levels.

Longer term theoretical needs

The general theoretical and empirical work on the structure and political economy of food systems should be expanded. Relatively little work done in this area has focused primarily on national and international issues, and the research would benefit from a multilevel analysis of local and regional issues. When the project team sought to do this, it learned of the great need for a practical theory. Such a theory would be aimed at helping local food-security practitioners to better understand their communities and the food needs of their communities and develop appropriate policies and programs to deal with them. Practical theories and concepts to guide organization and planning would also complement the many existing how-to manuals.

Key areas for a practical theory would be profiling, planning, organizing, and evaluation. Our resource guide (MFA 1997) provided readings and guidelines on the first three of these topics. The fourth, evaluation, was a most valuable tool for us. We used formative evaluation throughout to try to assess our progress and further objectives. In developing the final evaluation form for our six sites, we structured it to encourage the community workers to do some formative evaluation as they reviewed their progress and future goals.

At this stage, we especially realized how much we needed a practical framework or matrix to describe the key contextual parameters and organizational variables for the sites. It is hoped the following lists of these parameters and variables will benefit other groups and communities working on food planning and policy.

Key contextual parameters

1. *Scale* — One needs to find and show the area covered, plus its total population. These affect the prospects for intervention (distances to be traveled to meetings, numbers and types of people or organizations that need to be involved, etc.).

2. *Landscape patterns* — Any work with an urban–rural spectrum soon suggests that landscape patterns tell us very little about the patterns of people and land use important to local food systems. We need more useful descriptors and typologies.

3. *Population patterns* — These varied considerably between communities. Among the LFSP sites, Los Angeles and Pittsburgh were very concentrated; Austin was fairly concentrated; the Berkshires and West Virginia were very dispersed, and the New York site was dispersed but had one major population concentration. The question to ask in connection with this parameter is what types of organizing approach these variations suggest.

4. *Socioeconomic patterns* — These include the role and importance of the general economic structure of the community (whether it is diverse and to what degree it is autonomous), agriculture, various food enterprises, and social structures (patterns of race, class, poverty, etc.).

5. *Food organization patterns* — One needs to examine such patterns in both food-system and other food-related organizations in the community. One also needs to assess the linkages among them.

Key organizational variables

1. *Leadership* — It is helpful to work with more than one recognized community leader when dealing with food issues. When several leaders come from different sectors (public, private, nonprofit), they need to be aware of each other's orientations and work styles. Ideally, leaders can work together over a long enough time to develop collaborative leadership, where tasks can be rotated or delegated with relative ease.

2. *Work styles of groups* — These can be seen across three somewhat-overlapping spectrums. One of these goes from an emphasis on ad hoc responses to one on strategic planning; another shows the relative emphasis given to specific projects versus developing a process to pursue change; finally, the last ranges from a project emphasis to a policy or policy-development emphasis. Experience suggests that the more community workers pursue planning, process, and policy, the more effective they will be.

3. *Staff funding* — All observers agree that it is crucial to have funding for full- or part-time staff exclusively devoted to food-systems work. Without this, staff time tends to be consumed in dealing with other, more immediate issues of employment.

4. *Administrative approaches* — The administrative approaches of key staff (and their location) are important. In some cases, key staff are also key leaders. In others, they may be different people. Administrative questions include the degree of centralization and the types of delegation preferred. Relations between leaders and staff are of obvious importance.

Various combinations of these contextual parameters and organizational variables yield different results. With a set of matrices or a typology illustrating these, local communities would be in a much better position to identify their key issues, challenges, and opportunities.

The need for capacity-building

The need for capacity-building for the food-systems community emerges out of the generally increasing interest in food systems, sparked in part by the United States Department of Agriculture's *Community Food Security Act.* Six crucial elements are discussed below. The overarching challenge, however, is to find enough financial and organizational support to carry out this capacity-building.

- *Networking* — Few nonprofits have the resources to daily track the range of activities relevant to their interests. A web page dealing with food-systems issues would be most useful (keeping in mind that less affluent groups don't have web access), along with support for key people to attend regional, state, or national meetings.

- *Technical assistance* — Whereas a web page might offer some technical assistance, a national or a set of regional hotlines would be useful to answer questions on local food systems and policy. One model for this is ATTRA (Appropriate Technology Transfer for Rural Areas). A more modest approach would be to develop directories or databases listing the experts on various topics.

- *Leadership training* — Leadership training should be recognized as both a key next step and part of longer term capacity-building, including systems thinking and practical skills in planning, organization, and policy development.

- *Ongoing strategic evaluation* — One or more groups should monitor the many current programs and experiments to develop summary descriptions. These should be regularly analyzed for lessons learned. Both the summaries and the lessons learned should be disseminated in print or electronic forms or both. This would require not only financial support but also a group of analysts with both theoretical and practical knowledge.

- *Research on a practical theory* — Nonprofits in diverse regions could do such research, but they would need staff and more general organizational support. Regional centres would be in a good position to seek interns and graduate-student assistants from area academic institutions.

- *Longer term research on food systems* — The two most likely locations for longer term theoretical and empirical research are academic institutions and think tanks. They each have a great deal to offer if a critical mass of knowledge can be established and the problems of disciplinary specialization (academia) and shorter term policy focus (think tanks) can be avoided.

Conclusions

Meeting the larger challenge of finding financial support for capacity-building ultimately requires the diverse groups involved in food-systems work to establish a community of interest. Separately and jointly they need to consciously think about how to strengthen the capacities of the community, particularly in terms of building common organizational infrastructures and capacity-building programs. Only as a community, with a strategic vision and new organizations and common programs, will we make progress toward more equitable, sustainable, and democratic food systems.

References

Dahlberg, K.A. 1996. World food problems: making the transition from agriculture to regenerative food systems. *In* Pirages, D., ed., Building sustainable societies. M.E. Sharpe, Armonk, NY, USA. pp. 257–274.

Gottlieb, R.; Fisher, A. 1996. Community food security and environmental justice: searching for a common discourse. Agriculture and Human Values, 3(3), 23–32.

Hancock, T. 1993. How to facilitate a vision workshop. Healthcare Forum Journal, 36(3), 33–34.

MFA (Minnesota Food Association). 1997. Strategies, policy approaches, and resources for local food system planning and organizing. MFA, Minneapolis, MN, USA. 378 pp.

Community Agriculture Initiatives in the Metropolitan Borough of Sandwell, United Kingdom

Laura Davis, John Middleton, and Sue Simpson

Introduction

In agriculture, as in everything else, associated labour is the only reasonable solution. In such a case they would probably first of all associate for permanently improving the land which is in need of immediate improvement, and would consider it necessary to improve more of it every year, until they had brought it all into perfect condition. ... The labour that would be required for such an intensive culture would not be the hard labour of the serf or slave, it would be accessible to everyone, strong or weak, town bred or country born; it would have many other charms besides. ... From the technical point of view, there is no obstacle whatever for such an organisation being started tomorrow with full success. The obstacles against it are not in the imperfection of the agricultural art, or in the infertility of the soil, or in climate. They are entirely in our institutions, in our inheritances and survivals from the past — in the "Ghosts" which oppress us.

— Peter Kropotkin (1974 [1899])

In 1899, in his book *Fields, Factories and Workshops Tomorrow*, Peter Kropotkin estimated that intensive biological horticulture could supply about 40 households from each acre of land under cultivation (Kropotkin 1974 [1899]). Today, in the United Kingdom, many organic producers on small land holdings, operating rural and peri-urban direct food link (DFL) schemes, are achieving these levels of output; providing stable, feasible lifestyles for producers; and creating local training and employment. As John Middleton (in Middleton et al. 1996) remarked, "Sandwell as the garden of England is a bit far fetched, but it is not impossible for Sandwell to increase the food we can supply to ourselves."

Regenerating Health: A Challenge or a Lottery, the 8th annual report of the director of public health for the Borough of Sandwell (Middleton et al. 1996), recognized that the idea of urban areas growing more of their own food has recently been gathering pace. Allotments of course are not new. But in Sandwell, people are using available allotments, gardens, big and small derelict plots, and other urban land spaces to grow food for consumption by the growers themselves, the local market, and more distant markets (Middleton et al. 1996).

This paper explores the issues raised in a 1996 study of the practical, legislative, and economic feasibility of community agriculture. The study focused on general issues of health and sustainability and economic inequality and how to tackle these at a local level. It asked why Sandwell is the kind of place to try to tackle them and explored the potential role of community agriculture and DFL schemes if they were integrated with existing initiatives in community development. This paper explores problems and the ways forward.

Creating a healthier local economy

Many of the principles of sustainable development policy are also found in the World Health Organization's (WHO's) Health for All by the Year 2000 strategy (WHO 1978), for example, equity, democracy, participation, and multiagency and international cooperation. Underlying these principles is the need to seek local solutions in partnership with local communities and to seek environmental solutions to problems associated with social services, crime prevention, health and safety, and economic development.

The United Kingdom's public-health tradition has sought to protect its own people (one can argue its wealthier classes, particularly) from physical, chemical, and climatic risks, to meet their essential biological needs, supply food, water, and clean air, and prevent contamination from harmful wastes. However, in the United Kingdom, it is still possible to dispose of waste under water or soil, flush it away, or deposit it in someone else's back yard. The targets for the European region (developed as part of WHO's Health for All by the Year 2000 strategy) (WHOEURO 1985), and even the environmental charter (WHOEURO 1989), largely reinforce the view that a public-health policy exists to protect Europeans from the by-products of their way of life. This approach to public health, however, clearly fails to comprehend the interactions among human, animal, and environmental health. Unless these are taken into account, the sustainability of some ecosystems may be compromised through short-sighted pursuit of human health.

The Acheson report, "Public Health in England" (DOH 1988), rediscovered the definition of public health as "the science and art of the prevention of disease, the prolongation of life and the promotion of health through the organised efforts of society." According to Sandwell's director of public health, the report brought public health back into the mainstream of health-service planning and development (Middleton 1995b). People working in health-promotional activities in Sandwell see the local economy as currently a powerful force for poor health but as potentially a force for good health (Middleton 1995a).

Why Sandwell?

The Metropolitan Borough of Sandwell was formed in 1974 through the amalgamation of the county boroughs of West Bromwich and Warley in the West Midlands. Birmingham forms its eastern border. Sandwell has a population of about 300 000 and has the seventh-largest housing authority outside London. Sandwell's history dates back to the Industrial Revolution. In the past and, to a lesser extent, in the present, it has depended on heavy industry — foundries, metal working, chemicals, limestone, and steel. Its landscape is postindustrial, with the remains of its heavy industry and much industrial dereliction. Its local wards are joined (or fragmented) by arterial roads.

Submissions by the Inner Area Programme Team of Sandwell Metropolitan Borough Council (SMBC 1987/88–1989/90) revealed a not-very-encouraging economic-health diagnosis. The reports highlight problems such as

- High unemployment, particularly long-term joblessness;

- Low levels of job creation;

- Industrial contraction;

- A narrow economic base, with a lack of diversity in industry;

- A low proportion of people working in the service sector;

- A poor image (from the perspective of industrialists, visitors, and tourists);

- Extensive derelict land and an industrial-land shortage, with much of the land being difficult to reclaim because of chemical contamination and old limestone workings;

- A mismatch of workforce skills, requiring extensive retraining programs;

- Poor educational performance;

- Obsolete transport networks;

- Poor housing in public and private sectors; and

- Limited financial resources to tackle these problems.

The public-health diagnosis, set out in the annual reports of Sandwell Health Authority, described patterns of physical, social, and mental illness in the borough. The borough falls in the top 15% of health districts in the United Kingdom for houses lacking a basic amenity, overcrowded housing, unemployment, and ethnic-minority population. In 1988, more than half of the people in Sandwell were living in low-income households (Middleton 1990). Sandwell's disease indicators reflect the poor health associated with high levels of poverty and deprivation (Townsend and Davidson 1982; Whitehead 1987). Perinatal and infant death rates are above regional and national levels. Standardized mortality ratios are above the national standards for all ages.

Such reports demonstrate the extent to which the public-health diagnosis reflects the economic-health diagnosis and show how the Public Health Department is attempting to describe the causes of poor health in the methods and relations of production, the goods produced, and people's environmental and social circumstances. Sandwell and the surrounding Black County present a legacy of more than 200 years of unsustainable development, Middleton wrote (1996), and now face the consequences of industrialization going back to the start of the industrial revolution, compounded by postwar town planning and modernization, which seemed immune to community participation. Economic forces are powerful determinants of health and disease. Sandwell is a clear example of the reality that, at a local level, inequalities in health are an economic problem, not a health-service problem.

In response to the local Agenda 21 (UNCED 1992) and Health of the Nation targets (set out in a Department of Health White Paper [DOH 1992]), the Sandwell Regeneration Partnership (SRP) was formed with central-government single regeneration-budget funding.[1] Its role was to coordinate urban-regeneration strategy for Sandwell. It is clear that the regeneration policy affects health and that health services can improve regeneration. Community agriculture may have an important role to play in this regeneration policy and the SRP's regeneration strategy.

[1] A number of organizations and agencies arose from central-government regional-planning and regional-assistance policy instruments, beginning with the Urban Programme of the 1960s and continuing through the 1977 Inner Cities White Paper to the emergence (in the late 1970s) of a more explicit policy, one that involved expanded resources, specific (if modest) legislation, and new arrangements intended to bring about collaborative work between central and local governments. However, in the 1980s and early 1990s, funding for inner-city-regeneration programs actually declined. The new organizations came into being in the 1980s as a result of a policy to phase out the "traditional" Urban Programme.

DFL schemes

To transform ideas about community agriculture into achievable goals and practical applications, one needs to learn from examples. Initiatives such as city farms, community allotments, local-exchange and -trading systems, food cooperatives, and DFL schemes are emerging models of community development and economic diversification rooted in a bottom-up approach. These initiatives seek local environmental and social solutions to the health and economic problems of communities.

During the late 1980s, frustrated by the limitations of wholesale- and multiple-marketing routes and encouraged by news about community-supported agriculture from Europe, Japan, and the United States (Pullen 1992), a small number of organic growers in the United Kingdom began to develop what were first known as "box schemes" and what are increasingly coming to be known as DFL schemes (Steele 1995). Fruit and vegetables are produced in intensive organic (or biological) systems; typically, 30–50 crop varieties are grown each season. Produce is distributed to individual households in rural and urban areas in a variety of ways: by door-to-door deliveries or through small food cooperatives.

The producer can supply a known group of customers with seasonal vegetables and fruit in a planned system of production. As DFL schemes are based on local production for local needs, overhead costs — particularly for packaging, transport, and distribution — can be significantly reduced. This gives greater security to the producer and creates new employment and training opportunities for new entrants into this business. Profitability is improved by the simple act of cutting out the middleperson. All sales income goes directly to the producer, which enables the producer to supply fairly priced, safe fruit and vegetables.

DFL schemes develop a relationship of trust and cooperation between producers and consumers and address issues of food production, processing, distribution, consumption, and disposal (through the development of community composting schemes). Some producers are actively developing a critique of the global food system and seek to demonstrate the feasibility of local alternatives. DFL schemes can address issues not only in the forces of production and consumption but also in their relations, which are of critical importance in developing descriptions of, and predictions for, a postindustrial society (Williams 1983).

Clearly, the success of DFL schemes in rural and peri-urban areas and the expertise they help to develop in production, organization, and management can be adapted and transferred to a variety of urban situations to meet a wide range of social, environmental, and health objectives. This knowledge and expertise informed the feasibility study that led Sandwell to develop community agriculture.

The feasibility study: process and outcomes

The aim of the consultancy was to help the SRP establish whether community agriculture would be practically, legislatively, and economically feasible in the Borough of Sandwell and benefit local people. The hope was ultimately to see a patchwork quilt of land parcels cultivated by and for the community.

The process began with a consultation meeting with participants from SMBC, Sandwell Health Authority, and a range of community and voluntary organizations, including special-needs, mental-health, and disability groups, community- and women's-enterprise groups, conservation organizations, and the Sandwell Food Co-operative. The consultancy team was surprised and encouraged by the response.

The report prepared following the consultations (Booth et al. 1996) proposed a range of projects, some of which were pilots for the areas identified, plus some complementary or supporting activities (three of these are explored below). These projects included

- The Tipton Market Garden, in which the Sandwell Food Co-operative would produce high-value crops for distribution through its existing networks;

- The Woodentops–Sandwell New Horizons Garden Project, a nursery centre with emphasis on quality of life through the provision of care or work-related training, or both, for people with special needs or mental-health problems;

- The Sandwell Grow Your Own scheme, which proposed the creation of a post for a support or extension worker in the borough; and

- The Friends of Sandwell scheme, creating links between Sandwell residents and local farmers and growers in the region to supply staple produce and develop training links.

Two of these projects were under way after the completion of the study. The Tipton Market Garden group negotiated a lease on a derelict allotment site and has been clearing and preparing the site for food production, with the assistance of the British Trust for Conservation Volunteers. The National Schizophrenia Fellowship (NSF) Woodentops project has also been converting an abandoned allotment site into a community garden for people with mental-health problems, which will operate alongside a range of other services. A third project, not included in the study, has been under discussion. Rowley Regis College of Further Education, which has a large area (about 5 ha) for sports and leisure, has been considering proposals for a project with strong educational links through the college curriculum and with a local housing estate via the tenants' and residents' association.

As a result of the final meeting during the study, a Community Agriculture Steering Group was formed. The borough's Food Policy Advisor coordinates it. This group is responsible for realizing the aims of the SRP.

Making progress: problems and the way forward

To coordinate the patchwork of community agriculture projects in Sandwell, the SRP would need a thorough appraisal of Sandwell's physical and human strengths and weaknesses. Many of these lie in its industrial base (Middleton 1990). The signs from within the local authority, especially the health authority, are encouraging. A process of discussion has developed political support for the idea of community agriculture, and some funding is being made available. The local authority sees its role as an enabling rather than controlling one. Clearly, further research and reflection on progress and problems would be required to identify the real obstacles to development.

The local authority and the private and voluntary sectors would need to take a coordinated approach to issues of infrastructure, such as patterns of land distribution and ownership in the borough, access to land, planning requirements, and legal constraints. Conflicts will inevitably arise over priorities for land use, and their resolution will determine opportunities for individual projects and their success or failure. Leases must be negotiated, and these will need to be of long enough duration to establish feasible projects, an outcome that may take several years and considerable investments in labour and finance.

Without suitable equipment for undertaking fallowing cultivations, the reclamation of derelict land is difficult, especially that of small land parcels. Infestation of derelict land by annual and perennial weed species is likely to be a significant obstacle, especially if groups adopt organic systems, which exclude the use of herbicides.

A fourth potential project has run into the problem of heavy-metal contamination of land, from its proximity to metal foundries. The report identified the possible health risks associated with growing food on contaminated land. Clearly, no food production can take place until the risks are quantified and understood.

One of the most critical aspects will be the provision of information, training, and support for participants in community agriculture schemes. People in these schemes need to develop and be supported in the skills of production, organization, finance, and management. People in the community already have many of these skills, such as the gardeners, the allotment holders, and the people in various community-enterprise initiatives.

Funding must be found and maintained to cover startup costs for all projects and to cover key staff and operating costs for projects that focus on social-service more than production objectives. In an urban situation, the cultivation of small land parcels will often incur significant startup costs but lacks the potential to achieve economies of scale. In these cases, voluntary labour will be a principal aspect of the successful operation of community agriculture schemes. Site security will be a significant additional startup cost in many cases, as it is can be anticipated that, at least until a site has a role and identity in a community, theft and vandalism will present a major challenge.

In March 1997, the Community Agriculture Steering Group circulated a project proposal among various groups, along with executives within SMBC. The proposal sets out the vision for a community agriculture network, based on the feasibility study and subsequent meetings and initiatives in the local authority, health authority, and voluntary sector. The steering group is considering potential sources of funding to recruit a full-time peripatetic worker and part-time technical officer with expertise in planning, legal, and transfer issues. Their role would be to develop the network in Sandwell and offer expertise and guidance to projects. The steering group also hopes to eventually establish a Sandwell Community Agriculture Support Team (Simpson 1997).

Initially, this team would provide technical support to flagship projects, such as the Tipton Market Garden and NSF Woodentops project and work to bring new projects into the patchwork. The team would also explore prospects for obtaining European funding and develop bids when appropriate opportunities arise to ensure the future of the project. Good progress has been made in raising the initial funds, with a significant contribution from the health authority.

Conclusions

Although it is still far too early to claim that community agriculture is a feasible option for Sandwell, much progress has been made in laying the foundations for achieving the objectives set out by the SRP in its original brief to the consultancy team.

Experience has so far suggested that community agriculture can make an important contribution to understanding that environmental regeneration is the key to improving the local economy and the health of Sandwell's population (Middleton 1990). But community agriculture is not an alternative to tackling the structural causes of poverty and poor health. Effective intervention in the government, public, and private–public spheres will be essential. Of course, benefit levels must rise. We have tried exhorting people to eat more healthily and found that it's actually more complicated than that. Poor families are eating high-fat diets as a matter of basic survival. They don't have enough money, or they don't have access to good fresh food in large enough quantities. Some redistribution of resources must occur (Middleton 1996).

However, if agriculture by and for the community is integrated with existing initiatives within the local authority and community in Sandwell, it may contribute to an emerging development model for local food production, processing, distribution, consumption, and disposal, as well as delivering a range of health, social, educational, environmental, community-development, and economic benefits in a postindustrial, urban society.

As Peter Kropotkin remarked in 1899, the obstacles to the success of an endeavour such as community agriculture in Sandwell are not the imperfection of the agricultural art, the infertility of the soil, or the poor climate but our institutions, inheritances, and survivals from the past — the ghosts that oppress us. Sandwell's economic, health, and social problems are firmly rooted in its industrial past, in the forces and relations of production that have shaped its landscape and society. Sandwell's being the "garden of England" is, indeed, a bit far-fetched, but it is clearly not impossible if Sandwell receives strategic support to increase the food it can supply to itself through community agriculture. Progress on this path can make a positive contribution to sustainable development in cities.

References

Booth, E.; Davis, L.; Michaud, M.; Redman, M. 1996. Community agriculture in Sandwell: a feasibility study. Report to the Sandwell Regeneration Partnership. West Bromwich, UK.

DOH (Department of Health). 1988. Public health in England [Acheson report]. Her Majesty's Stationery Office, London, UK.

———— 1992. The health of the nation. Her Majesty's Stationery Office, London, UK. Government White Paper.

Draper, P., ed. 1991. Health through public policy. Merlin, London, UK.

Kropotkin, P. 1974 [1899]. Fields, factories and workshops tomorrow. Allen and Unwin, London, UK.

Middleton, J. 1990. Life and death in Sandwell: where public health and economic health meet. Local Government Policy Making, 16(4).

———— 1995a. Sandwell's experiences researching a healthier local economy. Sandwell Health Authority, West Bromwich, UK.

———— 1995b. Public health and sustainability. Paper presented at the Royal Institute of Public Health and Hygiene Conference on Sustainability and Public Health, 8 Feb 1995, London, UK.

———— 1996. Bad food trap. The Observer, 21 Jan.

Middleton, J., et al. 1996. Regenerating health: a challenge or a lottery. 8th annual report of the Director of Public Health. Sandwell Health Authority, West Bromwich, UK.

Pullen, M. 1992. Farms of tomorrow: community supported agriculture linking farmers and consumers. Living Earth [the journal of the Soil Association, Bristol, UK], May.

Simpson, S. 1997. Community agriculture Sandwell: project proposal. Sandwell Metropolitan Borough Council and Sandwell Health Authority, West Bromwich, UK.

SMBC (Sandwell Metropolitan Borough Council). 1987/88–89/90. Inner Area Programme Team reports. SMBC, Sandwell, UK.

Steele, J. 1995. Local food links: new ways of getting organic food from farm to table. Soil Association, Bristol, UK.

Townsend, P.; Davidson, N. 1982. Inequalities in health: the Black report. Penguin, Harmondsworth, UK.

UNCED (United Nations Conference on Environment and Development). 1992. Rio declaration on environment and development and Agenda 21. UNCED, Geneva, Switzerland.

Whitehead, M. 1987. The health divide: inequalities in health in the 1980s. Health Education Council, London, UK.

WHO (World Health Organization). 1978. Health for all by the year 2000. Report of the International Conference on Primary Care (Alma Ata declaration). WHO, Geneva, Switzerland.

WHOEURO (WHO European Regional Office). 1985. Targets in support of health for all by 2000 in the European region. WHOEURO, Copenhagen, Denmark.

———— 1989. European Charter on Environment and Health. WHOEURO, Copenhagen, Denmark.

Williams, R. 1983. Towards 2000. Chatto and Windus, London, UK.

...❧ ❧ ❧...

Developing an Integrated, Sustainable Urban Food System: The Case of New Jersey, United States

Michael W. Hamm and Monique Baron

Introduction

Establishing more localized food systems, with the aim of achieving social-justice goals, is an important strategy for developing sustainable urban food systems. As individuals and organizations throughout the world try to develop such food systems, it is useful to consider their context and philosophical background. This paper briefly describes the global context, the precepts for action, the components of such a system, and a case study.

Global context

Globally, a number of environmental reasons support food production in closer proximity to the consumer. Also, patterns throughout the world suggest the need for regions to locally maintain and enhance their food-production capacities. The world is confronting the likely prospect of major food-related crises in the next 20 years. In addition, competition in the world food market will increase as developing countries increase their industrial base and developed countries experience a decline in farmland and in the number of farmers. Many developing countries, such as China, are undergoing various degrees of industrialization. The arable land base declines as it is used for industrial sites and housing and infrastructure, as well as increased meat production. Given China's projected population growth for the next 25 years, it may have to import more grain than all the world exported in 1990 (Brown 1995).

Developed countries have experienced a decline in the farming base. For example, Japan produces about 47% of its calories and imports the rest. In 1960, Japan had about 11.75 million farms, and in 1992, this number had decreased to 3.13 million. By 2000, one-third of Japanese farmers will be older than 65 (Mikishi Okada Association, personal communication, 1996[1]). Water is becoming increasingly scarce. A number of countries throughout the world experience water shortages, with 26 classified as water scarce (Nicholas 1994). Significant increases in urban agriculture might temper food instability (UNDP 1996), but the potential for increased global food insecurity implies that states, regions, and nations should maximize their local food production as a general strategy for stabilizing world food resources.

---

[1] Mikishi Okada Association, Ohito, Japan, personal communication, 1996.

Precepts for action

Within this worldwide context, the need for sustainable urban food systems is apparent. In the authors' opinion, it is necessary to develop these systems on the basis of the following precepts:

- An exclusively local food supply would be isolating, necessitate cultural denial, and be potentially unstable;

- Sustainable food systems will develop within the current social, political, and economic framework;

- Development of sustainable communities with sustainable food systems begins with the concept that people have value and that the production of life's necessities has value; and

- People have an inherent interest in having food produced locally.

These precepts helped to form a philosophical basis for the case study.

Components of a sustainable urban food system

To create a more localized food system, one must include several components: production, transportation, processing, distribution, preparation, waste management, and resource inputs. Resource inputs occur at all levels of the food system. In addition, a sustainable food system would

- Incorporate social-justice issues into a more localized system;

- Alleviate constraints on people's access to adequate, nutritious food;

- Develop the economic capacity of local people to purchase food;

- Train people to grow, process, and distribute this food;

- Maintain adequate land to produce a high proportion of locally required food;

- Educate people, who have been increasingly removed from food production, to participate in, and respect, its generation; and

- Integrate environmental stewardship into this process.

These components define a broad framework for examining approaches to creating food security, encompassing the entire food system — from field to fork.

Case study

A number of groups and individuals are creating food systems that are more responsive to social and cultural concerns and more connected to the local area than is usually the case. We attempted to incorporate the ideas outlined above in our work in New Jersey, United States — a state with 7.8 million people on 7 800 square miles of land

(1 square mile = 2.59 km²). Since 1950 New Jersey has lost 51% of its farmland (NJDA 1995) and is expected to lose an additional 12% over the next 20 years (ECAFE 1994). An estimated 600 000 people or more are at risk of hunger (WWFI 1989), and 19% of New Jersey's 567 municipalities have been classified as high-unemployment areas (Schevtchuk, personal communication, 1997[2]).

We estimated that to feed 100 people in New Jersey, a complete vegetarian diet for 1 year requires about 23.5 acres of land (1 acre = 0.4 ha) (McGlinchy and Hamm 1996). This translates into 1.83 million acres for the entire population. The meat-based diet of the typical American increases this to about 41 acres. New Jersey currently produces about 27% of the population's required vegetable servings. Producing the additional 63% would require about 115 000 additional acres planted in vegetables, 6.8 million gardens of 100 square feet (1 square foot = 929 cm²), or a balance between the two. Large increases in community and individually owned gardens may be a way to increase local food production. Increasing the amount of local, farm-based fruit and vegetable production would create opportunities to develop rural–urban linkages through pick-your-own harvesting and other initiatives (for example, farmstands).

A major question is who will grow the food. In New Jersey, the average food-producing farmer is older than the average nonfood-producing farmer. The primary mechanism of increasing the farming population will be to grow more farmers. This is particularly important — as Wes Jackson said, a "greater eyes to land ratio" is needed for ecological, sustainable agriculture (Jackson, personal communication, 1992[3]). To develop a strategy to tackle this issue, the Cook Student Organic Farm (CSOF) program was created in 1993. The CSOF's primary objective was to provide interested college students with organic-farming experience within the larger framework of their academic programs. The CSOF also provides an avenue for students to develop an understanding of urban food problems in New Jersey.

The CSOF operates on the model of community-supported agriculture (CSA). The CSOF also devotes a large amount of the produce to the local soup kitchen and food bank. Crops are grown on 3 acres according to the standards set by the Northeast Organic Farming Association of New Jersey for organic certification. Proceeds from CSA finance the operation of the farm and provide about 22 000 United States dollars (USD) for student internships. The students have academic majors ranging from English literature to natural-resource management, and none were raised on a farm. They are predominantly women of urban or suburban background. Each year, several students become interested in pursuing careers related to sustainable food production, with some altering their original career goals. Others see themselves producing their own food as part of their livelihood. The coupling of this experience with several courses at college allows a cadre of students to explore options in food production. With additional strategies to expand hands-on training, create land access, and develop financial resources, a program like the CSOF might be used to increase the farming population.

Another consideration is the production of food for emergency assistance. As the national and international food companies decrease waste and unwanted production, food banks in New Jersey have experienced a decline in food donations. Ideally, food banks would be unnecessary; however, they are unlikely to be abandoned in the near future. Community farms financed for the public good are potential avenues for partially solving such supply problems at the local level. A number of programs in New

[2] Kimberly Schevtchuk, Mercer Street Friends, Trenton, NJ, USA, personal communication, 1997.
[3] Wes Jackson, The Land Institute, Salina, KS, USA, personal communication, 1992.

Jersey are oriented to expanding urban gardening as a way to increase and sustain local food production. However, urban production should not be oversold as a panacea for declining social programs.

Production is only one component. Marketing to bring the farmers' produce to the urban population would also be essential. Farmers' markets or community-run farmers' markets (in which local residents run a farmstand, selling several farmers' goods) are vehicles to improve the economic sustainability of local fresh food while increasing urban access to it. Community-run farmers' markets are also a mechanism for seasonal job creation.

For these reasons, we established the New Jersey Urban Ecology Program (NJUEP). In 1993, NJUEP established three community gardening and nutrition projects. Through the summer of 1993, it became obvious that programs specifically targeted to youth were necessary and desirable. Therefore, in 1994, we developed the Youth Farmstand Project to provide at-risk youth with job training through the experience of owning and operating a retail farmstand business. Program objectives included

- Bridging the gap between rural and urban communities by creating city markets for farm produce and racial understanding and economic partnership between these diverse communities;

- Helping high-school students by giving them hands-on job training and education to improve their future employment opportunities; and

- Establishing a long-term, local source of fresh, affordable, and nutritious food for the community.

The NJUEP was initiated in New Brunswick, New Jersey, and it subsequently coordinated the development of youth farmstand projects in seven New Jersey cities during 1997. Students were trained to establish and manage several farmstands in their local communities, to purchase wholesale fruits and vegetables from local farmers, and to retail this fresh produce at affordable prices.

New Jersey has a 5-month growing season and therefore a substantial need for food preservation. Food can be preserved in local, community-run, small-scale processing ventures. These would have the effect of increasing markets for farmers, creating jobs in the local area, and preparing food products for off-season use. Creating small-scale, microenterprises of this sort in urban areas would stimulate food production in outlying farm belts by providing an opportunity for farmers to increase the economic sustainability of their operations; at the same time, it would provide jobs for urban residents. Such entrepreneurial activities, which are prerequisites for sustainable food systems, must be developed in a way that ensures that economic multiplier effects occur within the community.

Sustainable, urban food systems inherently enhance local ecosystems and come with a guarantee that all residents have the opportunity to benefit from them. However, many urban youth are denied access to educational or practical experience in growing food, as well as being denied an appreciation of local ecosystems. It is particularly important that educational programs enhance career opportunities in sustainable food systems and provide an understanding of the local ecology. The NJUEP has worked to develop such programs, including the Children's Gardening and Environmental Education Program (CGEEP) and the School Yard Ecology Program (SYEP).

The CGEEP establishes safe, structured, and supervised gardens for urban youngsters aged 5–12 years. The CGEEP provides other advantages:

- The children develop their gardening skills, creative-arts abilities, cultural awareness, and a knowledge of ecological concepts and nutritional information;

- The program provides an avenue for these youngsters to develop an understanding of the biosphere within the framework of New Jersey's natural and cultural history; and

- It improves literacy-and-communication, problem-solving, and social skills.

The interdisciplinary educational curriculum of this hands-on program encompasses horticulture, ecology, nutrition, language arts, crafts, and heritage storytelling. Gardening makes children develop a positive relationship to the natural world. The children use traditional planting systems to grow a diversity of fruits and vegetables and culturally significant crops. Examples of the latter that are easily grown in a children's garden include sweet potato and collard greens (traditional Southern foods) and corn, beans, and squash (Native American foods). The children create a garden beneficial to insects and butterflies and also leave a natural space uncultivated to encourage wildlife and to beautify the area.

SYEP integrates the themes of food, ecology, and the community and enhances learning for students through a diversity of educational approaches. This program has extensive benefits for children, school faculty, and the nearby communities:

- Schools and their grounds provide abundant opportunities for experiential learning, community building, and environmental rehabilitation;

- Students are actively involved in school site inventories and detailed habitat studies; and

- Learned skills are applied through the creation of an outdoor classroom.

The program establishes a living example of a developing ecosystem for experiential education.

These and other initiatives link up the themes of urban economic development, rural–urban connections, hands-on education, and environmental stewardship.

Conclusions

If food security means access to nutritious, affordable, safe, adequate, and culturally acceptable food on a daily basis and is to be a right, rather than a privilege, for ourselves and for future generations, then the broadest cross-section of our communities must meaningfully participate in efforts to ensure it. This creates beneficial relationships and opportunities for all members of the community, through improved health, social relations, education, and quality of life, and ensures collaboration among the widest range of people, institutions, and organizations.

References

Brown, L.R. 1995. Who will feed China? Wake-up call for a small planet. W.W. Norton & Co., New York, NY, USA. 163 pp.

ECAFE (Ecopolicy Center for Agriculture, Food and the Environment). 1994. Into the 21st century: strategic planning for New Jersey's agriculture future — a staff report to the New Jersey FARMS Commission. New Jersey Agricultural Experiment Station, NJ, USA.

McGlinchy, M.; Hamm, M.W. 1996. Local production of food needs for a hundred people: a strategy for food security. Paper presented at the Agriculture, Food, and Human Values annual meeting, 1996, St Louis, MO, USA.

Nicholas, R. 1994. US National Committee for World Food Day teleconference and study/action packet. US National Committee for World Food Day, Washington, DC, USA.

NJDA (New Jersey Department of Agriculture). 1995. New Jersey agriculture 1995. NJDA, Trenton, NJ, USA. NJDA Circular No. 540.

UNDP (United Nations Development Programme). 1996. Urban agriculture: food, jobs, and sustainable cities. UNDP, New York, NY, USA.

WWFI (WorldWorks Foundation, Inc.). 1989. Tending the garden state: ending hunger and homeless-ness in New Jersey. WWFI, Bridgewater, NJ, USA.

...❦ ❦ ❦...

Public Policy and the Transition to Locally Based Food Networks

Ellie Perkins

Introduction

Locally based food production and distribution systems are important for a number of reasons: they reduce fossil-fuel use in food trade and transportation, undercut monocultures and increase biodiversity, promote organic agriculture by keeping the side effects of food production close to home, protect and create jobs in agriculture and food processing, and encourage cultural variation based on local food preferences and ecological differences. Locally based food networks are a vital and fundamental part of any local economy.

This paper explores the topic of food networks from a local-economy point of view and provides some examples of institutions and policies that foster them.

Food and local economies

A local economy essentially supplies the basic needs of a local community — so it is appropriate to begin by discussing food. Besides being physiologically vital, food provides a down-to-earth way of measuring the localness of an economy: the extent to which people eat local food shows the degree of their economy's dependence on distant markets. A recent study in Germany found that the ingredients of a container of yogurt (including the milk, the strawberries, and the cardboard and ink for the container) moved more than 11 000 km before reaching the consumer but could easily have been produced within 80 km of the consumer (Norberg-Hodge 1994). Because all this transport depends on fossil fuel, which is in limited supply, rising transport prices will make food production and distribution systems more locally focused in years to come. And this is closely tied to other social and economic changes that reinforce and echo each other.

The farmland around Toronto in Southern Ontario, Canada, is some of the richest in the country, yet a large proportion of the food consumed in Toronto is now imported from other countries. A century ago, nearly all of the food in Toronto was produced close to or in the city. This is reassuring — it means that the Toronto area still has great potential to be self-sufficient in food. It also points to the importance of preserving Toronto's cushion of food autonomy by protecting farmland reserves near the city and encouraging food production within the urban area itself. If Toronto devoted its green spaces, backyards, and rooftop gardens to food production, it would be able to supply even more of its food needs (see Guberman 1995).

What other changes does this way of looking at food supply entail? Small-scale food-processing and -preserving plants would arise to meet local demand. These would have space to use in abandoned industrial buildings and would create a number of seasonal and some year-round jobs. Greenhouses would be built to stretch the local growing season, along with indoor production facilities for winter produce like mushrooms, endive, bean sprouts, and other vegetables. People would consume more in-season produce in summer and more root vegetables and storable produce in winter. Dairy and poultry decentralization would also shorten the distances between producer and consumer. Individual households might need to spend more time on food production, processing, and preparation, or this could be done communally. These food-related changes would create jobs for people with the needed skills, from canning to baking to child care. This sort of small-scale job creation, using locally available raw materials, requires relatively little outside capital or start-up expertise, beyond the interpersonal and specific job skills involved. But people would need to learn and transmit these job skills, which again would also happen locally.

Locally produced vegetables, poultry and dairy products, and processed foods like bread, tomato sauce, pickles, salad dressing, baked goods, and margarine might cost up to twice their mass-production prices if produced in Canada's climate in smaller plants, employing local people at fair wages. But the cost of fossil fuel needed to transport food from far-away fields is increasing food prices in any case, as are the costs (including environmental remediation costs) of fertilizers and machines in high-tech agricultural production. As fuel prices rise, a largely local food system begins to look like a competitive alternative. Food costs might increase as a proportion of people's total expenditure. But local food production would also employ more people, which would have many positive multiplier effects for the whole community. With a "green" local food-production system, the community would probably also have fewer health-care and environmental costs to pay.

A locally focused food-supply system is already growing in Toronto and in many other cities around the world (Guberman 1995). It includes alternative new approaches to food distribution via organizations like FoodShare, as well as several programs for community-shared agriculture (COMSA) and food-producing rooftop gardens. COMSA allows farmers to link up with nearby consumers at the beginning of the growing season. Farmers get the financial support they need at planting time, consumers get an assured source of good-quality food, and production-related risks are shared between them. At least five COMSA farms are now operating in the Toronto area. Rooftop gardens can mean much more than an urban food supply — they improve the appearance of buildings and help to insulate them, absorb carbon dioxide and other pollutants, and reduce stormwater runoff, among other benefits. They also provide opportunities for education in the design and lifestyle changes needed to create more locally focused economies.

Public policy, local economies, and food systems

I believe it is easier for local economies to grow when all people have access to a guaranteed basic income, health care, child care, and education. This allows people, even if they cannot find paid employment, to devote themselves to alternative forms of economic activity, with a safety net in case of illness or change in life circumstances. This is clearly a government policy issue.

But locally based economies and food systems are too important to be left to governments, and the public-policy process has too many loopholes and opportunities for co-optation by moneyed interests to inspire local activists with much confidence (Roberts and Brandum 1995). Governments have been known to interfere with and quash creative, progressive grass-roots movements, sometimes purposefully and sometimes via stifling rules and bureaucracies. However, public processes and public money can at times provide very useful support for grass-roots economic initiatives.

Many authors emphasize the importance of change starting from the grass roots, beginning at the local level, to build more ecological production processes and undermine globalization. Their emphases vary, but some give specific examples of how this process has already begun. Norberg-Hodge (1994) mentions

- Local-skills exchanges;

- COMSA and local-enterprise trading systems;

- Credit unions and informal credit groups;

- Urban gardens;

- Child-care and other cooperatives;

- Environmental housing-improvement programs; and

- Local enterprises that transform local resources into goods and services for local people.

For Morrison (1995), the steps involved in building an ecological democracy include

- Democratizing finance, through credit unions and community-based banks;

- Building community economies and, especially, local production and distribution cooperatives of all types;

- Instituting new ways of valuing and accounting for environmental goods and services;

- Creating a social wage, which would provide some income for all;

- Pursuing disarmament and demilitarization;

- Developing an industrial ecology;

- Dematerializing production; and

- Developing a solar economy.

Efforts in Toronto include

- The Community Economic Development Secretariat, established and run by the Ontario government from 1992 to 1995;

- The Green Communities program (started by the Ontario Ministry of Environment and Energy in 1994), which initiated self-sufficient energy-efficiency housing-retrofit systems in several Ontario communities;

- The Healthy House in Toronto, constructed using funds largely from the Canada Mortgage and Housing Corporation (a federal institution); and

- The Boyne River Natural Science School outside Orangeville, Ontario, where schoolchildren from downtown Toronto study ecology and environmentally aware design.

These initiatives, both institutions and facilities, have served as pilot projects and demonstrated both the potential and the pitfalls of such undertakings. This is useful in showing the way for future nongovernmental endeavours along the same lines.

Conclusions

Although examples can be found in Toronto and other places of progressive public policy relating to local economies and food networks, it is important not to overstate the potential of such policy in this context. No substitute can be found for the creativity and hard work of local people — usually volunteers — striving to build a better and more ecologically sustainable food system in their local economy. Somehow, often against high odds, this continues to happen, and the local communities deserve the credit.

References

Guberman, C. 1995. Sowing the seeds of sustainability: planning for food self-reliance. *In* Eichler, M., ed., Change of plans: toward a non-sexist, sustainable city. Garamond Press, Toronto, ON, Canada.

Morrison, R. 1995. Ecological democracy. South End Press, Boston, MA, USA. 279 pp.

Norberg-Hodge, H. 1994. Building the case against globalization and for community-based economics. International Society for Ecological Economics Newsletter, 5(2), 3–4.

Roberts, W.; Brandum, S. 1995. Get a life! How to make a good buck, dance around the dinosaurs, and save the world while you're at it. Get a Life Publishing House, Toronto, ON, Canada. 344 pp.

PART 3

URBAN AND COMMUNITY AGRICULTURE

...🌿.🌿.🌿...

Urban Agriculture in the Seasonal Tropics: The Case of Lusaka, Zambia

A.W. Drescher

Introduction

During 1992 and 1993, a research project on home gardening and urban agriculture was carried out in Zambia's capital, Lusaka, in peri-urban areas of Lusaka, and in rural areas of Zambia and Zimbabwe. The so-called household-garden survey concentrated on household gardens as an important part of the land-use system that seems to contribute significantly to household food security. The survey also focused on staple-food production in the city. The main objective of the household-garden survey was to clarify the role of household gardens for household food security in Zambia. In detail, the objectives were

- To determine the role of household gardens for urban households;

- To determine the contribution of the outputs of gardens to household diets and budgets;

- To draw up an inventory of the main problems encountered in preserving household gardens; and

- To find out why certain households are and others are not able to garden.

Urban development of Lusaka

Like many other cities in the developing world, Lusaka is growing fast. It had a population of 1.192 million in 1991 (CSO 1992). Since 1980 the population of Lusaka has nearly doubled. The growth rate between 1980 and 1990 was 6.1%, and the population density was 2 728 people/km^2 (CSO 1990). Figure 1 shows the development of the population of Lusaka since 1950.

As Figure 1 indicates, Lusaka's future need for food will be much higher. During the same period, the built-up area will increase and agricultural land will further decrease (Schlyter 1991; Drescher 1998). No township in the Western world would be able to handle growth rates of 70 000 persons/year and provide housing, education, and infrastructure. How will it be possible in the developing world? Only recently were first steps taken in Lusaka to stimulate interest in urban agriculture.

NB: This paper is based on field research for the African Homegarden Project carried out in 1992 and 1993 in Zambia and Zimbabwe. The research project was partly supported by the Food and Agriculture Organization of the United Nations' Early Warning Project and the Zambian Central Statistical Office.

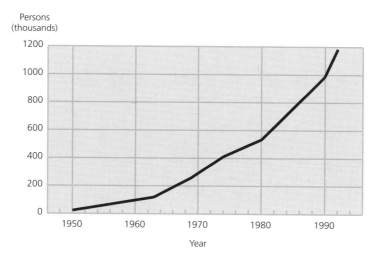

Figure 1. Population development in Lusaka, Zambia, 1950–92.
Source: CSO (1990, 1992).

Current nutritional status of Zambia's population

Among all the countries in southern Africa, Zambia shows the highest rates of malnutrition. Survey data indicate a higher prevalence of underweight individuals and stunted growth in the rural areas, both indicators of chronic malnutrition. However, wasting is significantly more prevalent in the urban areas, indicating current poor nutritional status (NFNC 1993a, b).

Protein–energy malnutrition is the most important of Zambia's major health problems, with impacts on morbidity and mortality and other long-term consequences. Iron deficiency (anemia) is also a serious health problem, as is vitamin-A deficiency (FAO 1993). Vegetables from household gardens and mixed cropping in the fields can contribute to nutrition, especially through vitamin-A content and microelements. In many cases, indigenous vegetables, gathered wild or grown, are more nutritious than foreign exotic plants (Table 1).

Where does Lusaka get its vegetables?

Agricultural activities in townships (gardening and rainy-season cropping) provide a source of vegetables of the traditional type, such as the very widely distributed *Amaranthus* spp. In 1989, a group of researchers carried out a survey of the vegetable supply of urban townships in Zambia (Ogle et al. 1990). They found that nearly 50% of the respondents practiced vegetable gardening (Table 2), mostly in the dry season.

The household-garden survey, carried out in 1992/93, showed that nearly 40% of the respondents in Lusaka still gathered wild vegetables for additional food or income (Figure 2). All of these families have gardens to augment their gathering activities. Urban households are more vulnerable during food shortages because they are unable to compensate for this through gathering. Plant resources have vanished around the urban centres.

Table 1. Nutritional value of some widely grown or gathered vegetables, Zambia.

Food	Moisture (%)	Protein (g)	Fat (g)	Ca (mg)	Iron (mg)	ß-carotene equivalent (µg)	Vitamin C (mg)
Brassica oleracea var. *capitata* (cabbage)[a]	93.0	1.6	0.3	55.0	0.8	280.0	46.0
Amaranthus spp. (cooked)	84.5	4.0	0.9	506.0	1.7	ND	ND
Manihot esculenta (cassava: dried leaves)	27.4	32.5	1.5	313.0	8.0	ND	ND
Ipomoea batatas (sweet potato: raw leaves)	83.0	4.6	0.2	158.0	6.2	5.9	70.0
Curcubita pepo (marrow: leaves)[a]	89.0	4.0	0.2	477.0	0.8	3.6	80.0
Adansonia digitata (bao-bab; dried leaves)	11.8	12.3	3.1	2.2	24.0	9.7	tr.
Beta vulgaris var. *cicla* (Swiss chard)[a]	92.0	2.0	0.2	132.0	0.7	600.0	50.0
Lycopersicon lycopersicum (tomato)	93.0	1.0	0.2	10.0	0.6	450.0	26.0

Source: FAO (1990), except as noted below.
Note: ND, no data; tr., trace.
[a] Data from Tindall (1992).

Table 2. Main source(s) of vegetables in urban areas, Zambia, 1989.

Source	Respondents (%)[a]		
	Lusaka	Kabwe	Ndola
Council market	79	95	70
Street vendor	62	69	57
Own garden	49	50	50
Bush	5	24	12

Source: Ogle et al. (1990).
[a] Number of households: Lusaka, 82; Kabwe, 42; Ndola, 58.

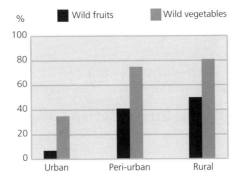

Figure 2. Gathering wild vegetables and wild fruits in urban, peri-urban, and rural areas, Zambia (*n* = 85 owners of household gardens).
Source: household-garden survey, 1992/93.

Urban agriculture in Lusaka in the 1980s and 1990s

In Lusaka, as in many other tropical urban centres, gardening and agriculture receive little support from the local authorities. In fact, the city councils often prohibit these activities. Even in the drought year of 1992, with the extreme shortage of food, Lusaka City Council suppressed urban agriculture, forcing the people to slash down maize.

People practice four types of agriculture in Lusaka: gardening for food, semi-commercial and commercial gardening, and rainy-season agriculture. Rainy-season agriculture is only practiced between the end of October and mid-May. Gardening is a permanent activity, but only with a permanent water source (natural wetlands, rivers, small dams). Sanyal (1985) carried out a survey of agricultural activities in Lusaka in May–June 1980. His survey covered five of Lusaka's townships: Jack-Extension, Mtendere, Kalingalinga, Matero, and Chilenje-South. He showed that an average 13% of households practiced both rainy-season agriculture and dry-season gardening. Comparing this with data now available, one can conclude that gardening in Lusaka has increased since 1980, except in high-density areas, where no space is available for gardening.

The role of women in household food security deserves special attention. In sub-Saharan Africa, women's labour is more important than that of men in all parts of food production (Fresco 1986). Women must provide the agricultural labour needed in every phase of the food cycle to guarantee the family's nutrition, without neglecting their other tasks: food preparation, child care, fetching water and fuelwood, washing, house cleaning, and looking after the small animals. In addition, women often generate more than half of the total household income (Due 1985; Fresco 1986). The literature shows, for example, that women's income has a greater impact than that of men on the health and nutrition status of children (Maxwell 1990).

Figure 3 shows the proportion of involvement of women and men in agricultural activities in the urban environment of Lusaka. When asked about their involvement in agricultural activities in Lusaka, 42.6% of the 648 persons surveyed answered "yes, we practice gardening." And nearly 30% practice irrigation or watering in the dry season, which means gardening. Nearly 50% of the women but only 35% of the men are involved in agriculture. As Figure 3 shows, differences among the townships of Lusaka are significant. In all townships, women are more involved in agriculture and gardening than men. Involvement in agriculture means both dry-season gardening and rainy-season agriculture. The differences between dry-season gardening activities and rainy-season agriculture become obvious when one compares Figures 3 and 4. In total, only 31.6% of women and 24.3% of men practice gardening. Whereas in Chilenje and Matero, nearly 50% of the women practice gardening, their involvement in other townships like Matero, George, and Chawama is only about 25%.

Rainy-season agriculture in Lusaka

Jaeger and Huckabay (1986) found medium-sized rainy-season plots of 300 m³ in the urban area of Lusaka. The field survey carried out in 1992/93 showed that the average size had increased significantly to 423 m³ ($n = 46$) (Table 3). The need to compensate for the deteriorating economic situation since 1980 might be one reason for the increase in cultivated area. The limited land resources are fully used during the rainy

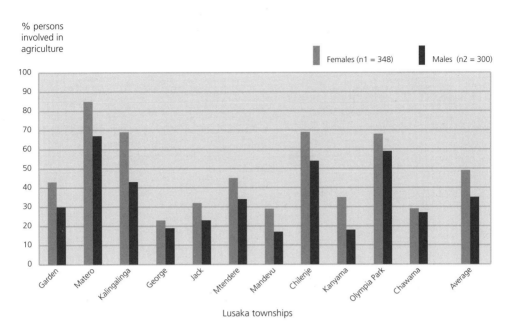

Figure 3. Involvement of women and men in agriculture in the townships of Lusaka, Zambia.
Source: household-garden survey, 1992/93.

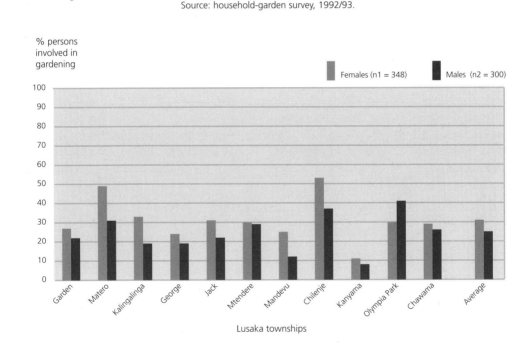

Figure 4. Involvement of women and men in gardening in the townships of Lusaka, Zambia.
Source: household-garden survey, 1992/93.

season. Public property, such as the university campus, areas around hospitals, and road strips, is used illegally for agricultural purposes.

Intercropping systems have up to four types of crop. The combination maize, beans, and pumpkin was most frequently observed. Sweet potatoes are cultivated

Table 3. Size of rainy-season plots in central Lusaka, Zambia, 1992/93.

Location	Average plot size (m²)
Kalingalinga–Fridays Corner	571
Kalingalinga–Old City Airport	475
Great East Road, "Chainama Hill"	666
Great East Road, "Chainama Hills Hospital"	273
Ibex Hill	231
Great East Road Campus, "Dambo"	321

Source: field survey, 1992/93.

Table 4. Rainy season crops recorded in central Lusaka, Zambia, 1992/93.

Maize	Beans
Pumpkins	Sweet potatoes
Bananas	Okra
Tomatoes	Cucumbers
Groundnuts	Cassava

Source: field survey, 1992/93.

separately, on ridges. It seems that sweet potato is becoming an increasingly important crop, probably as a substitute for other staples. The household garden plays an important role as a dry-season nursery for sweet potatoes. Sweet potatoes were planted in nearly all the gardens observed. Ten types of crop were recorded for the 1992/93 rainy season: maize, pumpkins, bananas, tomatoes, groundnuts, beans, sweet potatoes, okra, cucumbers, and cassava (Table 4).

According to Sanyal (1985), urban rainy-season agriculture is practiced in Lusaka mostly by people with the lowest per capita income. But this part of the population shows the lowest percentage of involvement in gardening (according to the 1992/93 survey). This shows once again that the poorest part of the population lives in high-density housing areas, where no space is available for gardening. Other factors that prevent gardening are

- Unreliable water supply in the townships;

- Plant pests and diseases;

- Human diseases and family problems;

- Lack of time; and

- Lack of human labour.

Understanding urban agriculture — the household-gardening model

The household-gardening model (Figure 5) helps to explain at least some of the factors that influence gardening. The household itself is in the centre of the model. Internal and external factors (for example, labour availability, access or entitlement to resources, education, occupation) determine the vulnerability of the household.

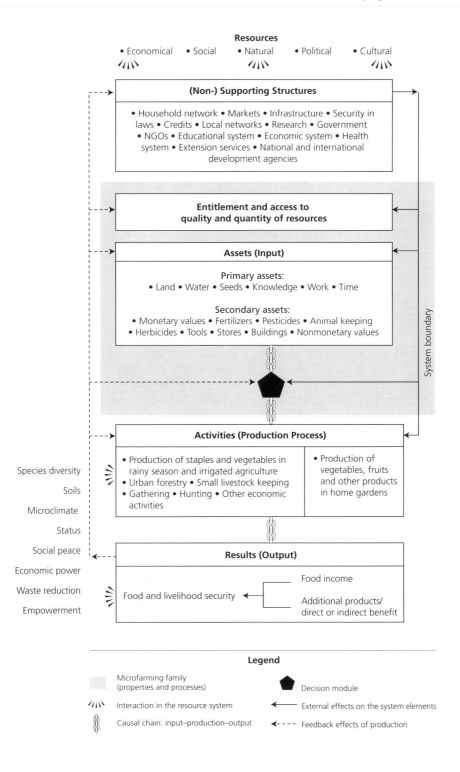

Figure 5. Household-gardening model.
Source: developed by A.W. Drescher and F. Bos (Bos 1994),
stimulated by Hardon-Baars (1990), greatly altered and revised.

Undefined land tenureship and the illegality of some of the townships explain the lack of available resources such as land and water. This is a constraint on agriculture, shown by Jaeger and Huckabay (1986). Eventually, agriculture will be limited by the expansion of official and unofficial residential land use and commercial activities in the peri-urban areas. Schultz (1979) pointed out that the ring of cultivation around the central urban zone of Lusaka is likely to be pushed outward by this process of urbanization.

Analyzing the strategies and resources of households can provide more information about their vulnerability. For example, a household's access to assets is often a good determinant of its vulnerability (Chambers 1989). Kanyama is an example of limited access to basic resources like land and water. This township is one of the most densely populated residential areas of Lusaka. It was originally designated a medium–low-cost area (Jaeger and Huckabay 1986) but without outdoor space and water for gardening and, as a result of rock outcrops, very limited land resources for rainy-season agriculture. This case also shows how the poorest of the poor can be without the means to meet their basic needs, such as through gardening, because of limited resources. Household gardening, as a coping strategy for survival, cannot be practiced in Kanyama, even given the needed tools, money, and seeds. Vulnerability increases with limitations on land and water resources.

Diversity of food and income resources (cash and kind, farm and nonfarm) is one of the main buffers against vulnerability in agrarian environments. This is also true of urban environments with poor economic development and little diversity. Household gardening creates a buffer for households in three ways: it generates income, saves resources, and creates a food supply. It is vital, therefore, to any understanding of household coping and survival strategies and, ultimately, to the effective design of food-security strategies to thoroughly understand the relative importance of different income sources, their seasonal fluctuation, sustainability, etc., and the responses of individuals and households to these characteristics (Maxwell 1990).

Conclusions: recommendations for future action and development strategies

The findings of the research project showed that the basis for urban agriculture is the availability of resources. The potential for development of the urban-agricultural sector is great. The formal economic sector in urban centres of developing countries is mostly underdeveloped. Consequently, it does not provide adequate income for the urban population. Urban agriculture can act as an alternative income-generating activity and as a buffer for household food security. Policymakers should therefore consider the following recommendations:

1. Strengthen rural development.

2. Use a self-help approach to resource management.

3. Decentralize.

4. Conduct appropriate town planning.

5. Improve the water supply in urban townships.

6. Support urban composting and waste management.

7. Support programs for urban agriculture and gardening.

8. Provide support for, and research on, indigenous vegetables and crops.

9. Extend services for urban smallholders.

10. Strengthen the role of women.

11. Provide support for existing gardens and other agricultural land uses, like animal husbandry and rainy-season cropping.

12. Provide research on and extension services for the sustainable use of wild food resources.

References

Bos, F. 1994. The role of household gardens in household food security. University of Wageningen, Wageningen, Netherlands. Reeks publikaties van de vakgroep Huishoudstudies, No. 14.

Chambers, R. 1989. Editorial introduction: vulnerability, coping and policy. IDS Bulletin, 20(2).

CSO (Central Statistical Office). 1990. 1990 census of population, housing and agriculture. CSO, Lusaka, Zambia. 15 pp.

—— 1992. 1992 census of population, housing and agriculture. CSO, Lusaka, Zambia.

Drescher, A.W. 1998. Hausgrten in Afrikanischen Rumen — Bewirtschaftung nachhaltiger Produktionssysteme und Strategien der Ernhrungssicherung in Zambia und Zimbabwe [African home gardens — self-management of sustainable production systems and strategies of food security in Zambia and Zimbabwe]. Centaurus-Verlagsgesellschaft, Pfaffenweiler, Germany. Soziokonomische Prozesse in Asien und Afrika.

Due, J.M. 1985. Women made visible: their contributions to farming systems and household incomes in Zambia and Tanzania. Urbana, IL, USA. Illinois Agricultural Economics Staff Paper.

FAO (Food and Agriculture Organization of the United Nations). 1990. Utilisation of tropical foods: fruits and leaves. FAO, Rome, Italy. Food and Nutrition Paper 47/7.

—— 1993. Technical Co-operation Programme; prevention of vitamin A deficiency. Terminal statement prepared for the Government of Zambia. FAO, Rome, Italy.

Fresco, L. 1986. Vrouwen en voedselvoorziening Hoofdstuk 6. In Honger op ons bord over politiek en voedselveiligheid. Evert Vermeer Stichting, Amsterdam, Netherlands.

Hardon-Baars, Ir. A.J. 1990. Household systems perspective to agricultural research and development: a missing link. User's Perspective with Agricultural Research and Development (UPWARD), Los Banos, Laguna, Philippines; International Potato Center, Los Banos, Laguna, Philippines; Benguet State University, La Trinidad, Benguet, Philippines. pp. 152–173.

Jaeger, D.; Huckabay, J.D. 1986. The garden city of Lusaka: urban agriculture. In Williamson, G.J., ed., Lusaka and its environs. Associated Printers Ltd, Lusaka, Zambia. ZGA Handbook Series, No. 9. pp. 267–277.

Maxwell, S., ed. 1990. Food security in developing countries: issues and options for the 1990s. IDS Bulletin, 21(3), 2–13.

NFNC (National Food and Nutrition Commission). 1993a. Aggregate description of national nutrition situation. NFNC, Lusaka, Zambia. Priority Survey Policy Brief 2.

—— 1993b. The geographic distribution of malnutrition. NFNC, Lusaka, Zambia. Priority Survey Policy Brief 4.

Ogle, B.A.; Malambo, L.; Mingochi, D.S.; Nkomesha, A.; Malasha, I. 1990. Traditional vegetables in Zambia: a study of procurement, marketing and consumption of traditional vegetables in selected urban and rural areas in Zambia. Sveriges Lantbruksuniversitet, Uppsala, Sweden. 77 pp.

Sanyal, B. 1985. Urban agriculture: who cultivates and why? A case-study of Lusaka, Zambia. Food and Nutrition Bulletin, 7(3), 15–24.

Schlyter, A. 1991. Twenty years of development in George, Zambia. Byggforskningsradet, Swedish Council for Building Research, Stockholm, Sweden.

Schultz, J. 1996. Land use in Zambia. Part I: The basically traditional land use system and their regions. Part II: Landuse map. Welstforum Verlag, Munich, Germany. Afrika Studien 95.

Tindall, H.D. 1992. Vegetables in the tropics. Macmillan Press, London, UK.

The Contribution of Urban Agriculture to Gardeners, Their Households, and Surrounding Communities: The Case of Havana, Cuba

Angela Moskow

Introduction

Urban agriculture is actively promoted in Havana, Cuba, to address the acute food-scarcity problems of the Special Period in Peacetime, which developed since 1989 as Soviet aid and trade were drastically curtailed. During the period of 1989–92, average daily per capita calorie consumption dropped an estimated 20%, and average daily per capita protein consumption dropped 27% (Torres 1996). A severe storm that destroyed much of the country's sugar crop in 1993, along with the tightening of United States' blockade in the early 1990s, further exacerbated these conditions (Deere et al. 1994).

In response to these conditions, the Cuban Ministry of Agriculture (MOA) began promoting urban food production in 1991. A number of urban agricultural activities have been under way. An important component of the government's program are gardens grown to provide for the gardeners' own needs. These gardens are cultivated on either private or state land. The gardeners can use state land at no cost. Havana has, according to an estimate, more than 26 000 such gardens (Paez Medina, interview, 1995[1]).

Research was conducted in Havana to trace the contributions of the gardens to the nutritional intake of the gardeners' households and the gardeners' sense of control of their lives and to determine the effects of these gardens on the surrounding communities. Much of the literature on urban agriculture focuses on food security, without much discussion of its aesthetic and therapeutic effects. The findings presented below may warrant a broader focus.

In-depth interviews were conducted with 42 gardeners during the period of July to September 1995. Nine of Havana's neighbourhoods were selected for the study. They represented a range of gardening conditions, from neighbourhoods with highly organized gardening efforts to areas known to have problems with their gardening programs. The researcher divided the neighbourhoods into three categories, based on the level of coordination between the gardeners and the MOA. Neighbourhoods in the first category lacked direct support from MOA. Neighbourhood activists were encouraging

NB: This research was conducted with funding from the Oberlin College Alumni Fund's Henry J. Haskell Fellowship, the Jastro-Shields Graduate Research Scholarship Fund, and the International Agricultural Development Graduate Group. Interviews were conducted by the author and Ana Himeley, who provided translation assistance and background information in conducting and transcribing the audiotaped interviews.
[1] Egidio Paez Medina, MOA, interview in Havana, Cuba, 1995.

and helped coordinate gardening activities, but they lacked assistance and coordination from MOA. The neighbourhoods of Los Angeles, Zayas, Pogolotti, and Alturas de Belem were assigned to this category. In the second category were neighbourhoods where gardening activities had just started to receive coordinated assistance from MOA or where MOA extension workers had been somewhat active, but not in a well-orchestrated fashion. The neighbourhood of Alamar was assigned to this category. The third category contained neighbourhoods where MOA activities were well developed. This included the neighbourhoods of Playa, Santa Fe, Diezmero, and La Lisa. Every interview was arranged by an individual involved in gardening promotion, usually one of the MOA's extension workers. No attempt was made to randomize the sample, as the logistical challenge of simply arranging the interviews precluded such a step.

At the time of the study, the MOA was hiring and training agricultural-extension staff to work at the community level in Havana. The MOA was hiring 67 workers to develop agricultural productivity with various types of urban agriculture. Additionally, every municipality in Havana had a staff member to oversee the extension activities. The extension workers helped gardeners to obtain land, encouraged the gardeners to form clubs, answered technical questions about gardening, acquainted the gardeners with available resources, and reported to the MOA. The MOA also worked with a number of Cuban and foreign organizations to coordinate training for gardeners and extension workers and provide materials to the gardeners, such as tools and hoses (Paez Medina, interview, 1995[2]).

This paper presents the results of the study on what nutritional benefits accrued to the gardeners and their households, what psychological benefits accrued to the gardeners, and the contributions of the gardens to their surrounding neighbourhoods.

Study findings

Characteristics of the gardeners

The average age of people for the study sample was 58 years; the age range was 28–80 years. Twenty-eight of the gardeners (67%) reported that they had learned to garden from relatives when they were growing up in the countryside. Eighteen gardeners (43%) indicated that the garden was their first direct experience with horticulture, although some had acquired gardening skills by observing others.

Thirty-eight (91%) of the gardeners were men, and 4 (9%) were women. The agricultural background of many of these men was presumably a factor in the high level of male participation in gardening. Additionally, a Cuban study found that women's household responsibilities in the Special Period in Peacetime allowed little or no time for gardening (Cruz 1997).

Characteristics of the gardens

Most (26) of the gardeners' parcels were individual gardens, although the largest garden in the study included 72 gardeners on 53 parcels. Garden sizes ranged from 18 to 40 000 m². Usually, more than one gardener tended the larger plots.

---

[2] Egidio Paez Medina, MOA, interview in Havana, Cuba, 1995.

Half (21) of the gardeners had plots adjacent to their homes. Additionally, five gardeners (12%) with distant plots cultivated a second, smaller plot adjacent to their homes. The longest distance a study participant had to travel to his or her garden was 1 km. However, another researcher spoke with gardeners who lived in neighbourhoods that had very little available land. They had to travel across town to reach their plots (Chaplowe 1996).

Thirty-four gardeners (81%) used their land through a system of *usufructo gratutito* (free usufruct); the other 8 owned the land they cultivated. Having the right to *usufructo gratutito* allows the gardeners free use of state land for the rest of their lives (Paez Medina, interview, 1995[3]).

Gardeners chose the crops they grew, constrained only by growing conditions and seed availability. Plantains were the most popular crop, cultivated by 98% (41) of the gardeners, who grew both fruit and viand types of plantain. Other popular crops were cassava, peppers, squash, and yams. Sixty percent of the gardeners (25) raised animals, including chickens, pigs, goats, ducks, rabbits, geese, *guanacos* (similar to llamas), and turkeys.

Food and economic security

The production of plant and animal products was found to significantly increase the quantity and quality of the food available to gardeners' households. An average 5.83 people ate in the gardeners' households, and 9.52 people in their extended families received food from their gardens. If this pattern is true throughout Havana, then more than 1 of every 10 people in the city received some food from these gardens. However, as the sample was not random, no generalizations can be made.

The gardens also had a profound impact on household budgets: they reduced weekly food bills, and gardeners could earn money selling their garden products. Forty one gardeners (98%) indicated that they saved 10–250 CUP per week with their gardens, with the average at 50 CUP/week (in 1998, 20 Cuban pesos [CUP] = 1 United States dollar [USD][4]). This is a striking figure, as the average household salary reported by the gardeners was 125 CUP/week. Thus, the average savings from the garden was 40% of the average household salary.

Control

A number of themes emerged from the study related to the gardens' role in enhancing the gardeners' sense of control of their lives. Many gardeners spoke about the ways the gardens increased their self-sufficiency, in terms of both household food needs and a direct sense of greater control of one's life.

Produce from the garden represented 5–100% of the households' fruit, vegetable, and viand intake. On average, the garden provided 60% of the households' produce needs. Gardeners from households in which the percentage was lower than this average gave a lower rating than others to the Likert-scale[5] question "I feel more in control of my life now that I am gardening." Further, a chi-square analysis found a

---

[3] Egidio Paez Medina, MOA, interview in Havana, Cuba, 1995.
[4] Cuban pesos are not normally sold outside Cuba. The rate for Cubans is 20 CUP per USD; that for foreigners is 1 CUP per USD.
[5] "Likert scaling is a measurement technique based on the use of standardized response categories" (Babbie 1995).

statistically significant relationship between responses to this and the Likert-scale question "Gardening increases the amount of food available to my family." A sense of increased control was also associated with the belief that the garden enhanced the family's nutrition. Lastly, awareness of information sources for gardeners was related to a greater sense of control. Thus, the findings indicated that both the ability of the gardeners to meet household food needs and their success in doing so were linked to their feelings of being in control of their lives.

The gardeners also considered their gardens entertaining and aesthetically appealing environments. Thirty-six of the gardeners elaborated on features of their gardens related to stress reduction, spiritual satisfaction, entertainment, and aesthetic value. Francis (1989) discussed Kimber's 1973 study of Puerto Rican gardeners, which found that "gardens ... represent social territories in which persons define their own places and express their self images." The most powerful story about the importance of the gardens, from this standpoint, was told by an individual with severe health problems, who was using the garden to help feed the 10 people in his very modest household. He was gardening where a road had been, so the soil was compacted and difficult to work. After discussing what he grew, he spoke at length about the aesthetic aspect of gardening and stressed its significance.

Many of the respondents indicated that gardening helped them relax. Study of the data revealed that these respondents gave relaxation two different but interrelated meanings. First, it meant that the gardens relieved their anxieties about meeting the family's food needs. Second, it meant the gardens were restorative. One respondent expressed both of these concepts: "Sometimes you have a lot of psychological pressure and the garden is a place to relax. Also, the worry of the *canasta familia* [household food supply] is less." Thus, given a measure of control of their families' physiological needs, the gardeners were also able to control their anxiety and experience the additional therapeutic properties of the gardens. Said one, "My nerves are better. I feel more agreeable." Another responded to the question "Are there other reasons why you garden here?" by noting "If you relax beneath a *mata* [grove], it restores you."

Many who had gardens next to their homes spoke of the pleasure of spending time in the garden watching the plants. Kaplan and Kaplan (1989) discussed this notion in *The Experience of Nature*: "Observing is an important form of involvement with nature. ... Much of the pleasure that people derive from nature comes from such occasions to observe." One gardener expressed this sentiment: "I came today just to watch the garden." Another respondent noted, "Seeing the plants grow makes me feel good." A third commented, "It's a distraction to watch the garden. At sunset it's relaxing." Thus, the gardeners conveyed a fascination with the elements of nature in their gardens.

Many of the older gardeners spoke of the importance of gardening to their health and social life. Those who grew up in the countryside were using skills they had neglected for years. They also spoke of the feeling of being useful in helping to provide their families and communities with food, and they contrasted their gardening days with an earlier, more idle time. One elderly gardener remarked, "You have to put love into agriculture. It's great to be able to help the family this way." In response to the question "Are there other reasons why you garden?", another gardener remarked, "I have been retired for 11 years and needed a way to feel useful." A number commented that if they had not been gardening they would be sitting in a corner drinking rum.

The findings illustrate that the gardeners' perceptions of control were strongly connected to their ability to meet their household needs and their success in doing so. The findings point to a number of ways in which the gardens afforded the gardeners a greater sense of control of their lives: gardening helped to meet food needs and helped the gardeners relax, connect with nature, and experience solitude. Further, the study determined that for the elderly participants, the ability to meet household needs was an especially important benefit of the gardens.

Community enhancement

The benefits of the gardens could also be traced to the surrounding neighbourhoods. Five types of community benefit were identified: a greater food supply, contributions to the country, neighbourhood beautification, improved safety, and enhanced urban ecology.

Greater food supply

The gardeners contributed and sold food to their local communities, enhancing local food supply. Fourteen (33%) of the gardeners sold some of the food they produced. Thirty-three gardeners (78%) donated food to the community, in some cases through their gardening clubs. Donations were often made to schools, nursery schools, and nursing homes. Gardeners also gave to neighbours, especially those who were not very well off.

Contributions to the country

Some of the gardeners characterized the gardens as having the power to contribute, in a variety of ways, to the country at large. A number of individuals spoke of gardening as an important way of solving Cuba's problems. They indicated that their work in their gardens was a way to help the revolution. One commented that he wanted a farm to "help the revolution with a huge harvest." Another observed that "work is good for health, spirit, and the revolution." Asked if gardening had been a positive experience for him and his family, another gardener responded, "Yes, for me, for my family, for the country." Three gardeners quoted José Martí, a 19th-century Cuban writer, poet, and revolutionary, when they spoke of their work in the garden.

Neighbourhood beautification

Quite a few of the gardeners indicated that they started their gardens in abandoned lots or trash dumps. Gardeners in one of the municipalities in the study constructed impressive walls, usually about 1 m high, with the rocks removed from the once-vacant lots that many of the gardens occupied. A number of the gardens in this area were quite lovely and contained multiple plots.

Improved safety

The gardens also improved neighbourhood safety. A number of gardeners indicated that before the gardens were planted lots were unsafe areas, where people had previously been afraid to walk. Two participants in the study mentioned that the area they gardened had previously been called the "hill of fear." It had been restored to a series of beautiful gardens. Turning unsightly landscapes into beautiful gardens was one of the many unintended benefits of a program designed to deal with the country's food crisis.

Enhanced urban ecology

Gardens are a prominent feature throughout much of Havana. Although many more gardens appear in the peripheral areas than in the city centre, food gardens are a common sight in many parts of the city. Also, farm animals, often kept close to houses as a precaution against theft, are much more conspicuous in Havana than in many capital cities. Thus, food production is very transparent. It is also environmentally sound because it has few transportation and storage requirements. The gardens also bring the multiple aesthetic and environmental benefits of increased vegetation. Further, gardeners who compost their food scraps and garden residue transform them into soil nutrients and divert them from the waste stream.

Cuba has been heralded for its green agricultural practices, which the Cubans developed in response to the striking drop in agricultural inputs and fuel during the Special Period in Peacetime. Much of the success of this approach is attributable to the country's impressive research capabilities, as well as to the commitment of many Cuban scientists to environmentally sound farming methods (Rosset and Benjamin 1994). Also, MOA, along with many of the organizations it works with, promotes ecologically sound growing techniques. For example, a 1995 request for proposals for *autoconsumos* (gardens for the gardeners' own needs) from the Consejo Ecumenico de Cuba (ecumenical council of Cuba) listed as one of its objectives "fomenting organic agriculture and application of ecological technologies in the processing of food."

The food gardens in the study were organic by default. Chemical inputs are not sold on the open market in Cuba (Consejo de Administración de la Provincia de la Ciudad de la Habana (council for the administration of the province of the City of Havana), interview, 1995[6]). The gardeners showed varying levels of attachment to the environmentally benign gardening methods they practiced. One reason for this appeared to be the variation in their skills in managing soil fertility and insect problems. A number of educational efforts were ongoing under MOA and other organizations. Gardeners who knew of composting and pest-control techniques were far more enthusiastic about organic gardening than those who had little or no such knowledge. For instance, when asked about soil conditions, gardeners who had been to training sessions on composting techniques spoke glowingly about the importance of compost in maintaining soil fertility. One gardener explained, "Through enriching the soil I am fostering beneficial organisms." Other gardeners spoke of the hardships caused by the lack of chemical inputs.

Ten (24%) of the gardeners used compost in their gardens. The gardeners were not asked about the materials used in the compost, but some indicated that they used garden and household food waste. Gardeners who lived in the vicinity of a sugar-processing plant indicated they used sugar by-products in their compost. Twelve (29%) of the gardeners used manure, and 13 (31%) used organic matter, including green manure, on their gardens.

---

[6] Consejo de Administración de la Provincia de la Ciudad de la Habana, interview in Havana, Cuba, 1995.

The gardeners were asked how important improving the environment was as a reason for gardening. The average response was 3.14 on a scale of 1 (not important) to 4 (very important). When asked this question one respondent noted, "I am aware that the environment has to be protected." Another gardener spoke about his plans to develop a living fence around his garden.

Discussion

Many Cubans recognize the importance of Havana's food gardens and are committed to continuing to work with them. Thirty-nine of the gardeners (93%) indicated their intention to continue gardening when the Special Period in Peacetime ends. Government officials interviewed for the study indicated the government's strong support for gardens and their intention to continue the gardening program.

The role of the Cuban government in promoting and supporting urban agriculture is unique from a global perspective and surely accounts for much of the success of the program (Marsh, interview, 1996[7]). The commitment and considerable effort of the gardeners must also be recognized. The study found gardeners' perceptions of control were strongly connected to their ability to meet their household needs and their success in doing so. The findings point to a number of ways the gardens gave the gardeners a greater sense of control of their lives, through improved household nutritional intake and relaxation, connection with nature, and experience of solitude. The study also traced the gardens' roles in enhancing the surrounding communities. The gardens provided patriotic inspiration and enhanced the community's urban ecology, landscape, and food supply. The impressive scope and achievement of Havana's gardening program should be a inspiration to all adherents of urban agriculture.

References

Babbie, E. 1995. The practice of social research (7th ed.). Wadsworth Publishing Company, Belmont, CA, USA.

Chaplowe, S. 1996. Havana's popular gardens and the Cuban food crisis. Geography Graduate Group, University of California at Los Angeles, Los Angeles, CA, USA. MA dissertation.

Cruz, M.C. 1997. Urban and community agriculture: cases from Cuba panel. Paper presented at the International Conference on Sustainable Urban Food Systems, 22–25 May 1997, Ryerson Polytechnic University, Toronto, ON, Canada. Ryerson Centre for Studies in Food Security; FoodShare Metro Toronto; International Development Research Centre; Oxfam Canada; Toronto Food Policy Council; Toronto Food Research Network.

Deere, C.D.; Pérez, N.; Gonzalez, E. 1994. The view from below: Cuban agriculture in the "Special Period in Peacetime." Journal of Peasant Studies, 21(2), 195.

Francis, M. 1989. Control as a dimension of public-space quality. In Altman, I.; Zube, E., ed., Public spaces and places. Plenum Press, New York, NY, USA.

Kaplan, R.; Kaplan, S. 1989. The experience of nature — a psychological perspective. Cambridge University Press, Cambridge, UK.

Rosset, P.; Benjamin, M., ed. 1994. The greening of the revolution. Ocean Press, Melbourne, Australia.

Torres, R. 1996. Cuban agromarket study. Geography Graduate Group, University of California, Davis, CA, USA.

---

[7] Robin Marsh, Senior Research Associate, North American Integration and Development Center, University of California at Los Angeles, Los Angeles, CA, interview at El Cerrito, CA, 1996.

...❦ ❦ ❦...

Agriculture in the Metropolitan Park of Havana, Cuba

Harahi Gamez Rodriquez

An overview of current work

The Metropolitan Park of Havana (PMH) is an urban, ecological, and social project being developed around the last 7 km of the Almendares River, the most important river of the Cuban capital. It overlaps four of the capital's municipalities — Playa, Plaza, Marianao, and Cerro — an area of great cultural, racial, and social diversity.

As an urban project, the PMH will have 18 attraction sites spreading over its 700 ha of land in the centre of the Havana. Whereas preexisting structures were eliminated to create the other big parks in Havana — Lenin Park and the Botanical Gardens — the PMH will retain the dense urban network of industries, military entities, and population centres currently occupying the territory.

As an ecological park, the PMH will address the deforestation problem in the zone, the uncontrolled social and industrial waste, and the general lack of care of the region that threatens the area's flora and fauna and the Almendares River itself. The development of the PMH depends on recovering and, in many cases, re-creating natural habitats, as well as developing mechanisms for these to coexist with the city and its inhabitants. As a social project, the PMH will provide a space for a population of nearly 9 000 inhabitants. The program takes a participatory approach: through collective planning and a reliable process of consultation the residents will have an integral role in planning the development of the park.

The PMH is committed to integrating development, environmental recovery, education, and participation — concepts that are frequently addressed independently in large urban-development projects. Investment plans for the park take into account its environmental impact and the objective of real participation.

Objectives

The objectives of the PMH are to

- Create a "green lung," with multiple functions, and improve the environment by integrating the park with the Almendares River;

- Demonstrate a sustainable and participatory approach in which problems are converted into opportunities;

- Promote contact between the park's inhabitants and nature and elevate the quality of the environment;

84

- Contribute to environmental education at all levels, from the most basic to the highest scientific level;

- Create sources of employment;

- Offer various forms of recreation and tourism;

- Raise the standard of living by improving the environment and level of cultural conscience, as well as preserving and promoting historical sites;

- Promote sports activities for people in Havana as an integral part of a broad conception of culture;

- Maintain the park's most important factories in production, such as the brewery, the paper manufacturer, and the lumberyards, while minimizing their environmental impacts;

- Develop an urban, holistic, ecological, and self-sufficient form of agriculture; and

- Organize the park's economy to guarantee that it is self-financing and sufficiently profitable.

Today the PMH has gone past the stage of analysis and is in the planning phase; the fundamental mission, objectives, and goals have been determined, and a process of strategic planning has been developed with community participation.

Interdisciplinary team

PMH's interdisciplinary technical team is currently being consolidated. The philosophy of the team is that practice is the criterion of truth. Its composition will be determined in due course as members attain a greater degree of understanding of the constraints on the program and the feasibility of alternatives. This means approaching reality with holistic, not sectoral, vision and ensuring that each specialist is well rounded and knows the fundamentals of every discipline involved. The technical team has been divided into working groups focused on different programs and different suburbs.

The agricultural program

In 1960, revolutionary legislation introduced the notion of cooperative property. However, only in 1975 did the idea gain acceptance. As a result of the cooperative movement, the farmers in the area decided to form the Agriculture/Livestock Productive Cooperative (CPA), named *Vincente Perez Noa* and founded on 7 May 1988.

Owing to numerous problems, this cooperative did not have a long or fruitful life. A lack of clear delimitation of properties encumbered the productive process. From its inception, the CPA exhibited serious organizational and functional problems as a result of several changes in the directorship and the instability of its membership, which had various causes, including the lack of interest in, and love for, the work and difficulties in managing to do the work with good results. Economically, the cooperative could not keep up with production plans because of the scarcity of inputs (which is not to say that they did not exist) and because unstable and unmotivated contract workers made up much of its work force.

As a result of these problems, the Ministry of Agriculture (MOA) decided to dissolve the CPA and confer these lands on the PMH administration, which was to elaborate a holistic development strategy. The principal goal was to integrate agricultural production into the strategy of the PMH, because it was still not known what could be done for agriculture in the park. For this reason, the technical team decided to hold two workshops to coordinate efforts in thinking about and constructing a new agricultural strategy — one workshop with the technicians and specialists of different institutions and the other with the producers.

In the first workshop, the following fundamental objectives were proposed:

- To determine the prospects for an agricultural and livestock industry; and

- To come up with a coherent work strategy to develop this capacity.

Participants also emphasized that the PMH's agricultural and livestock activities should be fundamentally urban, agroecological, intensive, and sustainable. A plan of action was elaborated, and the immediate tasks were quickly executed to maintain continuity with this workshop and prevent certain serious problems. Incorporation of the development criteria of the producers was also a priority.

The second step was to set up a workshop with the agricultural producers in the area. Taking the first workshop as a base, the team elaborated three central thematic questions to guide the discussion:

- *Agricultural, livestock, and forestry production* — What would be the essential characteristics of a successful agricultural and livestock scheme in the PMH?

- *Commercialization* — How should commercialization be organized to secure the mutual benefit of the producers and of the park?

- *Organizational structure* — How should the organs of production interact? (What forms of association should the producers adopt?)

Both producers and experts participated at this workshop. They collectively identified the following barriers to the development of agriculture in the area and defined the goals of the project:

- *Organizational structure* — Organizational structures for agricultural production vary in Cuba, including the CPA, Basic Units of Cooperative Production (UBPCs), state ranches, farms, and private-land tenancy. Although private-land tenancy exists on a small scale in the park — and thus forms a part of the existing socioeconomic structure — private farming should not be promoted; rather, efforts should be directed to discovering the potential of other existing organizational structures. The UBPCs and state ranches, on the other hand, require major extensions of land unavailable in the park. The state ranches have a complex organizational structure, including an administrative apparatus. The experts, the farmers, and the PMH team agree that the best means of organization would be the progressive development of small farms integrating cultivation, livestock production, and reforestation. To solve problems of dispersion and the lack of personal incentive for production, separate farms of a reduced size will be created. Each family will get partial ownership of a plot and be in charge of production. Reducing the size of the farms will help to address technical problems — such as risk — and the problems of administration and directorship. The structure of small farms will also facilitate the integration of the PMH's lands: agricultural activity will become more closely interconnected with other activities of the park.

- *Deterioration of the soils* — One of the objectives of the PMH is to locate agricultural lands in the most fertile regions and support methods to protect and improve the quality of soil. Research is under way on this matter.

- *Shortage of a clean supply of water for agriculture* — The agricultural zone of the park is part of the hydrographic region of the Almendares River, specifically of the subregion of Santoyo Creek. Both of these sources of water are contaminated. The goal is to develop reliable sources of irrigation water for agricultural plots and for aquaculture.

- *Producers' lack of training and resources* — The level of technical training among the farmers varies. Some cultivate without using effective traditional methods, and others are prevented from obtaining better results by their limited access to resources. In general, obtaining supplies, such as seeds, fertilizers, and tools, is problematic.

- *Lack of physical protection of the agricultural area* — As a result of Cuba's economic situation, farmers' crops are often stolen, which acts as a disincentive to production. It is essential to guarantee farmers' earnings and shield them from external threat by organizing an adequate system of protection.

- *Lack of mechanisms to commercialize agricultural production* — At the time of the research, the PMH had no plan for commercializing surplus agricultural production in the park. Producers have commercialized their own products through the agricultural and livestock market and in other ways. Commercialization takes time and energy from the productive activity of the farmers, so the farmers asked the PMH to organize this activity.

In the medium term, the agricultural program's goals are to deal with each of these problems. The program's objectives are to achieve a better organizational structure of the agricultural area through

- The organization of small organic farms of 2–4 ha (five are planned for the first 3 years);

- The creation of an organization or institution to provide services to farmers in the area;

- The organization of farmers by zone; and

- Joint participation of the farmers and the PMH in planning production and commercialization.

The project proposal

We propose that Oxfam Canada assist the PMH team during the initial stages of the project. This proposal combines key aspects of agricultural planning in the area with the implementation of three specific subprojects: creation of the first integrated farm; development of mechanisms to facilitate the participation of the farmers; and development of an organization to provide services to the PMH's agricultural producers.

The project zone covers about 151 ha in the municipalities of Marianao and Cerro. The proposed organic farm will be in Santa Catalina (population: 528), a suburb of Pogolotti (population: 11 200), in the municipality of Marianao.

Although developing agriculture in a park could be seen as self-contradictory, the PMH team proposes to develop this activity for the following reasons:

- Agriculture in urban zones would be fundamental to improving the food security of some sectors of the capital. This fits in with a national policy of recuperating urban spaces for agricultural cultivation to supplement the basic food supplies of urban residents at a low cost.

- The PMH needs to organize ecological, integral, and self-sufficient agriculture, integrated with the park's other activities and objectives, including economic sustainability for the farmers, recuperation of the environment, and the aesthetic compatibility of agriculture with other park activities.

- The park's agricultural community needs to be motivated to solve its problems, and this motivation needs to be consolidated in a voluntary and participatory approach to agriculture. Some proposals to generate participation are to create the mechanisms for consultation and dissemination of information about the park's projects and plan and execute a program of environmental education and reforestation.

Specific goals

1. *Organize the 53 producers of the area into four zones to facilitate the dissemination of information, environmental education, and training* — This idea emerges from farmers' and producers' meetings and workshops. Such an organizational structure would be used to develop an education program for environmental and technical capacity-building. The participatory process would rest on the agricultural producers' already established structures of association, such as the participatory local governments in the park. Those involved will determine the priorities of environmental education in their areas.

2. *Create an integral experimental farm of 4.3 ha* — The proposed farm would be located in the suburb of Finlay and Marianao, an area selected for its good soil quality. Single crops would be rotated with multiple crops. All of its waste products that are primary materials would be recycled to sustain the productive system. Self-sufficiency would be the goal: both the produce consumed by the farmers and the majority of the supplies needed by the farm's animals and crops would be produced on the farm. This farm would be the first of five planned for the next 3 years and would serve as a model for the organization of the rest of the land parcels.

3. *Create a centre to provide services (work supplies and assistance teams) to the producers* — In the first years, 16 workers dependent on the labour centres would be employed by a service centre. Once the service centres disappear, the independent farmers would become the park's focus of attention, and they would have access to the equipment and tools that had been administered by the service centre.

4. *Complete three essential studies needed to plan and organize agriculture in the park* — Three essential studies would be needed: one on wastes and the quality of the water, one on agricultural supply and the market, and an evaluation of the organizational forms of the integrated farm and service provider. In each case, the approach would be to integrate the results and findings of the study into the planning process.

As the interdisciplinary team is new to urban agriculture, it is receptive to all suggestions, ideas, and advice.

···ᴡᴇ. ᴡᴇ. ᴡᴇ···

People at the Centre of
Urban Livestock Projects

Alison Meares

Introduction

Organizations and professionals committed to promoting environmentally sound and
economically rewarding agriculture are just beginning to understand the significance of
farming in cities for long-term sustainability of agriculture and human settlements.
People worldwide are asking these questions: How can we help urban livestock and
crop production become a force to alleviate poverty and improve human nutrition and
welfare? How can urban agriculture reach beyond beautification and environmental
improvement, particularly in North American cities, and become a vehicle for the social
and economic development of disenfranchised communities?

Heifer Project International (HPI) has for more than 50 years developed livestock projects in predominantly rural areas to improve the economic and social welfare
of low-income families and communities. Seeking to apply its model for development
in urban areas, it launched its first North American urban animal-agricultural initiative
in Chicago in September 1996. Working with community groups, HPI provided training
and assistance for agricultural projects in three neighbourhoods in Chicago with the
highest levels of poverty, the most food banks, and no grocery stores.

The Robert Taylor Homes is the largest public-housing project in the United
States. It covers 92 acres (37.2 ha) in Chicago's South Side and has more than 20 000
residents. Considered one of the bleakest, most violent public-housing sites in Chicago,
it is plagued by crime and poverty. Gangs control many of the 27 high-rise buildings. In
this environment, a resident-run youth group constructed a vermi- and aquaculture
system in the basement of one of the high-rises, establishing some 30 pounds (more
than 13 kg) of worms and two barrels of fish. Worm castings are used in the planting
season as a soil additive in the group's small market garden or packaged for sale to
other city gardeners. Every 7 months, the participants harvest the fish for their families.
In neighbouring Cabrini Green public-housing complex, with large tracts of blighted
land just minutes from the glittery business district, a small herd of dairy goats will soon
be grazing and providing milk and raw materials for a goat-cheese microenterprise.

With these inroads barely paved, HPI is beginning to learn that urban agriculture can improve people's lives and natural surroundings. However, agricultural practice alone cannot improve nutrition, create a skilled and responsible work force, and
reclaim land. These depend on the approach taken to urban agriculture. What combination of elements brings about long-lasting change? How can people climb out of
poverty, instead of just temporarily dodging it like mines in a cornfield in a never-ending
war? In its work around the world, HPI has learned that any approach to development

must be people centred and responsive to a community's self-evaluated needs and assets.

In this paper, I will present the core elements of HPI's model for planning urban agricultural projects, which enables communities to define and shape their own development goals. The model has four principle components: the interdependence of the land- and lifescape, full participation of intended beneficiaries, a planning and evaluation process rooted in the community's values, and a method called "passing on the gift," designed to ensure that families and communities maintain the project through practical care and sharing.

Weaving together the land- and lifescape

The landscape has the biophysical qualities of a geographical region. The lifescape has the social, cultural, and economic qualities of the community. They come together in a whole-system view of an urban agricultural project or setting. Because change is never linear, thinking about change must be process oriented and holistic (Aaker et al. 1996). In urban agricultural projects, it is not enough to consider the health of the land, the species of plants or animal species that might live there, and the steps to environmental rehabilitation. We must also consider the lifescape: the market or local economy, the cultural setting, and the local need for such a project — in effect, the people who will build, benefit from, and maintain the project.

Urban agriculture provides intangible gifts, such as teaching these teenagers to take responsibility for sustaining life. It also provides economic opportunity and entrepreneurial capacity-building, such as in selling worm castings as fertilizer to the other city gardeners, making goat cheese, value added from herbs from their garden, and selling goat cheese to city restaurants or at local farmers' markets. Urban agriculture improves city residents' lifescape. A worm and fish farm in the basement of the Robert Taylor Homes provides an education. Urban agriculture also improves the landscape. Worm castings and composted goat manure enhance the soil fertility of nearby vegetable gardens.

HPI's city projects embrace several interconnected goals:

- *Environmental* — Urban animal-agricultural projects work in concert with organic agriculture (manure and worm castings to increase soil fertility, bees for crop pollination, and chickens and rabbits to heat a greenhouse);

- *Economic* — Opportunities are provided to earn income through the sale of animal products (cheese, honey, poultry, eggs);

- *Education* — Opportunities are provided to learn new skills while learning about and reconnecting with one of our food sources;

- *Empowerment* — Urban agricultural projects help people gain control of community and family food security (establishment of local markets, production and consumption at home, participation in community food kitchens or processing centres).

Participatory development

Participation in development has fallen into the same camp of popular rhetoric as sustainable development. It is discussed more often than it is put into practice or even understood. Fundamentally, participation is rooted in meaning, in what people care about. Participatory approaches to project development seek to identify people's values and to make these values explicit to these people and their partners in the project.

Through participatory development, project partners can begin to acquire skills and motivation to challenge their economic, social, and political place in society, think strategically about change, and make progress. As Freire (1970) wrote in his pioneering work on pedagogy, the only valid transformation in a community is one in which people are not just liberated from hunger but made free, or enabled, to create, construct, and produce.

Experience has taught HPI that participation is not easy and takes time but is ultimately rewarding. It can increase a project's longevity and improve the use of resources, both those existing within the community and those being introduced. For instance, a focus on livestock in city food-security projects presents a unique set of challenges, such as a perceived nuisance (odour, noise) and potential threats to the security of the animals. Having neighbours work with and educate neighbours has proven to be the most effective way to overcome those challenges. Participatory approaches to project development build relationships and trust over time, diminish the donor–recipient relationship, and emphasize the partner–partner relationship.

Most projects start with a needs assessment. Identifying a community's needs — what resources they are lacking — is an important element in a good project design. However, a singular focus on needs identification emphasizes what is wrong with the community. Although neighbourhoods are often beset with crime, economic depression, and urban decay, they are also full of good leaders, caring and skilful people, vacant land, and other resources critical to a project's success. A participatory-planning approach includes asset-mapping (Kretzmann and McKnight 1993). What is it about this community that is good and strong? What resources does this community have to build on? Participation must ultimately engender local ownership of the decision-making process and project management, a commitment of local resources, and a belief in people's capacities to bring about change (Aaker and Shumaker 1996). For a community-garden project, a truck-farming initiative, or an inner-city rabbitry to be successful, the process of engendering participation becomes, in effect, more important than the project itself. Participation is both a means and an end.

The idea that the process must precede the project has been a difficult one to promote or explain to people in HPI's urban initiative in Chicago. Introducing animals into the city as a way to address community food security through consumption of the products at home and economic gain is an intriguing idea. One year after planning began, the Cabrini Green goat and oxen project is finally getting off the ground, with the imminent arrival of the animals. Planning took the form of frequent meetings and research. They would need a barn. Where would they find it? Venturing out of the housing project and getting to know the neighbours led to the discovery of a nearby carriage-horse stable with empty stalls. What regulations apply to the production and selling of cheese? Relationships had to be built with local agricultural departments and restaurants. What did they want to accomplish in this project? Did they want to make money, educate children, improve the neighbourhood, involve the local schools? Goals were defined and redefined as new information was gathered. Who were their allies? How could they mobilize the city and their neighbours to support their project? Local city councillors and Chicago Housing Authority officials were invited to participate in discussions.

HPI field staff function as facilitators and participants. Community groups learn to organize themselves, develop a plan, get to know and trust each other, and engage in capacity-building. Building sustainable urban agricultural projects is first about engendering participation. The animals come later. "We're not a livestock development organization, but a people development organization. We use livestock as the tool; many wonderful things happen as a result of people in a community coming together and working on a livestock project" (HPI 1996 p. 32).

Values-based planning

With a holistic perspective and the goal of full participation firmly in mind, the partners can begin planning the project. Values-based project planning begins with a vision of a future that grows out of the community's shared values (Aaker and Shumaker 1996). Values that communities or project groups choose to identify collectively as central to their hopes and plans for the future are called the project's cornerstones, the brick and mortar that support the structure as it develops, grows, and changes. Values-based planning, as HPI practices it, incorporates envisioning the future and evaluating the project.

The key to values-based planning is that it is a dynamic process. Managing the project often leads to redefining the situation, which leads to a different or slightly altered vision of what the community or group hopes to accomplish. HPI collaborates with groups that have been managing projects for more than 20 years. As new participants become involved, the project is encouraged to accommodate the personal visions that new participants bring with them. For instance, regional participants' meetings occur annually in HPI's USA–Canada Program. Project participants meet to share experiences of failure and success, stretch each other's imagination, and support the process of questioning their own project's effectiveness. In the early stages of a project, for instance, a group might identify learning to successfully maintain the health of dairy goats and their milk production as a way to achieve economic self-sufficiency; in later years, the activity grows to involve training in effective niche marketing to local restaurants and neighbours to reach the same value-based goal of economic self-reliance.

Values-based planning is like providing a group with well-made, time-tested, uncomplicated tools. The project participants are both the architects and the carpenters, drawing their own blueprints and crafting their own structure. This planning process is not foolproof and it takes time, but this gives it the potential to build ownership and project longevity.

Passing on the gift

Passing on the gift is one of the cornerstones that HPI relies on to govern its own vision for a world in which local agriculture is a vehicle for eradicating hunger. As an act, passing on the gift refers to the contract between HPI and its project partners. Project participants are required to pass on some form of the gift they have received from HPI.

The Robert Taylor Homes youth will provide to new youth entering the project a pound of worms for each pound they received. They will also serve as mentors, passing on the knowledge they gained in their training and experience. For instance, Robert Taylor Homes youth will conduct a hands-on training for youth in Milwaukee eager to learn to raise *Tilapia* spp. indoors in their inner city. Together, they will build the aquaculture system. By passing on the gift, HPI recipients become donors. As a value, passing on the gift captures the notion that we all have important resources to share, despite our circumstances, and that perhaps the greatest gift we can give someone else is the gift of life — metaphorically, in sharing something with and caring for another or, literally, in giving animal life.

Passing on the gift is an important management tool. It is a unique measure of accountability. The animals that HPI provides are a "living loan"; the contract is complete and the project partners have full ownership of the animals once they are passed to other project participants. Passing on the gift also contributes to the longevity and sustainability of the project. The project has less chance of becoming static as more people are brought into the circle to receive training and prepare for their animals, broadening the project and introducing their personal visions for a better life. For instance, the goat and oxen project in Cabrini Green will begin with six youth caring for two goats and two oxen. Four years later, 24 youth will be caring for and benefitting from at least six goats and two oxen. Passing on the gift helps to weave together the land- and lifescape. At its core, an animal relies on the land and also fortifies it. But the impact is also felt in the lifescape as neighbours organize, share a vision, work together, and enrich their economic and social lives.

References

Aaker, J., ed. 1994. Livestock for a small Earth: the role of animals in a just and sustainable world. Heifer Project International, Little Rock, AR, USA.

Aaker, J.; Shumaker, J. 1996. The cornerstones model: values-based planning and management. Heifer Project International, Little Rock, AR, USA.

Freire, P. 1970. The pedagogy of the oppressed. Continuum Publishing Company, New York, NY, USA.

HPI (Heifer Project International). 1996. Can Mrs. O'Leary's cow come home? Explorations in urban animal agriculture. HPI, Chicago Field Office, Chicago, IL, USA.

Kretzmann, J.P.; McKnight, J.L. 1993. Building communities from the inside out: a path toward finding and mobilizing a community's assets. ACTA Publications, Chicago, IL, USA.

Measuring the Sustainability of Urban Agriculture

Rachel A. Nugent

Introduction

What can agriculture add to a city's sustainability? Beyond the immediate benefits of fresh food, dietary variety, and landscape diversity, do cities gain in the long term from growing food within and nearby? Research suggests that it is worthwhile to look beyond traditional views of urban dwellers as consumers and rural dwellers as producers of food, especially in developing countries. Urban planners and policymakers seek practical, feasible solutions to infrastructure problems and environmental degradation while trying to address the social and economic ills of the inner city. Urban agriculture may have something to offer these policymakers. (See FAO [1996] and Smit et al. [1996] for detailed descriptions of urban agriculture.)

Food production in cities and that in the surrounding densely populated areas are called urban and peri-urban agriculture, respectively. Definitions of *city* vary by settlement characteristics and the laws of different countries. Regardless of the legal definition, every city contains some urban agriculture, in backyards, rooftop containers, public open spaces, community gardens, greenhouses, and bona fide commercial farms on the periphery. Common to these diverse agricultural activities are limited space, products that are of high value or perishable (or both), and products often consumed by the growers themselves or by nearby populations. This study presents a framework for measuring the economic, social, and environmental benefits and costs of urban agricultural production.

Because urban agriculture has only recently become the object of policy and academic interest, no standard method of quantitative analysis has yet been established to evaluate its effects. The most detailed discussion of urban agriculture to date is "Urban Agriculture: Food, Jobs, and Sustainable Cities" by Smit et al. (1996).

The present study, however, rather than being descriptive, offers a method to systematically quantify the costs and benefits of urban agriculture across a spectrum of cities.

Framework for analysis

Economists and policymakers have used cost–benefit analysis for years to assess the overall and distributional impacts of projects and policies. It has only recently been extended to environmental impacts (Hanley and Spash 1993; Schulze 1994). The present study presents an extended cost–benefit approach to identifying and quantifying the economic, social, and ecological impacts of growing and distributing food to local consumers in an urban environment. It is important to extend traditional cost–benefit-analysis techniques to recognize the nonmonetizable and nonquantifiable values and impacts (Hanley and Spash 1993) of urban agriculture.

Although methods have been devised to measure nonmarket values (see Pearce and Turner 1994), applications to urban agriculture are virtually nonexistent, and many of the impacts are still being defined. One promising way to measure ecosystem and other complex effects is to develop indicators — proxies that suggest impacts on underlying features of concern. The proxies are more observable and measurable than the features of concern and provide indirect indices of changes in these features. For instance, quantities of total particulate matter in the air or poverty rates among populations can indicate the state of otherwise unrecordable ecological and social conditions (see *Urban Quality Indicators* [Yoakam n.d.][1] and related Internet-based publications).

The results obtained using this approach are less precise than those of a standard cost–benefit project study, but they are more representative of the full range of impacts of urban agriculture. As research progresses and data improve on both urban agriculture and ecosystem impacts, this framework can be used to develop a more precise understanding of costs and benefits.

The purpose of a cost–benefit analysis is to provide a clear accounting framework for any increase or decrease in society's welfare (with society defined as the affected population). Impacts that improve society's welfare are assumed to be those that increase consumption levels of market and nonmarket goods or services (including decreases in price) or those that increase the quality of goods or services already being consumed. These impacts are called benefits. The impacts that lower society's welfare are assumed to be those that decrease the quantity or quality of consumed goods or services, increase the price of consumed goods or services, or use resources that cannot then be used for other purposes. These impacts are called costs.

A cost–benefit analysis offers policymakers and participants important information about urban agriculture. The primary purpose of such an analysis is to ascertain whether an activity is beneficial. The careful accounting required by a cost–benefit analysis also provides insights into the nature of the impacts, their distribution throughout the population, and their timing. For example, a cost–benefit analysis of urban agriculture in one location may show large short-term economic benefits. But it may also show long-term environmental costs from, for example, the deterioration of water quality from the use of chemical fertilizers. Costs and benefits of agriculture have been more extensively defined and quantified in the rural than in the urban context. Further, the same activity will often have different impacts and consequences in the urban environment. Thus, it is useful to identify differences between urban and rural agriculture to clarify the scope of the impacts.

Urban food systems

Typically, urban economies import labour and export goods and services; urban ecological systems import natural resources and export waste and pollution (import–export model). Cities cannot be self-sufficient in meeting many of the needs of their

[1] Yoakam, C. n.d. Urban quality indicators. Indicator discussion and archives (1997–present), available at RP-Cinet@RP.org.

populations, and it would be unwise to create policies to divert resources with such a goal in mind. However, urban agriculture suggests some ways to reorganize urban food systems to make them more of a closed loop, reducing both the importation of natural resources and goods and the exportation of waste and pollution. In the process, cities may derive other economic and social benefits from diverting resources to meet a broad set of citizens' needs.

A careful cost–benefit analysis can help urban planners, consumer advocates, poverty groups, and others understand how to integrate urban agriculture with local needs and conditions. For instance, an urban area in a developing country may be faced with growing numbers of poor residents who cannot purchase adequate quantities of food but are eager to engage in part-time agriculture to provide for themselves. A cost–benefit analysis can reveal that specific factors impede their engaging effectively in agricultural production, such as lack of proximity to available vacant land or scarcity of seeds. In this case, a cost–benefit analysis makes the solutions readily apparent and helps to realize the full potential of urban agriculture.

A city facing decisions about solid-waste disposal may have an incentive to develop more urban agricultural production, as it can productively use compost produced from solid waste. In Hartford, Connecticut, urban gardeners used both yard and animal wastes from horse stables for fertilizer. Although a city would not develop urban agriculture simply to dispose of compost, cost–benefit analysis of the activity can reveal that it is worthwhile to use resources in a certain manner from an economic, social, or environmental perspective.

Economically relevant impacts of urban agriculture

Under the traditional import–export model, food production and urban food consumption are separate activities or systems. They have some overlapping functions but in general are specialized and isolated from each other. Production occurs in one locale, consumption occurs in another, and each system has very little knowledge of the other. However, it is possible, by changing the location of some agricultural production to the consumers' locale, to reduce the consumers' dependence on outside sources of inputs and to reduce the disposal of waste into outside sinks (certain parts of an ecosystem, for example, wetlands, that have a biological capacity to receive and neutralize toxins or other pollutants).

The framework presented in this paper takes into account how agricultural production in cities alters the urban food system. Table 1 lists the benefits of urban agriculture, and Table 2 lists the costs. Empirical measures of these benefits and costs are presented elsewhere (Nugent 1999).

The benefits and costs of urban agriculture are put into three major categories: economic, social, and ecological. This categorization stems from the common illustration of sustainability as a "three-legged stool". A cost–benefit accounting of all the impacts in the tables would reveal the level of sustainability of urban agriculture in a selected city. A process of assigning weights to different factors could be used to account for local conditions or needs. For instance, a city with a large number of food-insecure residents may assign a heavier weight to the benefit of food production. Such

Table 1. Benefits of urban agriculture.

Agricultural production
- Marketed
- Nonmarketed

Indirect economic benefits
- Multiplier effects
- Recreational
- Economic diversity and stability
- Avoided disposal costs of solid waste

Social and psychological benefits
- Food security (available and affordable)
- Dietary diversity
- Personal psychological benefits
- Community cohesion and well-being

Ecological benefits
- Hydrologic functions
- Air quality
- Soil quality

Table 2. Costs of urban agriculture.

Inputs	Outputs
Natural resources • Land, rented or purchased • Land, vacant or donated • Water	Pollution and waste • Soil-quality impacts • Air-quality impacts • Water-quality impacts • Solid-waste and wastewater disposal
Labour • Wage and salary labour • Volunteer, unemployed, and contributed labour	
Capital and raw materials • Machinery and tools • Fertilizer and pesticides • Seeds and plants • Energy (fuel oil and electricity)	

weights would have to be derived from a process of stakeholder involvement to elicit overall community values.

Like rural agriculture, the urban production process requires inputs (land, labour, natural resources, know-how) and produces waste. In an urban environment, however, some of those inputs are provided by recycling resources that have already been used in the urban environment, thus avoiding or delaying disposal. Examples of these recycled and unused resources are vacant land; unemployed and volunteer labour; household "gray" water (water that has been used for washing dishes, etc.); and composted yard waste, wood chips, and manure. Other inputs within the urban environment may go unused for other purposes (zero opportunity cost) but be productive as part of agricultural production.

As in rural agriculture, major components of urban agriculture are packaging, transporting, and marketing of food products. However, the products of urban agriculture are frequently transported only short distances (to a farmers' market or local grocery store) or not at all (sold on site at farmstands or through pick-your-own schemes). This locational advantage obviates the need for heavy packaging and reduces the amount of energy consumed by these processes. Locally grown food products are marketed more directly to the consumer, or they are not marketed at all but given to family, friends, and neighbours.

As in rural agriculture, modern urban food production carries some health and environmental risks. This is especially true if potentially toxic chemicals are used in proximity to people or if other human activity exposes food to contamination. However, growing food in urban environments also creates documented social and health benefits, such as greater food security, nutritional diversity, community cohesion, and psychological well-being.

Future research should strive to create a better understanding of the impacts of urban agriculture and its potential for ameliorating some of the problems faced by growing urban populations. A necessary first step would be to employ a common framework for assessing the nature and distribution of costs and benefits. Using this framework, policymakers can discuss the sustainability of urban agriculture and develop appropriate policies.

References

FAO (Food and Agriculture Organization of the United Nations). 1996. State of food and agriculture. FAO, Rome, Italy.

Hanley, N.; Spash, C. 1993. Cost benefit analysis and the environment. Edward Elgar Press, London, UK.

Nugent, R. 1999. Is urban agriculture sustainable in Hartford, CT? In Furuseth, O.; Lapping, M., ed., Contested countryside: the North American rural urban fringe. Avebury, Aldershot, UK. pp. 207–230.

Pearce, D.; Turner, R.K. 1994. Economics of natural resources and the environment. Johns Hopkins University Press, Baltimore, MD, USA.

Schulze, P.C. 1994. Cost–benefit analysis and environmental policy. Ecological Economics, 9, 197–200.

Smit, J.; Ratta, A.; Nasr, J. 1996. Urban agriculture: food, jobs, and sustainable cities. United Nations Development Programme, New York, NY, USA. Publication Series for Habitat II, Vol. 1.

PART 4

ACCESSIBILITY AND URBAN FOOD DISTRIBUTION

Food Banks as Antihunger Organizations

Winston Husbands

Introduction

Food banks in Toronto fulfil an extremely valuable mandate: they provide food on an emergency basis to people in need. Moreover, through experience over several years, the food-bank community in Toronto has developed a notably sophisticated understanding of the dimensions and immediate causes of hunger in Toronto. However, despite their stated intentions, these food banks have not succeeded in addressing the structural features of this problem. This failure, though understandable, reflects the limitations of the traditional food-bank system. Insecure access to food is now more entrenched in low-income households than in the early 1980s, when the Daily Bread Food Bank (DBFB) was established. It is now evident that Toronto's major food-bank network needs to transform itself into an antihunger movement, and the large food bank at the centre of this network (DBFB) should become an antihunger organization.

Background to organized food banks in Toronto

DBFB, the largest food bank in Canada, was established in Toronto in the recession of the early 1980s. In 1982, the year before DBFB commenced operations, Toronto's unemployment rate was 10%. Although a major restructuring of Canada's economy was then taking shape, DBFB was supposed to be an emergency response to the growing problem of hunger among jobless low-income people in Toronto. Unfortunately, the problem was not short lived. Despite the original idea being that DBFB would work to put itself out of business (that is, work to eradicate hunger), it is now solidly institutionalized.

Today, almost 15 years since its inception, DBFB shows no sign of closing its doors. On the contrary, DBFB's operating expenses grew from $49 000 in 1985 to $960 000 in 1996. The increase in its budget supported a vastly expanded food-assistance program, in addition to programs designed to address food security more generally, as well as the human and other resources needed to administer them. DBFB assisted 75 000 people in 1985, but by March 1997, 133 000 people had already been assisted through 140 affiliated agencies administering 160 food programs. In a similar fashion, the quantity of food distributed rose from 800 000 kg (1985) to 24.2 million kg (1995/96). Over the last few years, DBFB also improved its efforts in research, public-policy analysis, and public education. Consequently, since the mid-1980s DBFB's staff has expanded from 5 to 22.

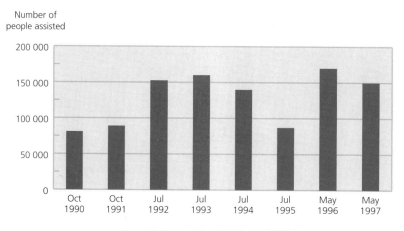

Figure 1. Toronto food-bank use, 1990–97.
Source: Daily Bread Food Bank's annual surveys of people assisted by food banks in the Greater Toronto Area.

DBFB now recognizes that acute hunger is not a transient feature of Toronto's economic life. Although DBFB has diversified its programs over the years, in 1996 it commissioned a major study to assist in transforming the agency from a food bank to an antihunger organization. It is now acknowledged that this transformation would involve rather more effort and thought than previously imagined, especially in public education and community development and mobilization.

Clearly, the initial optimism (wanting to put itself out of business) represented a fundamental misunderstanding of the problem of hunger in the early 1980s, as well as some confusion about how to respond effectively to this problem then and since.

The problem at a glance

The rising long-term trend in numbers of people assisted by DBFB and its member agencies masks significant fluctuation from one period to another — periods of increase invariably follow periods of declining food-bank use (Figure 1). This wavelike sequence, driven by fluctuations in economic activity and changes in welfare-related public policy, indicates a structural fragility in household food security. When times are good, the incidence of hunger appears to diminish, but an economic downturn or paring down of welfare benefits exposes the underlying fragility of low-income people's access to food.

Less noticeable, however, is how much more entrenched the problem of hunger is becoming.[1] This is evident in the increasing proportion of food recipients who experience the most critical level of hunger (Table 1); the large proportion of parents who cannot adequately feed their children (Table 2); and the increasing proportion of food recipients who require assistance more frequently (9% of households were assisted more than once a month in 1997, up from 5% in 1995). Moreover, the proportion of long-term recipients of food-bank assistance almost doubled between 1995 and 1997: in 1995, 9% of recipients had been food-bank clients for more than 5 years; by

---

[1] The data used to illustrate the circumstances of food recipients are derived from Daily Bread's annual survey of people assisted by food banks in the Greater Toronto Area. These surveys involve structured, face-to-face interviews with 800–1 000 randomly chosen food recipients in 30–40 hamper programs.

Table 1. Hunger among food recipients, Toronto, 1995–97.

	Respondents (%)			
	1995[a]	1996[a]		1997[b]
At least once/day	15.4	24.9	At least 2 days/week	29.2
At least once/week	15.4	19.7	About 1 day/week	15.4
At least once/month	18.3	11.8	At least 1 day/month	17.9
Seldom or never	50.9	43.6	Seldom or never	37.4

Source: Daily Bread Food Bank's annual surveys of people assisted by food banks in the Greater Toronto Area.

[a] Survey question was as follows: "How often do you go without a meal because of a lack or shortage of money to buy food?"

[b] Survey question was as follows: "During the last three months, on average how often are you hungry because you can't afford to buy enough food?"

Table 2. Parents whose children are hungry, Toronto, 1995–97.

	Respondents (%)			
	1995[a]	1996[a]		1997[b]
At least once/day	4.9	4.4	At least 2 days/week	25.1
At least once/week	6.0	10.8	About 1 day/week	12.3
At least once/month	6.7	6.1	At least 1 day/month	13.7
Seldom or never	82.3	78.7	Seldom or never	48.9

Source: Daily Bread Food Bank's annual surveys of people assisted by food banks in the Greater Toronto Area.

[a] Survey question was as follows: "How often do children in your household go without a meal because of a lack or shortage of money to buy food?"

[b] Survey question was as follows: "During the last three months, on average how often do your children eat less than they should because you can't afford to buy enough food for them?"

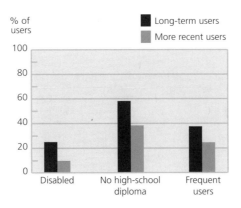

Figure 2. Long-term and more recent food recipients, 1997.
Note: long-term = >5 years; frequent users = once or more per month.
Source: Daily Bread Food Bank's annual survey of people assisted by
food banks in the Greater Toronto Area.

1997, the share of long-term recipients had risen to 15%. In addition, the circumstances of these long-term recipients are particularly worrisome (Figure 2). For example, long-term recipients are much more likely than others to be disabled or to be without a high-school diploma, which makes long-term recipients least able to benefit from employment opportunities.

At least three sets of factors explain these trends:

• Notwithstanding the upward trend in employment in Toronto since the early 1990s, the high level of food-bank use is consistent with generally high unemployment in the first half of the 1990s (Figure 3). However, clear sequences of expansion and decline in the numbers of people assisted reflect changes in unemployment to some extent. The increase in food-bank use from 1991 to 1993 corresponded to a period of particularly high unemployment, whereas the decrease from 1993 to 1995 reflected a lower unemployment rate.

• Although the unemployment rate continued to fall, food-bank use actually increased in late 1995 and 1996 after the Government of Ontario cut welfare benefits by more than 21% in October 1995. Food-bank use increased after the cuts because a larger proportion of welfare recipients could no longer pay their rent from the reduced shelter portion of their welfare payment (Figure 4) and had to draw on their basic allowance for this (that is, their food money). Food-bank use declined to some extent by May 1997, but the extent to which this represents a trend is still unclear.

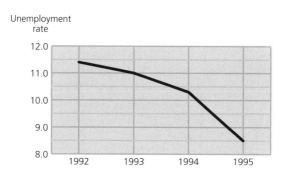

Figure 3. Unemployment rates in Toronto, 1992–95.
Source: Board of Trade of Metro Toronto, 1996.

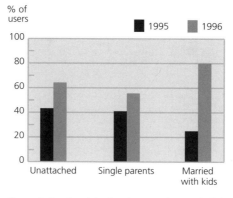

Figure 4. Food recipients whose rent exceeded the welfare shelter limit, 1995 and 1996.
Source: Daily Bread Food Bank's annual surveys of people assisted by food banks in the Greater Toronto Area.

- A rising trend toward part-time rather than full-time work hampered the reduction in food-bank use normally expected from greater employment opportunities. Only a minority of food recipients have jobs (9% in 1995; 12% in 1997). Although 40% of employed food recipients had full-time jobs in 1995, the full-time complement fell to 26% in 1997. Ideally, employed food recipients gradually recover their ability to pay for their own food, thereby causing a gradual decline in the total number of people requiring food-bank assistance. However, the shift to part-time work means that recently employed food recipients are unable to withdraw from food-bank assistance over the short or medium term because of the insufficiency of part-time wages.

Clearly, the traditional food-bank system has not in 15 years made any difference to hunger or insecurity of access to food in Toronto. DBFB has failed not only to put itself out of business but also to get a public-policy agenda entrenched to systematically address hunger and insecurity of access to food. This is largely attributable to the organization's singular (though not exclusive) focus, until recently, on the traditional food-bank system.

The problem with the traditional food-bank system

DBFB's early optimism was fundamentally in conflict with its focus on the traditional food-bank system. Traditional food banks are geared to providing emergency assistance (hunger alleviation) but not to addressing hunger as a structural phenomenon.

Food banks solicit food from the public and corporations, in addition to purchasing food from producers. The food banks then distribute the food to people in need (Figure 5). In so doing, food banks assist people in meeting their immediate needs only and are unable to accomplish much else. Because food banks depend on public and corporate goodwill, they are often unwilling to pursue social change in any determined way. Also, food banks rely to a large extent on volunteer labour and very low-key fundraising, so they often do not have the human or financial resources to undertake the research, advocacy, and community mobilization needed to systematically address

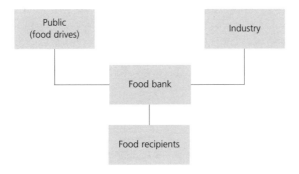

Figure 5. Hunger-alleviation model.

hunger. Of course, the relative importance of different sources of food and methods of food solicitation may change without influencing the basic philosophy or practice of a traditional food bank.

DBFB has recognized the limitations of the traditional food-bank system. In fact, over the years the organization has moved beyond the traditional system, but it remains essentially a traditional food bank, rendering emergency assistance. DBFB's agenda still does not fully incorporate the functions of an antihunger organization.

An antihunger perspective

To a considerable extent, large food banks such as DBFB, which act as a central resource supporting several dispersed programs, have reached the limits of the alleviation and emergency-assistance model for responding to hunger. If they want to address the structural issues driving hunger and insecurity of access to food, they must transform themselves into antihunger organizations.

This expanded role is difficult to define straightforwardly, but the goal of antihunger organizations is to severely reduce the incidence of hunger and eliminate the need for food banks as welfare agencies. This "eradication" model forces food banks to become antihunger organizations or at least to fulfil some of the functions of an antihunger organization. This includes some combination of research, public education, public-policy advocacy, one-on-one advocacy, and community mobilization. This transformation should not necessarily lead food banks to jettison their current alleviation and emergency-assistance programs and services — after all, people's basic needs still have to be addressed. In any case, the basic principles underlying an antihunger perspective include the following:

- The notion of a human right should be meaningfully extended to include access to food;

- Marginalized people should be empowered to insert their interests into public-policy agendas; and

- Social-service agencies, including food banks, should be challenged to render services in ways that uphold the dignity of their clients (that is, low-income people).

However, to function as antihunger organizations, food banks face some important challenges. People mostly view food banks, as the food banks present themselves: rather benign charities. Because food banks depend on individuals and corporations donating food for hungry people, they depend on the sheer goodwill of others for their success. Consequently, when they engage governments and various elites in discussions of appropriate public-policy initiatives and programs, they risk alienating the goodwill that actually makes food available to hungry people. In general, antihunger organizations also risk the charge of acting as special-interest lobbyists, and some may even perceive antihunger advocacy as the self-interest of another set of talking heads. Moreover, with respect to hunger, the term *eradication* is apt to be misunderstood, because it raises expectations that may not be fulfilled in any known time frame. These challenges suggest that research and public education, in addition to strategic alliances, would be instrumental in any rigorous antihunger agenda.

Food banks and public policy

People should not have to regularly forgo food because they are unemployed or on welfare. In other words, governments have a duty to protect their constituents from hunger. This does not, however, imply that everyone can always satisfy their food needs by normal means; however, public-policy initiatives should always promote secure access to wholesome food, rather than jeopardizing some people's ability to feed themselves. Although food banks have a vested interest in the latter, they currently have limited capacity to pressure governments or hold them responsible for substantively addressing the problem of hunger.

As it stands, food banks enter public-policy debates after the fact. Obviously, they have no direct access to or influence on government policy and program decision-making processes. Food banks have to struggle to be heard. They cannot afford to undertake the sophisticated and concerted lobbying that other types of organization frequently pursue.

Yet, antihunger organizations have no alternative but to force governments to put hunger on their public-policy agendas. To do this, the organizations have to identify a set of core ideas and proposals and then market them relentlessly in the public sphere. DBFB and similar organizations have already accomplished part of this difficult task, being storehouses of accumulated practical experience and insight into hunger and food security. Nonetheless, the credibility of their antihunger proposals must be demonstrated through research, consultation, and building and maintaining an antihunger movement, including mobilization of low-income people.

Conclusions

Joblessness and less social security have exacerbated the problem of insecurity of food access for low-income people in Toronto. In response, Toronto's food banks satisfy a limited but important mandate — they provide emergency food assistance. In pursuing this limited mandate, food banks have taken on the institutionalized role of a social-welfare agency. However, food banks need to reconstitute themselves as antihunger organizations so that they can more substantively address the problem of hunger. This new mandate would entail new services and new functions for food banks, along with improvements to their traditional emergency food programs.

...❧ ❧ ❧...

Bottlenecks in the Informal Food-transportation Network of Harare, Zimbabwe

Shona L. Leybourne and Miriam Grant

Introduction

One of the outcomes of rapid urbanization in many developing countries has been the evolution of informal (that is, unenumerated and untaxed) rural–urban and intraurban food-transportation networks. Contrary to the assumptions of policymakers and the elite, urban commercial marketing systems are beyond the reach of the vast majority of the urban poor. The combination of rising unemployment and retrenchment, escalating costs of living, increased user fees, and inadequate salaries — usually in countries with structural-adjustment programs (SAPs) — forces an ever greater number of people to seek alternative sources of food.

In Zimbabwe, urbanites have four options to meet their subsistence food needs (Drakakis-Smith 1994; ENDA–ZW 1994; Horn 1994a, b; van Zijll de Jong 1995):

- Relying on food remittances from family members in rural areas;

- Cultivating their own urban gardens;

- Creating and patronizing an alternative cheap retail system; or

- Being pushed into the cash-based commercial food-marketing system.

In and around Harare (formerly Salisbury), food-supply linkages have been established since 1927: African farm women bring their produce to town on the rural–urban buses and sell it at Harare's central wholesale market, Mbare Musika; female vendors purchase this produce and resell it throughout Harare's townships and high-density residential areas (HDRAs), 5–20 km away (Horn 1994b).

During our 1994 fieldwork, it became clear that 1.25 million people (80–90% of Harare's population) rely on informal rural–urban and intraurban food-distribution networks. These networks transfer food from producer to consumer, using everything from scotchcart to bicycles to buses to emergency taxis (Jamare 1993).

Given Harare's heavy dependence on the informal food-distribution network, fluctuations can have a critical impact on people's food insecurity. Food insecurity, or people's fear (according to Maxwell 1996) that they will not have food in the near future, is exacerbated in an informal economy. People become increasingly fearful that their long- and short-term food needs will not be met. The reasons for this are extensive: income-generation opportunities are uncertain; the informal food-transportation system may encounter impediments; and the price of food may escalate beyond people's means.

This paper argues that the transportation of small quantities of foodstuffs within a broad network of producers, transporters, retailers, and consumers enhances food security for the vast majority of the urban poor. Despite this significance, one of the prevailing forces of the network's operation is fear: drivers' fear of being punished by the police, vendors' fear of their produce spoiling or of their losing their investment, and consumers' fear of the state's use of power aggravating rather than alleviating their food insecurity. We explore the mechanisms of state control and disenfranchisement in the informal food-transportation system and the ways people manoeuvre within the context of hardship and oppression and "help one another."

The case study: food vendors, emergency taxis, and official interventions

The purpose of the fieldwork, conducted between May and October 1994, was to explore the largely invisible and "illegitimate" informal food-transportation system in Harare and uncover the layers of collaboration and negotiation among actors and their reactions to official regulations and enforcement. Interviews with various agents, such as bus conductors, emergency-taxi drivers, rural–urban food traders, and fresh-produce vendors, revealed the silence of actors in the illegitimate and invisible system. The state seemed unable to understand the linkage between increased crackdowns and fines on intraurban transport, on the one hand, and growing bottlenecks in the informal food-distribution system, on the other.

Although Cheater (1979) tangentially discussed Zimbabwe's informal food-transportation system, most local scholars (for example, Ndzombane 1982; Kwinjo 1983; Ziupfu 1988; Nyahunzvi 1992; Mutizwa-Mangiza 1993) have concentrated on formal and informal modes of transportation without acknowledging their use in transporting agricultural commodities. Within Harare, the illegally operated pirate taxis, which emerged in the 1960s, were finally legalized under the label of "emergency taxis" in 1981. However, taxis that persisted in operating without the required registration or specific passenger insurance were still considered as being pirate taxis (Kwinjo 1983).

Over the years, the economic and political vulnerability of transporters, vendors, and consumers has provided the social impetus for a grudging sense of collaboration. At the end of each month's pay period, the local economy expands. Because the urban poor often spend 50% of their income on food (CSO 1992), this is a critical time for food vendors. Most will ask friends for small loans so they can increase their stock. Because the food could perish before it is sold, efficient transportation to the market is a critical factor in the vendors' economic well-being.

The vibrant market of Mbare Musika is a dynamic terminus of rural–urban and intraurban informal food-distribution networks. Emergency-taxi drivers solicit business from vendors who have purchased large quantities of produce and require transport, usually to the HDRAs. Transporting large, bulky bags of maize, onions, tomatoes, and *rape* (a local leafy green) is a cumbersome chore. The difficulties are exacerbated when consumer, vendor, and transporter are increasingly vulnerable to the whims of authorities enforcing the transport regulations, such as the police, whose options include ignoring, harassing, or fining people for their illegal activities.

October 1994 proved to be a difficult month for pirate-taxi drivers: fines rose overnight from 150 ZWD to 400 ZWD for those illegally transporting passengers and produce (in 1998, 33 Zimbabwe dollars [ZWD] = 1 United States dollar [USD]). This sub-stantially affected the dynamics of Mbare Musika. Police harassment increased along with the fines. Drivers were admonished for carrying more than seven passengers, for not having passenger insurance, and for not registering with the Controller of Road Motor Transport. Deeper investigation identified that these small trucks were not allowed by the city council to register as commuter vehicles. This situation was wors-ened by involvement of the commuter-omnibus operators (COOs). Because the COOs are legal and compete with the pirate taxis, the COOs encouraged authorities to enforce the laws.

This major crackdown had a considerable impact on vendors, of course. Vendors' comments emphasized their increasing difficulties and frustrations with transportation:

> Transport on the working days is no problem ... . Saturday and Sunday the police are waiting, people are scared to ferry [transport] us. Police are asking drivers with the people and parcels to go to the office. We wait there for 3–5 hours. The transporters do not want to ferry us.
>
> Transport is many problems. The price is too high, higher than before. Now there is no profit [selling the produce] because of the transport and we use the bus because [with] the ETs [emergency taxis] ... there is problems with the police ... they will be waiting on the way ... they don't want the ETs to carry the vendors ... .
>
> Transport is more dangerous problem. We don't get transport in time, so we sell our things late in the afternoon, so there will be no business ... . If we can get a straight transport to where we sell our things, things would be better ... .

These comments illustrate three key points. First, the transportation problem affects the vendors' ability to sell their fresh, highly perishable produce. Second, the time the ven-dors spend waiting for transportation is longer than the time they spend ultimately sell-ing their produce. Third, up to this point, emergency taxis were convenient to the vendors, because if the vendors chose to take the bus instead, they always had to wait for a bus with an empty boot (space underneath), which increased the amount of time they were investing. However, the vendors then had to deal with the increase in the cost of emergency taxis as a proportion of their investment, the increasing unpre-dictability of this mode of transportation (48% cited police-related delays), and possible losses incurred from produce spoilage.

At the heart of the process of gaining access to transportation was multilevel negotiation between vendors and bus drivers or conductors or emergency-taxi drivers, between vendors and authorities, and between transporters and authorities. Although everyone was aware of the significance of transporting the food, especially to HDRAs, negotiations significantly increased the costs of getting the food to the customer. For pirate-taxi drivers, harassment included spending 3–5 h in the police station or the Vehicle Inspection Depot, negotiating with authorities and often, even then, paying the full fine. Vendors could be abandoned by the roadside. Indeed, many were forced to take a bus back to Mbare Musika to search for another willing emergency-taxi driver.

To deal with this heightened harassment, the pirate-taxi drivers formulated three strategies. The first and most effective way to avoid police confrontation was to refuse to transport the vendors, which left many vendors stranded and angry. The sec-ond strategy was to leave Mbare Musika before 09:00, even though it was a miscon-ception that fewer police were on the road between 06:00 and 09:00. The third strategy was economic. As transport to the HDRAs was scarce, prices could be raised to offset financial negotiations with police. Vendors reported that emergency-taxi prices had doubled over the past year, and this took place in conjunction with increases in the cost of produce.

All this has had a serious domino effect, reaching each actor in the system. Increased transportation costs, which often translate into higher produce costs, have resulted in the collapse of many of the support systems for the segment of urban poor with little or no income. Excessive transportation costs have also left many vendors without sufficient capital to operate the next day. This has affected their own food security. Rising produce costs (410% from 1990 to 1995 [EIU 1996]) have increased the amount of bribery going on inside and outside the marketplace and heightened security problems within Mbare Musika.

The location of some of the residential areas is another problem for the vendors. As Table 1 illustrates, the vendors who serve the low- and medium-density residential areas, closest to the market, spend the least on transportation, and those who service the HDRAs have the highest range of transportation costs. Because the supermarkets are located closer to central Harare and its suburbs, the majority of HDRA residents need the vendors to supply them with fresh produce, particularly soup ingredients (for example, tomatoes, *covo*, *rape*, and onions), as most lack refrigerators. Also, as most lack both the means of transportation and the cash to patronize formal supermarkets (Drakakis-Smith 1994), they have come to rely heavily on the informal food-retail system, which has met their needs sufficiently over the years.

Conclusions

Often people in the informal sector suffer food insecurity because the state in no way protects their jobs. A strategically oriented dialogue is crucial to the survival of the urban poor, and it should involve the state's recognition of the key roles played in the informal food-distribution system; policies should facilitate, rather than punish, involvement in the network. This network of local structures has been created by the people for the people to ensure basic food security.

As a baseline study, this has captured how nonfood policies affect people's food security and interpersonal lives. It has shown how official restrictions had the effect of initiating collaboration among transporters, vendors, and consumers, with levels of affinity corresponding to degrees of economic vulnerability. Different interests at each link of the chain are soon negotiated, depending on the importance of each actor to the survival of the informal food-distribution community. A common interest exists

Table 1. Average daily transportation costs of vendors by residential area, Harare, Zimbabwe, 1994

ZWD	Proportion of vendors		
	LDRAs	MDRAs	HDRAs
0–5.49	71	43	43
5.50–10.49	29	57	37
10.50–14.99	0	0	15
>15.00	0	0	5

Source: van Zijll de Jong (1995).
Note: HDRA, high-density residential area; LDRA, low-density residential area; MDRA, medium-density residential area; ZWD, Zimbabwe dollars (in 1998, 33 ZWD = 1 United States dollar [USD]).

inasmuch as they are all subject to policies that ignore each actor's role in ensuring local food security. Authority figures manipulate the criminalization approach, usually to gain financially. Attempts by individuals to petition or politically influence the state have, for the most part, been unsuccessful.

Until the state recognizes the actors within the informal food-distribution system in cities such as Harare and stops harassing them, it will continue to exacerbate the food-insecurity problem for a large proportion of the urban poor. Without formal recognition of the contribution of the informal food-distribution network to the food security of the city, these people's "margin to manoeuvre" (Campbell and Parfitt 1995, p. 6) will continue to decline, alongside the socioeconomic–political well-being of Zimbabwe, which is held in the grips of an SAP.

References

Campbell, B.; Parfitt, T. 1995. Virtual adjustment: whose reality? Review of African Political Economy, No. 63.

Cheater, A.P. 1979. The production and marketing of fresh produce among Blacks in Zimbabwe. University of Rhodesia, Salisbury, Rhodesia. 41 pp.

CSO (Central Statistics Office). 1992. Quarterly digest of statistics. CSO, Harare, Zimbabwe.

Drakakis-Smith, D. 1994. Food systems and the poor in Harare under conditions of structural adjustment. Geografiska Annaler B, 76, 3–20.

EIU (Economist Intelligence Unit). 1996. EIU #1. EIU, London, UK.

ENDA–ZW (Environment and Development Activities – Zimbabwe). 1994. Urban agriculture in Harare. ENDA-ZW, Harare, Zimbabwe. IDRC 93-0024. 47 pp.

Horn, N.E. 1994a. Still invisible: women microentrepreneurs and the economic crisis in Zimbabwe. Paper presented at the 1994 annual meeting of the African Studies Association, Toronto, ON, Canada.

――― 1994b. Cultivating customers: market women in Harare, Zimbabwe. Lynne Rienner Publishers, Boulder, CO, USA. 186 pp.

Jamare, J. 1993. Public transport user behaviour analysis: a focus on the city–Canaan route. University of Zimbabwe, Harare, Zimbabwe. Hons BA thesis.

Kwinjo, C.T. 1983. The informal transport sector in Harare. University of Zimbabwe, Harare, Zimbabwe. Hons BA thesis.

Maxwell, S. 1996. Food security: a post-modern perspective. Food Policy, 21(2), 155–170.

Mutizwa-Mangiza, N.D. 1993. Urban informal transport policy: the case of emergency taxis in Harare. In Zinyama, L.; Tevera, D.; Cumming, S., ed., Harare: the growth and problems of the city. University of Zimbabwe, Harare, Zimbabwe. pp. 97–105.

Ndzombane, N. 1982. A time–movement study using Harare as the centre. University of Zimbabwe, Harare, Zimbabwe. Hons BA thesis.

Nyahunzvi, D.K. 1992. Urban–rural linkages: a case study of travel patterns. University of Zimbabwe, Harare, Zimbabwe. Hons BA thesis.

van Zijll de Jong, S. 1995. Rural–urban and intra-urban food distribution networks of Harare, Zimbabwe. The University of Calgary, AB, Canada. MA thesis.

Ziupfu, C. 1988. Road traffic accident analysis in Harare, 1986. University of Zimbabwe, Harare, Zimbabwe. Hons BA thesis.

From Staple Store to Supermarket: The Case of TANSAS in Izmir, Turkey

Mustafa Koc and Hulya Koc

Introduction

The notion of self-regulating markets is a myth. Even in advanced industrialized countries, the state has always intervened in or regulated the market to some degree. The level of intervention varies with the regime of accumulation, the dominant discourse about the state–society relationship, and the nature of that society's social, political, and ideological struggles. State intervention is particularly significant in the primitive accumulation phase of capitalist development, during times of economic recession, and in certain accumulation regimes, such as import-substitution industrialization. The recent tendency to privatize, deregulate, and decentralize the public sector has reduced the role of the state in the economy and made certain segments in society increasingly vulnerable. This paper examines the role of local government in shaping food policy and improving access to food, specifically in the case of TANSAS, a municipally owned staple-store project that turned into a supermarket chain in Izmir, Turkey.

From the time when Turkey was founded, in 1923, the modern Turkish state has played a very active role in forming the country's food and agriculture policies. As well as encouraging industrialization and modern agriculture, the state has intervened in the economy directly, through various policy measures, and indirectly, through the activities of state economic enterprises. State economic enterprises have sought to create favourable conditions for the accumulation process in Turkey by offering essential services, infrastructure, and products that the private sector is unable to supply. Parallel to the actions of state enterprises are regulatory measures to protect producers through support pricing and protectionist customs policies and the consumers through subsidies or price regulations on major staples. State interventions and regulations have also been introduced at the local level. Municipal Law 1580 (item 15/43), for example, required local governments to take measures to lower the cost of living through such devices as offering basic consumer goods to consumers without intermediaries.

Industrialization in Turkey gained momentum after World War II. Production of nondurable consumer goods, such as textiles and processed food, dominated the manufacturing sectors in the 1950s. This gave way in the late 1960s and throughout the 1970s to a new emphasis on consumer durables, including household appliances and cars. Turkey's endeavour to modernize agriculture was particularly instrumental in the success of this domestic industry. From the early 1950s on, Turkey mechanized and commodified its agriculture. This resulted in a major rural–urban population movement. Between 1950 and 1960 alone, the rural portion of Turkey's total population declined from 81.3% to 74.1%. This migration continued without interruption in the decades that followed. The rural "surplus population" constituted the basis for the urban proletariat and the informal sector and served as a captive market for domestic industry.

The conditions of workers with steady jobs and those of Turkish migrant workers employed in Western Europe improved considerably. Real wages increased steadily throughout the 1960s. Changes in labour laws gave people the opportunity to retire with a significant pension and severance pay after 20–25 years of work. For the majority of new pensioners, these payments offered the chance to open a workshop in their trade or a retail store. A new social class of petty bourgeoisie emerged out of the ranks of retired proletarians and public-sector employees. Even for the marginalized masses, the semiemployed, and the subproletariat who were unable to find jobs in the formal labour market, the urban boom offered new opportunities. Thousands of pedlars and petty traders responded effectively to the gap created by rapid urbanization, industry's indolence, and government's inability to provide effective services.

By the 1970s, thousands of small retailers and people operating service shops of all sorts were competing for a share of the urban market. Favourable customs barriers, resulting from import-substitution policies, enabled industry to dictate prices to the owners of small shops. Shop owners, in turn, in the attempt to maintain living standards for their families through commercial or service activities had no choice but to pass these costs on to their customers by increasing prices to whatever level competition would allow.

The nation's economic situation declined dramatically in the mid-1970s, as a result of increases in energy and input costs that followed the oil crisis. Spiralling inflation and a serious foreign-exchange crisis required continuous devaluation of the lira and battered the Turkish economy throughout the 1970s. By the late 1970s, annual inflation was running at around 100%. Major staple items were in short supply. The rapid increase in prices encouraged retailers to keep some of the most desired items off their shelves, either to avoid losing in the inflationary environment or to benefit from it. Governments often accused retailers of contributing to inflation by hoarding or black-marketing items in short supply. Big line-ups would appear in front of stores where people believed they could buy such items as margarine, rice, sugar, cigarettes, or coal.

Emergence of staple stores

Throughout the 1970s, local governments in many municipalities intervened in the market, to penalize hoarders and regulate prices, by supplying major staples at a lower price. In 1973 the municipal government of Izmir authorized the city abattoir to sell meat and coal at a low price. In 1976, the Regulation Sales Directory (RSD) opened its first store in downtown Izmir and started selling basic staples, as well as meat and coal. In 1977, the RSD had eight stores carrying such items as meat, milk products, margarine, vegetable oil, pulses, rice, pasta, flour, soap, and detergents and a variety of food items produced by cooperatives and public enterprises. In 1977, the local government boasted of selling a kilogram of rice for 6.90 lira, whereas it sold for as much as 35 lira in the market. Despite such prices, the staple stores' rate of profit that year was 14.3% (Izmir 1977). In a short time, staple stores became very popular among working- and middle-class urban residents. The success of these stores and the demand for regular supplies and low prices led to the emergence of TANSAS, in 1978, as a wholesale supplier for municipal staple stores.

Izmir had a series of social-democratic municipal governments throughout the 1970s, with a political commitment to intervene in and regulate the market to protect "consumers." Despite the government's best efforts in the inflationary environment of the late 1970s, real wages began to decline. Strikes, work stoppages, and political demonstrations became commonplace. In January 1980, the Turkish government adopted a set of stabilization policies recommended by the International Monetary Fund. These policies favoured a neoliberal course of action with the following emphases:

- Removal of price distortions through elimination of price controls and subsidies;

- Liberalization of trade through elimination of import quotas, reduction in tariffs, and implementation of realistic exchange-rate policies; and

- Reduction of the role of the state in the economy through privatization, deregulation, and reductions in government spending.

The new austerity package was designed to integrate Turkey more closely into the global economy and redirect economic resources to those sectors of the economy most able to adapt to this orientation. The success of this strategy depended on increasing the profitability and productivity of Turkish industry. This meant further reducing workers' wages, as well as suppressing trade-union activity. The military coup of September 1980 made it possible to implement these policies without democratic opposition.

During its first 3 years, the military government outlawed strikes and scrapped existing collective-bargaining agreements. It introduced restrictions on the right to strike, the establishment of new unions, and the collective-bargaining process, as well as putting restrictions on severance pay, seniority rights, and social-insurance benefits. These measures were accompanied by a severe decline in real wages (about 50%, by some calculations) between 1977 and 1984. In this economic environment, affordable food became an important issue of political legitimacy and public policy.

In 1981, under orders of the martial-law authorities, the staple stores were transferred to the newly formed Staple Sales Directory. The number of staple stores increased to 14, and 4 new stores on wheels were introduced to improve accessibility in working-class neighbourhoods. By 1985, the number of stores was 32. They claimed to offer 25% savings to consumers, and they did offer services to about 70 000 families (about 14% of total households).

In 1986, TANSAS was incorporated as a retail enterprise and meat combine. This transformation of a public corporation into a profit-making enterprise was compatible with the dominant neoliberal discourse of the time and drew no noticeable public reaction. TANSAS started to expand its line of products and services. It introduced fresh fruits and vegetables, registered itself as a fresh-produce wholesaler at the city's food terminal, and created a packaging company and a sausage factory. It also became the city's food caterer.

By 1989, TANSAS had 66 retail outlets, three cafeterias, and a modern bakery, producing 20 000 loaves a day. TANSAS continued to play a role in regulating prices in the city. In 1990, it started putting ads in local newspapers, displaying prices of 100 staples, to control price increases. TANSAS was now a large price-setting enterprise in direct competition with local corner stores. In fact, by the early 1990s, TANSAS started offering wholesale products to independent grocery stores, claiming to be the "grocer of grocers." Turning local corner stores and independent grocers into TANSAS outlets was defended as public policy.

Observing the success of TANSAS, new supermarket chains initiated food-retailing and supermarket ventures. Independent chain stores, supermarkets, and hypermarkets started to expand into the Turkish market with 15 000–30 000 different products and with discount prices for bulk items. By 1996, Turkey had about 40 hyper-markets and 400 supermarkets. Major Turkish corporate ventures entered the super-marketing business, either independently or in joint ventures with major European chains, such as Metro Gross Market (Germany), Carrefour and Promodes (France), and GIB (Belgium).

The expansion of supermarkets during the 1990s greatly changed food access, pricing, and consumption. First, the independent corner stores; groceries, green gro-cers, butchers, and bakers started to feel the pinch. Many could no longer survive as family enterprises, and others ended up becoming small retail outlets of the major supermarkets. Second, the supermarkets, with their wholesale to retailers and retail or bulk sales to consumers, became the price- and trend-setters in the marketplace. Finally, as store sizes expanded, space limitations in the inner-city neighbourhoods pushed the supermarkets to suburban locations. The change in location, combined with bulk bargains, started to alter shopping and food-consumption patterns, particularly those of the urban middle class. Buying daily from local neighbourhood stores became a habit of the past, replaced with weekly shopping trips and bargain hunting for bulk items. Cars became increasingly popular, despite the traffic chaos, as they gave con-sumers easier access to better bargains and more choices. Unable to compete against supermarkets, more and more inner-city grocers changed over to specialty stores to serve wealthier middle-class clients. Interestingly, all of these changes occurred in par-allel with the law-and-order initiatives of local-government authorities. Crackdowns on illegal pedlars selling food made access to cheap food even more difficult for a larger segment of the population. TANSAS continued to boast that it was still playing a regu-latory role in the marketplace, but now the causes of the access problems were com-pletely different. Operating as a supermarket chain, TANSAS was itself one of the problems (Table 1).

TANSAS continued to expand its operations and number of stores throughout the 1990s. By 1996, it had become one of the two biggest supermarket chains in Turkey. It had 91 stores, 13 of which were located in major resort towns outside the city limits. TANSAS stores were carrying about 14 000 different items, with 28–29% of these bear-ing the company's label. Store sizes continued to increase, and TANSAS gradually expanded to suburban or out-of-town locations. Seven stores with more than 1 750 m^2 of space were responsible for 22% of sales (Table 2). TANSAS also owned shares in

Table 1. Market share of supermarkets and hypermarkets in various European countries, 1980–95.

	Share (%)		
	1980	1990	1995
United Kingdom	81	87	89
Germany	58	60	62
Italy	26	40	51
Turkey	3	9	16

Source: TANSAS (1996).

several other municipally operated companies specializing in such diverse fields as tourism management, insurance, computer consulting, and printing and publishing (Table 3).

Despite its claim to being a publicly held company, until recently, 94.27% of TANSAS was owned by the municipal government. In 1988, 5.22% of the shares were offered to the public. A TANSAS advertisement in the municipal government periodical, *Izmir Buyuksehir Belediye Dergisi* (1987), was highly reflective of the new notion of public enterprise:

> TANSAS RETURNS TO THE PUBLIC WHAT IT TAKES FROM THEM
> Corporations are formed to make profits. If this is not so, they will be in unfair competition with other enterprises, which is a crime according to law. TANSAS too makes profits, but TANSAS is owned by the public. Naturally, its profits will also be returned to the public.

In 1996, TANSAS revealed its intention to offer another 32.98% of its shares to the public. This was partly a response to the national campaign for privatization of state economic enterprises. Changes in the corporate tax laws required that at least 15% of the ownership of a publicly held corporation be in public hands. A quick check of various Internet sites revealed that TANSAS shares were snapped up on the Istanbul stock exchange. Significant TANSAS shares in the portfolios of various European mutual-fund companies were also an indication that TANSAS's "public" was global, no longer just the citizens of Izmir.

Table 2. TANSAS stores by floor size, 1996.

Size (m²)	Stores (n)	Share of sales (%)
<250	36	18
251–500	24	19
501–750	9	10
751–1 000	5	6
1 001–1 250	5	14
1 251–1 500	2	5
1 501–1 750	2	6
>1 750	7	22

Source: TANSAS (1996).

Table 3. TANSAS investments in other ventures, 1996.

Company	Specialization	Shares (%)
Tansas Tarim Urunleri Tic. San.	Agricultural products	95
Izbeltur	Tourism management	90
Tansas Sigorta Aracilik Hizmetleri	Insurance	90
Unibel	Computer consulting	25
Teknopark	Technology research	16.9
Izmir Buyuk Sehir Belediyesi Yayincilik ve Tanitim	Printing and publishing	15
Ege Sehir Planlamasi ve Isbirligi Merkezi A.S.	Urban planning	7.2
Besyildiz Dis Ticaret Ltd Sti.	Restaurant management	5
Izmir Su ve Kanalizasyon Hiz. A.S.	Water and sewage treatment	3
Izulas A.S.	Public transit	2
Izmir Buyuk Sehir Belediyesi Bakim Onarim A.S.	Repair and service	1

Source: TANSAS (1996).

Finally, in the spring of 1998, a consortium of a private bank (Finansbank) and a holding company (Gucbirligi Holding) that had captured a 22% share of TANSAS, following the earlier privatization campaign, purchased another 29% of TANSAS shares from the municipal government. With this, the city's share declined to 10% of the total. This was the end of the first municipally owned supermarket chain in Turkey (Turkmen 1998).

Lessons to learn

1. Local staple stores can play a vital role in improving food access, particularly for the urban poor and middle classes. Such stores, with their bulk buying capacities, limited shelf space, lack of concern for advertising and store appearance, and smaller profit margins, can offer cheaper effective alternatives to typical private retail distribution systems. Unlike food banks, they offer better selection and choice and more dignified access to affordable food and they operate independently of continuous private or corporate donations. Customers in staple stores choose items they need and prefer, without losing their self-respect. Staple stores can also indirectly regulate price levels in the marketplace, especially in highly inflationary environments. In these environments, they protect a large segment of the population from hoarders and speculators. These operations do not offer unfair competition to the existing retail systems but only complement them when they fail.

2. There are, however, no easy solutions for improving access to food. Often the cure becomes a problem. Although it protected consumers from high inflation and speculation in the 1970s, TANSAS inadvertently played a role in introducing and spreading supermarket chains in Turkey. The small neighbourhood stores that have been the livelihood of tens of thousands of small family operations are disappearing. Consumers have to travel longer distances, change their shopping habits (buy less frequently items that are less fresh in larger quantities), spend more time traveling, and store food items longer. This turns their households into a storage space for supermarket chains. Although what happened in this case was somewhat affected by a unique combination of events, expansion beyond the original purpose of improving access and regulating prices is potentially self-defeating for all staple-store operations.

3. Intense global economic pressure and international regulation have eroded certain powers of nation-states, shifting more and more responsibility to regional and local governments. This shift partly reflects recent tendencies toward the decentralization and restructuring of the nation-state and partly reflects the increasing demand from local populations for effective and representative government. Both the increasing vulnerability of certain segments of the urban population and the new roles of urban regions in the globalized economy highlight the importance of local-level policy-making. The neoliberal restructuring schemes, however, not only erode the nation-state's role in the economy but also attempt to re-create the state on a corporate model. This creates a serious threat to the future of public enterprise and public policy. Using populist jargon, such as "less state," elected governments can easily and irreversibly destroy years of effort in a very short time (Koc 1995). We challenge this vision and believe that governments should keep public agencies at least within arm's length to create their capacities to serve the public interest, with or without the support of the state.

References

Izmir Belediyesi. 1977. Izmir 1977, Belediye Calismalari. Karinca Matbaaclik ve Ticaret Kollektif Sirketi, Izmir, Turkey.

Izmir Buyuksehir Belediye Dergisi. 1987. Izmir Buyuksehir Belediye Dergisi, 11 (Oct). Inside back cover.

Koc, M. 1995. Global restructuring and communities. *In* Wolensky, B.; Miller, E., ed., Social science and the community. Proceedings of the Conference on the Small City and Regional Community. Vol. 11. University of Wisconsin–Stevens Point Foundation Press, Milwaukee, WI, USA.

TANSAS. 1996. Tansas Halka Aciliyor. Izmir Buyuksehir Belediyesi Ic ve Dis Ticaret Anonim Sirketi, Izmir, Turkey. Brochure. 30 pp.

Turkmen, H. 1998. 28 trilyonluk ozellestirme. Yeni Asir (2 May), 5.

A Nonprofit System for Fresh-produce Distribution: The Case of Toronto, Canada

Kathryn Scharf

Introduction

Every month, 4 000 boxes of fresh fruit and vegetables are delivered to 200 volunteer-run neighbourhood dropoffs in Metropolitan Toronto. The Good Food Box (GFB) project of FoodShare Metro Toronto is essentially a large buying club, based on many of the same principles and aspirations as Japan's Seikatsu Club, the United States' Share Box, and Brazil's Citizens' Action Against Hunger and Poverty and for Life. Since its inception in 1993 the GFB has grown steadily, and eight towns in Southern and central Ontario have adopted the model or variations of it. This paper provides a case study of the development, operation, and principles of the GFB as a successful community-based market-driven food-distribution alternative.

Development of the GFB project

The GFB was the eventual outcome of the Field to Table project, started in 1991 by the Toronto Food Policy Council (FPC). The members of the FPC recognized that food banks were an inadequate response to urban hunger and that hunger at the individual and household levels is not the only facet of food insecurity (FPC 1994). A feasibility study proposed alternatives for people with food-access barriers, such alternatives as small, preorder buying clubs and traveling fresh-produce markets. FoodShare, a Toronto anti-hunger organization, agreed to take over the actual operation and administration of the Field to Table project. An advisory group comprising Ontario farmers and antipoverty activists provided direction for the project.

Buying clubs and markets are designed to provide people with locally grown, nutritious, fresh food in their neighbourhoods, independently of the for-profit retail system. Although they succeed on one level, they are extremely labour intensive and expensive to run. They require a high number of staff hours and a lot of labour and faith from community members. Inspired by international models from Brazil and Japan, the FPC and FoodShare staff began to develop what they hoped would be a more efficient and sustainable system that would serve more people. In February 1994, staff packed the first 40 GFB food boxes at FoodShare's offices.

Operations

The GFB purchases the food for its boxes from the Ontario Food Terminal (the outlet for most imported and local produce coming into Ontario). As the project grew, it began to buy directly from farmers. The GFB distribution system developed into a partly staff-driven, partly volunteer-run project. Volunteers pack boxes twice monthly, then deliver them to any neighbourhood location in Toronto with 10 or more individuals or families who want to buy a box. Volunteer coordinators collect money in advance of delivery, call in orders, then make sure that customers get their boxes.

The GFB buys food centrally, based on the numbers of advance orders. The advance-order system minimizes waste and is designed to coincide with the income cycles of people on social assistance (orders and payment are made when money is available; food arrives when supplies and money are scarce). The boxes have standard contents, although items vary with each delivery, according to what is in season or what is a good deal at the time. Participants sacrifice choice for affordability and convenience.

Principles

Even at the planning stage, a top priority of the GFB was to ensure that the produce was very fresh and of the best quality, with a good balance of staples and luxury items. Centralized purchasing also permits a focus on other goals of food-security and health: buying locally and as directly as possible allows the GFB to provide in-season produce and offer more nutritious produce (for example, romaine lettuce versus iceberg lettuce). The GFB newsletter included in the box provides information on food preparation, nutrition, and food issues.

The GFB reflects a philosophy distinct from, though not incompatible with, other strategies to reduce hunger. On the one hand, traditional charity focuses on the individual and his or her immediate household food shortage; on the other, the GFB is an example of advocacy for systemic, long-term solutions on behalf of entire classes of people (for example, advocacy for income redistribution). The GFB is a response to problems recognized by most antihunger activists: that food banks are not a sustainable food-distribution mechanism and that food-bank recipients often feel that their self-esteem is damaged by having to rely on charity. Although unquestionably the emergency and advocacy approaches are vital, the GFB also challenges assumptions often shared by proponents of both these approaches — that the normal, or "ideal," food-distribution mechanism is the for-profit retail system and that if people had enough money to buy food, they would have no problem with the food system.

A food-security analysis shows that adequate income is a necessary but not sufficient condition for food security on either the individual or the societal level. The GFB challenges the premise that the oligopolistic retail food sector, so largely shaped by advertising and profit-making exigencies, is the healthiest way for everyone to obtain their food. Thus, even if everyone had enough money to buy food from a supermarket tomorrow, would our food supply necessarily be safe, stable, and geared toward community needs and individual health? Would we have the skills and nutritional knowledge needed to prepare food and have the socially rewarding and empowering food culture needed to enjoy it?

The GFB incorporates some elements of a traditional business. It is a "community business," which must survive in a marketplace dominated by powerful, "efficient" corporations. This means that the GFB must offer products, delivery, and service that are competitive with, or superior to, those offered by a supermarket. The market mechanism is thus a good indicator of whether the project works for people and avoids taking a top-down approach that fails to address real community needs.

In a capitalist society, without other types of meaningful social participation, people often find self-affirmation in being treated as "customers." This is partly because a retailer must treat people with respect and provide a good-quality product. If these are not forthcoming, customers will exercise their power of complaint and their prerogative to shop elsewhere. Aside from the real, practical nature of the consumer relationship, it has a symbolic dimension. A good-quality product and good service give customers the message that they are valued. Low-income people are often the recipients of inferior goods, either those they receive from food banks or those they are forced to select to save money (the "garbage food for garbage people" perception that Foley [1992] identified among food-bank recipients). The high-quality food in the GFB is intended to send the message that "you're worth it." This is confirmed by the professional evaluations of the GFB, which have consistently cited the good quality of the food in GFB as an important motive for purchasing GFB food boxes (SWC 1996).

One can speculate that this is one explanation for the lack of popularity of the Staples Box and the Basic Box, which were experimental versions of the GFB, providing basic dry goods and less expensive fruit and vegetables, respectively. Although it is difficult to identify all the variables that might explain their failure, the customers may well have been too used to shopping for the "no-name" and lower end food items and they therefore experienced them more negatively than they did the goods in the GFB food boxes, with their touches of extravagance (strawberries, cranberries at Christmas, etc.). On a purely practical level, the Staples Box and Basic Box may have made sense, but customers may have experienced them as simply no fun.

The GFB has never used a means test. This is to avoid the stigma attached to services exclusively for poor people. A recent study of food insecurity in Scarborough, a suburb of Toronto, found that 46% of low-income people surveyed had never used a food bank (SHC 1997). The stigma attached to the use of food banks (especially strong among some immigrant groups) appears to have been a primary reason for this. If the fear of stigma prevents people from using even a free service constructed only for low-income people, then a service charging a fee and requiring unconventional shopping practices must be even more wary of putting people off. The organizers' analysis of the failure of one GFB experiment in Windsor, Ontario, bears out the theory that the association with charity may cause people to avoid participating (Scharf and Morgan 1998). It would be impossible to administer a means test without sending the message that this service caters to "the poor." So the GFB has never used one. However, the GFB targets low-income neighbourhoods and groups.

The GFB's refusal to employ a means test is also justified because most people, regardless of income, consume inadequate amounts of fresh fruit and vegetables. Evaluation shows that GFB customers do increase their intake of fresh fruit and vegetables, possibly either because the GFB raises their awareness of the health benefits or because it fills the refrigerator with fresh food that must be eaten or left to spoil. Higher income people use the project at a much lower rate, perhaps because they have the transportation and money to access exactly the food they want at exactly the time they want it (SWC 1996).

The GFB competes in the marketplace of imagery as well. Early evaluations showed that low-quality publicity materials created an impression of a low-quality product (Saint Jacques 1994). So care has been taken to create bright, upbeat materials that acknowledge that low-income people are savvy media consumers and that they would prefer to be a part of a project with positive, uplifting imagery than one with a dingy or depressing aura.

Although the GFB seeks to be efficient and sustainable, it goes far beyond the traditional retailer's role in its response to community needs. Sometimes serving these needs is not the most efficient economic strategy. In this way, the GFB is more like a traditional nonprofit organization, governed by an ethic of service, rather than a preoccupation with the bottom line. The GFB organizers initially hoped that an economy of scale and centralized administration would entirely pay for the project. But a variety of other expenses have turned up, that is, for community development, environmentally sound practices, health promotion, volunteer support and development, nutrition and food-skills education, political education, and advocacy. Capital inputs needed to run a project of this scale are also high, along with the crossover expenses that go to support related FoodShare projects running with the same staff and equipment (a community economic-development catering project, a kitchen incubator, a food-skills training project for low-income women).

The payments made by customers for the GFB are roughly equivalent to the cost of the food itself, delivery, and the newsletter. FoodShare's funding mechanisms cover staff time, capital costs, and other expenses. These mechanisms include private donations and grants from foundations and government. Although one cannot be sure what motivates funders to support a given project, the government probably supports the GFB because it can reach into the community on a more grass-roots level than government-run projects can and the CFB's size and efficiency enable it to promote health on a reasonably large scale.

Private donors make an important contribution to FoodShare's funding. However, appealing to private donors is complex, as many are primarily familiar with more traditional charitable "feed the poor" appeals (including FoodShare's own appeals in the past). Care must be taken in the mailing campaigns and newsletters to avoid alienating private donors while honestly explaining the project and the difference between food security and food charity.

The GFB is more a community-development than a community economic-development project geared to job creation. The aim of improving food access for low-income people is to a great extent at odds with that of providing jobs. This latter goal must be left to projects that tap a wealthier market (for example, the Field to Table Catering Co., also a FoodShare project). The GFB relies on the volunteer labour of GFB packers and neighbourhood coordinators. Volunteers receive a free box, which appears to be an important incentive, but this is in no way a payment at a market rate. The volunteers' food "honoraria" require a subsidy, but not as large a subsidy as would be needed to provide salaries for the 500 volunteers who support the project. Theoretically, one can see the GFB as stepping over into a subsistence or barter economy, rather than seeing the free food box purely as a commodity with a market value. Ideally, food should not be viewed in relation to one's ability to pay for it, but as something basic to health and therefore as something qualitatively different from other commodities.

When viewed in this light, the acceptable relationship between volunteer time and food received, together with the community development achieved, is different from that of a simple work-for-money relationship.

As a community-development project, the GFB tries to mitigate some of the difficulties that such projects often experience. The traditional difficulty with community development is that it requires heavy buy-in and labour from the community. Unfortunately, the demand for this level of commitment often thwarts the success of the project — the labour of a few volunteers rarely seems to justify the rewards (hence the difficulty keeping small-scale buying clubs going). This has been FoodShare's experience with community gardening projects as well: groups are often shipwrecked by the grueling and difficult early stages of sod-turning or by disheartening learning-curve disasters. Where there is clearly a need, a little skilled help with garden design and labour can go a long way to creating success.

The GFB works on the principle that a project must meet demonstrated community needs and rely heavily on community input. Just as importantly, a project needs to have a good reception and abundant resources in its early stages. Starting with a fundamentally good idea with a concrete and visible benefit is better than having fruitless and endless meetings, with a "product" or benefit figuring only as an eventual payoff. The danger, of course, is that the project may become too undemocratic and centralized.

The way the CFB determines the box contents is an example of how it maintains a balance between democratic participation and central planning. Were one to strictly follow the community-development credo of asking the community what it wants, it is quite possible people would demand processed, brand-name items. However, rather than insulting popular taste, one should recognize that consumer desires are not created in a vacuum but in response to the many millions of dollars spent on advertising highly processed, nonnutritious foods. The health-promotion role of providing a countervailing influence through social marketing qualifies the community-development objective of working only for what the community articulates as its desires. So FoodShare has chosen to provide and promote only nutritious foods, knowing that people also need and desire these and that people still have the option of purchasing processed foods through other means. On the other hand, the GFB makes no attempt to stretch people's preferences too far in the direction of "health food" by including, say, seaweed in the box. Within these parameters, feedback on contents is welcome, and the GFB is constantly making adjustments based on this feedback.

Conclusions

The GFB has, from the very beginning, sought community input through customer service and detailed project evaluation. In terms of project design and control, early attempts to hold meetings and educational sessions showed that neither customers nor coordinators have much interest in project administration or in activities or politics beyond the scope of the project. However, a survey of coordinators indicated that many were starting to take an interest in networking, advising the project, and learning more about food issues and the food system (SWC 1995). Hence, a concerted attempt has been made to form a coordinators network to facilitate this.

The Toronto organizers have always hoped that the project would form the basis for some type of food action or consumer movement similar to those in Japan and

Peru. Low-income people in Toronto have historically proven difficult to organize (in this as well as any other type of collective action, for that matter). The GFB has operated on the principle of taking only baby steps into community and political development. Whereas a food bank, welfare office, or supermarket deals with the individual, the GFB will only deal with groups — a small way of encouraging community self-organization. As a first step into collective action, becoming a GFB coordinator or becoming a customer who purchases food in this novel way may be significant enough. FoodShare's hope is that in the longer term, the GFB's customers will show the same general inclination as the coordinators and become interested in complementary food-access initiatives, and possibly even consumer or political activism. The GFB newsletter continues to highlight these programs and issues.

The GFB is constantly negotiating the tensions between the need for efficiency, competitiveness, and health promotion and that for service and responsiveness to individual and community needs. The ability to be flexible and to constantly reassess progress is key to making the project a success. If we start from the premise that a food system that actually works for low-income people and promotes a stable, local agricultural economy is needed, we get a very different result than if we start from the premise that the task is to remedy food emergencies. In this case, the means and process of setting up this alternative system become as important as the objective of improving food access. But idealism can only take us so far. The project must be relevant to individuals, feasible, and sustainable. Thus, the hope is that the GFB can act as a catalyst to mobilize interest and action in working toward the social goals of improved health, building community capacity, reviving a healthy food culture, and gaining equitable control over food supply.

References

Foley, M.C. 1992. Beggars can't be choosers: an ethnography of a food bank. York University, Toronto, ON, Canada. MA thesis.

FPC (Food Policy Council). 1994. Reducing urban hunger in Ontario: policy responses to support the transition from food charity to local food security. FPC, Toronto, ON, Canada.

Saint Jacques, H. 1994. Field to Table social marketing program: an in-depth consumer evaluation of Field to Table services. Informa, Inc., Toronto, ON, Canada.

Scharf, K.; Morgan, M.L. 1998. The Good Food Box guide. FoodShare, Toronto, ON, Canada.

SHC (Scarborough Hunger Coalition). 1997. Food insecurity in Scarborough: a study of current reality and a report of recommendations for community action. SHC, Toronto, ON, Canada. Research Paper.

SWC (Smaller World Communications). 1995. Field to Table coordinators survey. SWC, Toronto, ON, Canada.

———— 1996. Field to Table program evaluation results. SWC, Toronto, ON, Canada. 50 pp.

PART 5

ECOLOGICAL AND HEALTH CONCERNS

Urban Food, Health, and the Environment: The Case of Upper Silesia, Poland

Anne C. Bellows

Introduction

In 1997, Poland celebrated 100 years of urban allotment agriculture. This represents a system of social survival woven into the economic transition from early industrialism, through socialism, and back to a market state. Typically conducted by women, retirees, and other reserve workers, local food production has provided a measure of autonomy or shelter from the vagaries of inefficient production and food distribution (characteristic of centralized socialist states) and from inaccessibly high food prices compounded by unemployment (characteristic of market systems). In some regions severely challenged by environmental pollution, however, the locally grown food is sometimes loaded with toxic contaminants that threaten health (Bellows 1999). Urban food sustainability is not just about local food production but also about local determination of food needs, experience with complications of environmental health, and site-specific food security.

The case study from Silesia, Poland, demonstrates ways to manoeuvre through intersecting food and health demands and offers strategies for adaptation and replication. These strategies require, in part, nonlocal realization. In this region for example, activists have determined that locally grown food has undermined health in their region. They are, therefore, establishing a system to import organic and chemically tested foods from cleaner regions of Poland to Silesia.

Contaminated agricultural land and human health

Upper Silesia is a geographic region under the administrative regional government of Katowice. Katowice is also the name of Upper Silesia's main city. With only 2% of Poland's land area, Upper Silesia has the highest population density in the country (900 persons/km^2) and 10% of the Polish population. It has 18% of the country's total industrial production. Of Upper Silesia's 3 000 factories, 300 are considered environmentally hazardous. Upper Silesia has the highest concentration of heavy industry in Poland, yet

NB: Research for this paper was sponsored by the Society for Women in Geography (research fellowship, 1995/96); the Kosciuszko Foundation and Polish Ministry of National Education (research fellowship, 1996); the Institute for International Education (travel and research grant, Poland, 1996); the American Council for Learned Societies (Polish language training, 1995); and, at Rutgers, by The State University of New Jersey, its Center for Russian, Central and East European Studies, and its Department of Geography.

up to 50% of the land is used for agriculture and urban garden allotments, and 40% of locally consumed vegetables are locally grown, despite warnings of health risks (Potrykowska 1993; Bellows and Regulska 1994; Kacprzak et al. 1996). The area produces 30% of national dust emissions, 40% of national nondust air pollution, and 60% of total national waste.

The most severe threat to health from soil pollution in Upper Silesia is food contaminated with lead, cadmium, and excessive concentrations of nitrogen compounds. The World Health Organization (WHO) and Polish researchers demonstrated that 60–80% of the heavy-metal toxins found in the human body in densely industrial urban areas are ingested from food, rather than from breathing polluted air (Kacprzak et al. 1996). Other health concerns include residuals of nitrosamines, polycyclic hydrocarbons, and pesticides (Wcislo 1995; Kacprzak et al. 1996).

Local residents of Upper Silesia acknowledge the problem of food contamination but are suspicious of "safe food," which they perceive as deceptive and overpriced. In 1994, a regional community survey ($n = 460$) (Bellows and Regulska 1994) showed that most people in this region believe that locally grown food is unsafe, yet they grow and consume this food and even reject data regarding the problem because

- They "know what they are doing" (tradition);

- They distrust nonlocal food sources and production procedures; and

- They want to maintain their buffer against problems with market cost or supply.

Integrating local and nonlocal solutions

Gliwice is an independent municipality within the Katowice industrial megalopolis in Upper Silesia. The Gliwice chapter of the national Polish Ecological Club (PEC–Gliwice) formally began its Tested Food for Silesia program with a grant from the local city council (*Gliwice Municipal Act*, No. 214, June 1992) (Bellows 1996). The work of the group has expanded, and its reputation has spread. PEC–Gliwice now oversees a national program, Tested and Organic Food for Residents of Densely Industrialized Urban Areas.

PEC–Gliwice seeks to identify and supplant hazardous locally grown foods and minimize risks where local production of these foods continues. It argues that contaminated foods impair human immune systems and that building up a resistance is the best defence against the endemic pollution in Silesia and other densely industrialized areas. PEC–Gliwice targets populations most vulnerable to toxins from contaminated food: the youngest children; pregnant and lactating women; and people with impaired health (Kacprzak et al. 1996).

PEC–Gliwice has built linkages in Poland between environmentally clean and environmentally contaminated regions. The major program elements are

- Organizing a quality-controlled system for acquisition, labeling, and market distribution for retail sale of chemically tested organic products, to link farmers to consumers;

- Distributing the chemically tested produce directly to schools and hospitals and creating subsidies for their purchase; and

- Educating community target groups on the connection between contaminated food and poor health, as well as on the benefits of organic foods and farming. (Kacprzak et al. 1996).

The program promotes the growers of organic and chemically tested foods. PEC–Gliwice conducts systematic chemical testing to screen produce for adherence to WHO and Polish standards for safe food. It prefers to support organic farmers but rejects some certified organic produce. Organic farming certification and practice cannot prevent airborne chemical toxins from contaminating fast-growing, typically green-leaf vegetables. Integrated pest management (IPM) farmers are also included (for example, for apples), as long as the produce meets stringent chemical-testing standards (field interviews, 1993, 1994, 1996).

Chemical testing is conducted for heavy metals (lead, cadmium, and sometimes zinc and nickel), pesticides, nitrates, and occasionally global radioactivity. Regular spot-check testing for heavy metals, pesticides, and nitrates is done at farms, wholesalers, and retail stores. The inspections monitor the integrity of the distribution system, especially the possibility of fraudulent substitutions of nontested for tested produce, and build consumer confidence at a time when suspect safe-food products flood the market.

The United Nations Commission on the Status of Women hailed PEC-Gliwice's unique labeling system (which displays the chemical test results) as a model to be disseminated. Consumers may inspect the test results for each new off-farm delivery. This technical information educates consumers on their ability and need to monitor and safeguard household nutrition and health. The system was proven effective in the first 7 or 8 years. However, PEC–Gliwice faces the practical challenge of maintaining system integrity as the program enlarges.

In the post-1989 market era, PEC–Gliwice quickly used the new legal, private-entrepreneurial sector in a strategy to develop a producer-to-consumer network to introduce and distribute tested foods in polluted urban centres. All participating growers farm in Poland. The club encourages them to convert to organic and IPM practices. The program focuses on foods in traditional Polish diets and aims to strengthen existing farmer–consumer relationships. PEC–Gliwice cooperates with an expanding network of growers north and northeast of Gliwice, wholesale food distributors, and retail stores in Gliwice and elsewhere in Upper Silesia. Some local municipalities, to minimize cost, have arranged for direct distribution from wholesalers to hospitals, nurseries, and kindergartens.

PEC–Gliwice has emphasized community education programs for urban and urban-area food producers, local NGOs, journalists, teachers, school administrators and dieticians, school children, their parents, hospitals, various branches of municipal governments (including City Council members), and the offices of environment, agriculture, and health. One exceptionally innovative and successful strategy was to lobby local city councils in Upper Silesia to subsidize kindergarten schools to purchase foods for midday meals. Specifically, city grants cover the cost differential between tested and conventional market foods. Thus, safer diets are made available to young children, regardless of income.

PEC–Gliwice is grounded locally through its practical strategies to minimize, even eliminate, risk. It knows that Upper Silesians will continue to grow and consume food from contaminated soils. Soil remediation is costly, and its effectiveness will be questionable as long as the environment remains severely polluted. Selective cropping,

**Table 1. Heavy-metal absorption through edible plants
(minimizing risk in regions of industrial agglomeration),
Upper Silesia, Poland.**

Locally grown crops that must not be eaten	Locally grown crops that may be eaten
Celery	Grains
Parsley	Poppy seeds
Leeks	Legumes (beans, peas, broad beans)
Lettuce	Gourds (pumpkin, squash, cucumber)
Spinach	Amaryllidaceous plants (onion, garlic)
Carrots	Tomatoes
Beetroots	Fruit from trees and bushes
Cauliflower	
Radishes	

Source: Kacprzak et al. (1996).
Note: Heavy-metal absorption ratio in plant parts fruits and
seeds to leaves and roots = 1 : 10.

for example, planting waves of protective plant cover is one remedial practice. Another is to encourage people to grow certain foods on the basis of the heavy-metal absorption ratio of plant parts: fruits and seeds to leaves and roots = 1 : 10. This means that fruits and seeds are 10 times safer to consume than leaves and roots. PEC–Gliwice discourages people from growing celery, parsley, leeks, lettuce, spinach, carrots, beets, and radishes. Better options are legumes, gourds, onions, garlic, tomatoes, and fruit trees and shrubs (see Table 1).

The work of PEC–Gliwice is astonishing. Committed individuals — mostly women who grew up together and share family stories of increasing illness — work collaboratively and form the sinew of this project. Many have backgrounds in chemistry and engineering. Some participated in the pre-1989 underground, which gave them experience in visualizing and demanding change. Most are retired, with small pensions and few alternative work opportunities. The heart of this model program lies in the participants' determination, common experience, and hard work. Although the program can be replicated, the sacrifices of these people, mostly volunteers, working in an underfunded project for more than a decade must never be romanticized.

Conclusions

The availability of affordable food is insufficient for urban food sustainability. Particularly in urban and industrialized areas, environmentally based contamination in locally grown food complicates any prospect of regional food autonomy. The 100-year history of urban allotment agriculture in Poland provides a prototype of an urban-based food system, as well as a warning. Addressing the issues of food safety and respect for the need for local food production requires a redefinition of local food sustainability. Under the combined duress and opportunity of the post-1989 social transition, PEC–Gliwice provides a model to be adapted, extrapolated, and replicated.

References

Bellows, A.C. 1996. Where kitchen and laboratory meet: the "Tested Food for Silesia" program. *In* Rocheleau, D.; Thomas-Slayter, B.; Wangari, E., ed., Feminist political ecology: global and local experiences. Routledge, London, UK. pp. 251–270.

———— 1999. The praxis and production of food security: urban agriculture in Silesia, Poland. Department of Geography, Rutgers University, New Brunswick, NJ, USA. PhD dissertation. (In preparation.)

Bellows, A.C.; Regulska, J. 1994. Setting the agenda: environmental management and leadership training for women in Silesia. Project report. Center for Russian, Central and East European Studies, Rutgers, the State University of New Jersey, New Brunswick, NJ, USA. 61 pp.

Kacprzak, H.; Sokolowska, J.; Staniszewska, M.; Sliwka, J.; Migurska, B. 1996. Tested and organic food for residents of densely industrialized urban areas. Gliwice chapter of the Polish Ecological Club, Gliwice, Poland. Program report. 17 pp.

Potrykowska, A. 1993. Mortality and environmental pollution in Poland. Research and Exploration, 9(2), 255–256.

Wcislo, E. 1995. Environmental pollution in the Katowice Province. *In* Seminar on Assessment of Garden Allotments' Contamination in Industrial Areas: published abstracts. Instytut Ekologii Terenow Uprzemyslowionych, Katowice, Poland. pp. 8–9.

Reuse of Waste for Food Production in Asian Cities: Health and Economic Perspectives

Christine Furedy,
Virginia Maclaren, and
Joseph Whitney

Introduction

Food production based on the principles of sustainable development can be enhanced if the nutrients and organic residues from urban consumption can be safely reused. Substantial interest has been shown in linking waste management and sustainable food production: municipal-waste managers have for decades hoped that composting would reduce the cost of waste disposal, and current proponents of urban agriculture suggest that compost from urban organics can be applied in urban and peri-urban plots and that human excreta can be used in fish farming (van der Bliek 1992; Lardinois and van de Klundert 1993; Hart and Pluijmers 1996; Smit et al. 1996).

Although no one has done a reliable comparative study, municipal solid waste in most Asian cities has fairly high organic content, even today, averaging well more than 50% in most cases (Stentiford et al. 1996). Traditionally, Asians have diverted substantial amounts of waste (including human excreta) for use in farming and aquaculture. This practice has been supported by factors such as the diversity of farming in and around cities; the large numbers of poor farmers; the scarcity and expense of chemical fertilizers; and the peri-urban farmers' ready access to urban garbage (owing to the casual supervision of solid-waste transportation and disposal). Municipal authorities have often endorsed waste reuse (most metropolitan cities invested in compost plants from the 1970s to the 1990s) (Stentiford et al. 1996).

Waste reuse in agriculture is everywhere underresearched, but widespread waste reuse in the region and paucity of research data (as against merely observational data) for Asian cities are notable. Furthermore, apart from projects on waste-fed aquaculture (Edwards and Pullin 1990; Edwards 1992), international agencies have supported few projects, especially for South and Southeast Asia. This paper briefly discusses health concerns and the economic feasibility of waste reuse in urban agriculture (WRUA). These are thought to provide constraints to waste reuse. The urban waste referred to here is the organic component in municipal waste streams, human and animal excreta, and wastewater and sewage sludges. The focus is on municipal, rather than commercial, waste sold for processing.

Waste-reuse practices in South and Southeast Asian cities

Table 1 summarizes the main WRUA practices in developing countries. Almost every conceivable reuse of organics from urban consumption can be found in Asia. In both South and Southeast Asia, one can find large and small peri-urban integrated farming systems using wastes. Fish farms draw on human and animal excreta; rice, vegetables, and fruit trees are irrigated with wastewater; and some feed for livestock and poultry is derived from aquatic plants grown in wastewater (Edwards and Pullin 1990; Ghosh 1990; Edwards 1996b). Urban areas can be ranked along a continuum from intensive to restricted reuse of waste in their economies. In places ranked intense, traditions of reuse persist, supported by low wages for agricultural labour, scarcity of chemical fertilizers, easy access to organic wastes, acceptability (if only to certain social groups) of waste handling, and little concern about health risks (for example, Calcutta). In restricted-reuse economies, contamination of organics, availability of chemical fertilizers, transportation expense, and labour costs have led to a decline in traditional reuse practices and a concomitant increase in solid waste requiring disposal (for example, Bangkok). International health research is raising awareness of the health risks associated with waste reuse. Governments may enact regulations, particularly in rapidly changing societies, to limit WRUA.

Areas of concern

To persist in the vicinity of large cities, WRUA must ultimately be made economical, safe, and acceptable (to urban authorities, farmers and farm workers, and the public). Currently, economic factors affecting the availability and cost of agricultural inputs (chemical fertilizers, organic wastes, water, labour) are more important in explaining the persistence or decline of WRUA than public-health considerations. Better urban management, higher levels of education, and more international attention to occupational health and consumer safety will, however, help to focus attention on health aspects of reusing urban organic waste and human excreta or sewage.

Health risks

Health concerns always surface in discussions of waste reuse (Mara and Cairncross 1989; Edwards 1992, 1996a; Lardinois and van de Klundert 1993; Khouri et al. 1994; Allison and Harris 1996; Furedy 1996; Hart and Pluijmers 1996; Shuval 1996; Smit et al. 1996; Cointreau-Levine et al. 1998). Although the general health risks for both wastewater and organic waste are well known (see below), substantial environmental health research has been done only in the areas of wastewater irrigation and waste-fed aquaculture (for Mexico, Indonesia, Israel, and Pakistan, see Blumenthal et al. [1989], Blumenthal et al. [1991], and Shuval [1996]; for Viet Nam, see Edwards [1996b]). Very little research has been done on the health risk of organic solid-waste reuse in developing countries. Some possible reasons for this are that the extent of waste reuse is unknown; disease outbreaks can rarely be traced to specific practices; few people can do this type of research; and developing countries have many other health-research targets.

Table 1. Main WRUA practices in developing countries.

Type and origin of wastes or site	Materials included	Practices	Comments
Land based			
Kitchen and yard waste	Kitchen waste, with some garden trimmings, leaves, grass cuttings	Backyard composting for home gardening, domestic-animal feed (poultry, pigs goats, cows); neighbour-hood composting	Kitchen wastes composted over long periods may concentrate pesticide residues in plants grown in home gardens; small-scale compost plants lack leachate infrastructure; rats, flies, etc., may cause problems
Restaurant and canteen food waste	Raw peelings and stems, rotten fruits and vegetables, and leftover cooked foods	Fed to household livestock; sold for auctioning to poultry, pig farms	Direct feeding of household livestock carries fairly low risk
Market waste	Organic waste from vegetable markets	Sold to farmers; separately collected for centralized compost plants	Potential for composting market wastes could be better exploited in some cities
Mixed municipal solid waste	Full range of local domestic, institutional, commercial, solid waste, with small industries' waste, bio-medical waste, human and animal excreta	In South and Southeast Asia, farmers buys MSW off garbage trucks and apply it to soil immediately or after 5–14 days	Where fertilizer and organics are scarce, composting is not carried out for long enough
Mixed municipal waste processed at centralized composting plants	Mixed municipal waste that may contain problematic levels of plastic film, small industries' waste, broken glass, batteries and fluorescent light starters, biomedical waste, human excreta	Compost is collected from centralized (municipal) plants by farmers, sold to farms, golf courses, or used in municipal parks, etc.	Most centralized composting plants have either failed or are operating at low capacities; products are hard to sell because of glass splinters and plastics
Kitchen and yard waste processed at VC projects	Same materials as for small-scale neighbourhood composting	Compost is sold or distributed from small vermiculture projects	Little is known about pathogen survival; VC bins must be protected by screens from rats
Compost removed from garbage dumps	Well-decomposed, mixed municipal waste	Nearby farmers collect compost from old dumps or closed sections of current dumps; sieves may be used at the site	Dust inhalation is a health hazard for compost miners
Compost cultivated on old garbage dumps	Most is well-decomposed garbage, often several years old; in areas of high recycling, extensive waste recovery, relatively few synthetic materials appear in the natural compost	Garbage farming represents the most extensive use of MSW for food production in the world today	The safety of the food produced depends on the nature of the original dump; workers are injured by sharp objects and develop respiratory illnesses
Night soil		Applied raw to fields; fed to animals (urban and peri-urban); co-composted in centralized plants; co-composted on farms informally	Excreta (from latrines, septic tanks) is deposited at most garbage dumps; multiple health risks to workers and consumers (of some crops) from night-soil reuse
Cow dung		Used as fuel, fertilizer and in mud plaster in South Asia	The women and children who gather dung do not have access to washing facilities

(continued)

Table 1 concluded.

Type and origin of wastes or site	Materials included	Practices	Comments
Animal waste	Bones, skin, intestines, horns, scrapings, etc.	Sold to fertilizer factories, rendered, composted	Little is known about risks (mad-cow disease?)
Water based			
Human excreta from latrines (night soil)	Vegetables, fruits, fodder, fish	Defecated into ponds, streams or lakes; deposited into water bodies; directly applied to fields; applied after composting or drying into cakes	Overhanging latrines are widespread in Indochina
Municipal sewage and peri-urban wastewater	Fish, shrimp, vegetables, fruits, fodder, aquatic plants, algae (for human consumption and fodder)	Fed into fish ponds, canals, lakes; agricultural irrigation	A variety of fish-, seafood-culture practices are found in the region; "polishing" in stabilization ponds and desludging wastewater are rare; east Calcutta system of wastewater-fed fishponds is the largest in the world
Urban wastewater	Fish, vegetables, fodder, aquatic plants, trees, shrubs	Irrigation; fed into moats, canals, municipal ponds	Where water is scarce, wastewater is used for irrigation and cultivation in water bodies

Note: VC, vermicomposting; MSW, municipal solid waste; WRUA, waste reuse in urban agriculture.

Multiple health problems can occur when mixed solid waste is processed, human excreta is applied to fruit and vegetable farms, or wastewater is used for irrigation or for fish farming. Pathogens, viruses, and parasites in waste can cause enteric infections, helminthic infestation, and skin ulcers. Fish farmers who use sewage can be exposed to the whole range of waterborne diseases. Poor management of compost piles increases disease-causing vectors. Particulates and gases are responsible for chronic bronchitis, tuberculosis, dysentery, chronic cough, headaches, and cancers. Leachates may increase the mobility of heavy metals (Olaniya and Bhide 1995). Workers are exposed to sharp objects, such as glass splinters in compost. Handlers and consumers of produce can be affected by crop-contamination disease links, such as diarrhea from fecal contamination of wastewater used in irrigation and cancers from heavy metals that plants absorb from the soil or wastewater. The food-chain path of transmission is also involved when animal-feeding disease links occur, such as enteric infections, whipworm infestation, and "mad-cow disease," linked to feed produced from animal parts (Shuval et al. 1986; Giroult et al. 1996; Cointreau-Levine et al. 1998).

One can assume that some health risks increase as industrialization and modern consumerism change the nature of both solid and liquid urban waste. Although legislation governing the disposal of industrial waste is improving throughout Asia, few special industrial or biomedical dumps or cells within dumps are in place, and in many places no legislation covers small industry (Cointreau-Levine et al. 1998). Aquaculture research frequently mentions industrial and domestic pollution from wastewater (Krishnamoorthi 1990; Zhang 1990). Edwards (1996a) recently argued that chemical pollution may pose an even greater threat to public health than pathogens and parasites. Hundreds of factories discharge effluent into Calcutta's wastewater, including highly toxic chromium from tanneries. One wastewater-fed fishpond system in Calcutta receives 70% industrial sewage. Hanoi sewage also contains about 30% industrial waste (Edwards 1996b). Both cities have extensive sewage-fed fish-farming systems.

A range of options can be used to reduce WRUA health risks to workers and consumers (Furedy 1996). Major interventions include the following:

- Reduce the contamination of the waste (for example, limit industrial waste in sewage; increase source separation of organics);

- Modify agri–aquacultural practices (for example, prohibit irrigation of leafy vegetables with untreated sewage; use holding ponds for fish);

- Monitor compost to ensure pathogens are inactivated;

- Regulate human consumption of certain products; and

- Educate handlers and consumers in protective practices.

Economic constraints

Numerous economic constraints may limit increased WRUA. Two important consider-ations in compost use — contamination and the cost of production — help to illustrate some of the issues.

The most common problem is contamination. Contamination is mainly due to the almost universal practice in the region of mixed-refuse collection and the subse-quent composting of mixed waste. Even with elaborate sifting, the compost product usually contains many splinters of glass and hard plastics, shredded plastic film, and toxic substances. Such contamination affects farmers' demand, mainly because farm workers suffer injuries, skin problems, and respiratory diseases (Allison and Harris 1996). Producers fear for the health of their animals if food waste is contaminated. Another consideration is that contaminated compost is a poor soil conditioner over time. Research in Hanoi and Bangkok showed that farmers are unwilling to pay for con-taminated compost, no matter how cheap it is (Kim 1995; Le 1995). Farmers in Viet Nam have noted that plastic film in waste leads to soil problems (Midmore 1994). Food-chain disease links, however, seem not to affect farmers' demand.

The relatively high cost of standard compost production is also cited as a con-straint. This is particularly so in places where chemical fertilizers are available and (often) subsidized. The estimated price differential between properly produced compost and chemical fertilizers depends on the scope of the analysis. If WRUA is considered as a waste-reduction strategy (less cost for municipal disposal), the overall economic assessment would differ from a simple cost analysis. Using an economic-appraisal approach, Le (1995) demonstrated that the cost of composting in Hanoi is almost half that of disposal of the waste at dumps. The efficiency of plant management (including marketing strategies) is important. Small-scale compost plants and private enterprises have met costs or been profitable in several places (Sharma 1995; Rosenberg and Furedy 1996; Lardinois 1997).

Interventions to minimize contamination can ameliorate both these econom-ic constraints, as well as being necessary to address health problems. The main options are discussed in the following section.

Minimizing contamination

Minimizing the contamination of organic waste and wastewater helps to alleviate both health concerns and economic constraints. If pure organics can be obtained, many public health risks can be reduced and the end product is more marketable. Two main procedures are available for obtaining relatively pure organic waste:

- Waste from special generation points (fruit, vegetable, and flower markets; restaurants and canteens) can be collected separately; and

- Organics from domestic and institutional waste generators can be segregated.

In intensive-reuse urban areas, the first option is widely practiced: municipal crews deliver the market waste to compost plants or directly to farms; livestock farmers arrange for collection of food waste (Furedy 1995; Giri 1995; Rosenberg and Furedy 1996). In many places, however, the relative purity of waste from these generation points could be better exploited.

Market waste is usually insufficient to meet the demand for organic matter, especially in intensive-reuse areas, and limiting reuse to this category does not substantially reduce the quantities that municipal authorities must dispose of. So to improve composting, a major challenge is to persuade large numbers of waste generators to cooperate in separating larger quantities of organics. This is an area requiring pilot projects (from which case-study information can be obtained) and a great deal of research. Projects undertaken so far in South and Southeast Asia include the following:

- Small-scale projects for the separation of wet and dry waste at the neighbourhood level in Bandung (Woolveridge 1995), Bangalore (Waste Wise 1995; Lardinois 1997), Ho Chi Minh City (Du 1995), and Jakarta (HIID 1992; Wawolumaya and Maclaren 1998);

- Divided street bins for wet and dry wastes in Bangkok and Surabaya (Furedy 1997);

- Composting of organics in schools in Manila (Comacho, personal communication, 1994[1]); and

- Composting at a waste-recovery station in Santa Maria, Philippines (Lardinois 1997).

Apart from the Manila school projects, the only other projects where even a very small degree of success has been reported are the Bangalore projects for neighbourhood separation of wet and dry waste. Other projects achieved no success with separation at source. However, these efforts have received minimal assistance. Considerable investment in public education and further commitment from urban authorities are needed to achieve suitable levels of cooperation for separation at source.

---

[1] L. Comacho, Chair, Metro Manila Council of Women Balikatan Movement, Inc., Manila, Philippines, personal communication, 1994.

Background research is also needed. The limited amount of research done on waste generators' practices and attitudes in Bangalore, Hanoi, and Ho Chi Minh City revealed the following:

- The more residents are aware of the farmers' need for organic matter, the more they are willing to separate waste at source (Rosario, personal communication, 1994[2]);

- Collecting organics more frequently and separately might be an important incentive for practicing separation at source (Le 1995);

- Food waste is extensively used in households where animals are raised. Such animal raising may contribute significantly to household income in places like Hanoi (Le 1995);

- Up to 35% of householders are currently separating food wastes (and some organics) to feed to animals or to sell (Ho Chi Minh City) (Du 1995);

- Up to 15% of organic waste is used for compost or animal feed in Hanoi (Grégoire 1997); and

- Lack of space in the living unit in cities like Hanoi is a constraint on thorough separation at source (Le 1995).

There is scope for much more research on attitudes and behaviours important to food consumption and the separation of organics at source (Allison and Harris 1996; Lardinois 1997). Economic analyses, including analyses of the costs and benefits of composting as compared with landfilling, are needed for all places where composting is considered. Information should be disseminated on ways to test compost for pathogens (Stentiford et al. 1996).

The main factor in contamination of wastewater and sewage sludge is urban authorities' inability to control the disposal of liquid wastes into sewers and canals. More emphasis should be placed on ameliorative production methods, such as crop selection, holding ponds, and careful monitoring. Bioremediation is also relevant.

Conclusions

At present, concerns that derive from health risks and scepticism about the economic feasibility of municipal waste-derived compost limit the potential of waste reuse in food production. However, the risks can be reduced by practicing separation at source to reduce the contamination of organics, amending agri–aquacultural practices, and educating workers and consumers. Composting less contaminated organic waste should help to market this compost.

Although limited in scope, recent research is laying the basis for a better understanding of waste reuse. Greater integration with research in related fields (for instance, integrating findings from wastewater research with those of work on solid waste) can strengthen the research on waste reuse.

Asian cities cannot be complacent about their waste-reuse practices, however, as higher urban densities, more industrialization, and waste-producing consumerism

---

[2] A. Rosario, Project Officer, Mythri Foundation, Bangalore, India, personal communication, 1994.

usually reduce urban and peri-urban food production, as well as contaminating organic resources. On the other hand, the prospects for WRUA's contributing to sustainable urban food production are stronger with improved urban management, higher levels of education, greater environmental awareness, and more community participation in environmental management.

References

Allison, M.; Harris, P. 1996. A review of the use of urban waste in peri-urban interface production systems. African Studies Centre, Coventry University, Coventry, UK.

Blumenthal, U.J.; Abiaudjak, B.; Bennet, S. 1991. The risk of diarrhoeal disease associated with the use of excreta in aquaculture in Indonesia, and evaluation of microbiological guidelines for use of human wastes in aquaculture. Proceedings, 3rd Conference of the International Society for Environmental Epidemiology. ISEE, Jerusalem, Israel.

Blumenthal, U.J.; Strauss, M.; Mara, D.D.; Cairncross, S. 1989. Generalized model for the effect of different control measures in reducing health risks from waste reuse. Water Science and Technology, 21, 567–577.

Cointreau-Levine, S.; Listorti, J.; Furedy, C. 1998. Solid waste. In Herzstein, J.A.; Bunn, W.B.; Fleming, L.E., Harrington, J.M.; Jeyaratnam, J.; Gardner, I.R., ed., International occupational and environmental medicine (1st ed.). Mosby, Inc., St Louis, MO, USA. pp. 620–632.

Du, P-T. 1995. The determinants of solid waste generation, reuse and recycling by households in Ho Chi Minh City, Vietnam: a case study of District No. 3. Asian Institute of Technology, Bangkok, Thailand. Masters thesis.

Edwards, P. 1992. Reuse of human wastes in aquaculture: a technical review. World Bank, Washington, DC, USA. Water and Sanitation Report 2.

⸻ 1996a. Wastewater-fed aquaculture systems: status and prospects. Naga (Jan), 3335.

⸻ 1996b. Wastewater reuse in aquaculture: socially and environmentally appropriate wastewater treatment for Vietnam. Naga (Jan), 3637.

Edwards, P.; Pullin, R., ed. 1990. Wastewater-fed aquaculture. Asian Institute of Technology, Bangkok, Thailand.

Furedy, C. 1995. One world of waste: should countries like India solve solid waste problems through source separation? In Tepper, E.; Wood, J.R., ed., Enriched by South Asia: celebrating 25 years of scholarship. Vol. II: Social sciences. Canadian Asian Studies Association, Montréal, PQ, Canada. pp. 87–107.

⸻ 1996. Solid waste reuse and urban agriculture — dilemmas in developing countries: the bad news and the good news. Paper presented at the Joint Congress of the Association of Collegiate Schools of Planning and Association of European Schools of Planning, Toronto, ON, Canada, Jun 1996.

⸻ 1997. Socio-environmental initiatives in solid waste management in southern cities. Journal of Public Health, 27(2), 141–156.

Ghosh, D. 1990. Wastewater-fed aquaculture in the wetlands of Calcutta. In Edwards, P.; Pullin, R., ed., Wastewater-fed aquaculture. Asian Institute of Technology, Bangkok, Thailand. pp. 251–266.

Giri, P. 1995. Urban agriculture: waste recycling and aquaculture in east Calcutta. Paper presented at the International Workshop on Urban Agriculture and Sustainable Development, Dec 1995, Calcutta, India. Urban Agriculture Network, Washington, DC, USA.

Giroult, E.; Christen, J.; Brown, A. 1996. Public health aspects of municipal solid waste management. In Rosenberg, L.; Furedy, C., ed. International source book on environmentally sound technologies for municipal solid waste management. International Environmental Technology Centre, United Nations Environment Programme, Osaka, Japan. pp. 395–406.

Grégoire, I. 1997. From waste generation to food production: development of a composting strategy for Hanoi, Vietnam. Department of Geography, University of Toronto, Toronto, ON, Canada. MA research paper.

Hart, D.; Pluijmers, J. 1996. Wasted agriculture: the use of compost in urban agriculture. WASTE Consultants, Gouda, Netherlands.

HIID (Harvard Institute for International Development). 1992. Enterprises for the recycling and composting of municipal solid waste in Jakarta, Indonesia. HIID, Cambridge, MA, USA. Discussion paper.

Khouri, N.; Kalbermatten, J.M.; Bartone, C.R. 1994. The reuse of wastewater in agriculture: a guide for planners. United Nations Development Programme–World Bank Water and Sanitation Program, Washington, DC, USA.

Kim, S-M. 1995. Demand and supply of waste derived compost in Bangkok Metropolitan Region, Thailand. Asian Institute of Technology, Bangkok, Thailand. MSc thesis.

Krishnamoorthi, K.P. 1990. Present status of sewage-fed fish culture in India. In Edwards, P.; Pullin, R., ed., Wastewater-fed aquaculture. Asian Institute of Technology, Bangkok, Thailand. pp. 99–103.

Lardinois, I. 1997. Organic waste recycling. In Reader for UWEP programme policy meeting. WASTE Consultants, Gouda, Netherlands. pp. 22–34.

Lardinois, I. ; van de Klundert, A., ed. 1993. Organic waste: options for small-scale resource recovery. Technology Transfer for Development; WASTE Consultants, Amsterdam, Netherlands. Urban Solid Waste Series, No. 1.

Le, T-H. 1995. Urban waste derived compost in Hanoi, Vietnam: factors affecting supply and demand. Asian Institute of Technology, Bangkok, Thailand. MSc thesis.

Mara, D.D.; Cairncross, S. 1989. Guidelines for the safe use of wastewater and excreta in agriculture and aquaculture. World Health Organization, Geneva, Switzerland.

Midmore, D. 1994. Social, economic and environmental constraints and opportunities in peri-urban vegetable production systems and related technological interventions. In Richter, J.; Schnitzler, W.H.; Gura, S., ed., Vegetable production in periurban areas in the tropics and subtropics — food, income and quality of life. Deutsche Stiftung für internationale Entwicklung; Arbeitsgemeinschaft Tropische und Subtropische Agrarforschung [German Foundation for International Development; Council for Tropical and Subtropical Agricultural Research], Feldafing, Germany. pp. 64–111.

Olaniya, M.S.; Bhide, A.D. 1995. Recycling of municipal solid waste on land and its impact — a case study. Paper presented at the International Workshop on Urban Agriculture and Sustainable Development, Dec 1995, Calcutta, India. Urban Agriculture Network, Washington, DC, USA.

Rosenberg, L.; Furedy, C., ed. 1996. International source book on environmentally sound technologies for municipal solid waste management. International Environmental Technology Centre, United Nations Environment Programme, Osaka, Japan.

Sharma, A.A. 1995. A methodology for locating small-scale composting plants with an application to the Kathmandu Valley, Nepal. Asian Institute of Technology, Bangkok, Thailand. MSc thesis.

Shuval, H. 1996. Do some current health guidelines needlessly limit wastewater recycling? Paper presented at a Consultative Meeting on Recycling Waste for Agriculture: The Rural–Urban Connection, Sep 1996, World Bank, Washington, DC, USA.

Shuval, H.I.; Adin, A.; Fattal, B.; Rawitz, E.; Yekutiel, P. 1986. Wastewater irrigation in developing countries: health effects and technical solutions. World Bank, Washington, DC, USA. World Bank Technical Paper 51.

Smit, J.; Ratta, A.; Nasr, J. 1996. Urban agriculture: food, jobs, and sustainable cities. United Nations Development Programme, New York, NY, USA. Habitat II Series.

Stentiford, E.I.; Pereira Neto, J.T.; Mara, D.D. 1996. Low cost composting. University of Leeds, Leeds, UK. Research Monographs in Tropical Public Health Engineering, No. 4.

van der Bliek, J. 1992. Urban agriculture: possibilities for ecological agriculture in urban environments as a strategy for sustainable cities. ETC Foundation, Leusden, Netherlands.

Waste Wise. 1995. The execution of field demonstration of small scale composting for the treatment of the organic fraction of municipal refuse. Status report and special report to Mythri Foundation. Mythri, Bangalore, India. Mimeo.

Wawolumaya, C.; Maclaren, V. 1998. Community composting in Jakarta, Indonesia. Department of Geography, Centre for Human Resources and Environment, University of Indonesia, Jakarta, Indonesia.

Woolveridge, C. 1995. An analysis of critical factors affecting the success of neighbourhood composting projects in Jakarta and Bandung, Indonesia. Department of Geography, University of Toronto, Toronto, ON, Canada. MA research paper.

Zhang, Z.S. 1990. Wastewater-fed fish culture in China. In Edwards, P.; Pullin, R., ed., Wastewater-fed aquaculture. Asian Institute of Technology, Bangkok, Thailand. pp. 3–12.

How Meat-centred Eating Patterns Affect Food Security and the Environment

Stephen Leckie

Introduction

With world population projected to increase by 50% to 8.8 billion by 2030, our ability to adequately feed people will face growing challenges (Brown and Kane 1994). Scaling back on heightened levels of resource-intensive meat production may be the best way to ensure food security for all people into the next century.

Essentially, the world is experiencing an overpopulation in farm animals. Between 1950 and 1994, global meat production increased nearly fourfold, rising faster than the human population. During this period, production rates jumped from 18 kg/person to 35.4 kg/person (Brown and Kane 1994; FAO 1997). The combined weight of the world's 15 billion farm animals now surpasses that of the human population by more than a factor of 1.5 (Table 1).

In many countries, the affluent are eating the most meat, often at the expense of poorer people who depend on grain supplies increasingly diverted to feed livestock. In China, grain consumption by livestock has increased by a factor of five since 1978 (Gardner 1996).

Any discussion of overpopulation should surely include domesticated animals that, like people, depend on food, water, shelter, and mechanisms for heating, cooling, and transport. The many farm animals are straining resources and causing environmental harm as a result of their voracious appetites for feed crops and grazing.

Land use

At Toronto's 1992 Royal Agricultural Winter Fair, Agriculture Canada displayed two contrasting statistics: "it takes four football fields of land (about 1.6 hectares) to feed each Canadian" and "one apple tree produces enough fruit to make 320 pies." Think about it — a couple of apple trees and a few rows of wheat on a mere fraction of a hectare could produce enough food for one person!

Many countries in the world use as little as 0.2 ha (half an acre) of farm land per person (see Table 1). This is equivalent to having 5.5 m² of land available to produce each day's food. In 1994, the average yield worldwide for cereal crops was 2 814 kg/ha, equivalent to 1.5 kg (14 cups of cooked grain) per day from 0.2 ha. For root crops, the average global yield in 1994 would have provided 6.8 kg of food per day from 0.2 ha (FAO 1997). As grains and roots are easily stored, it seems reasonable to

Table I. Per capita land use and food production in selected countries, 1994.

	Agricultural land Amount (ha)	in pasture (%)	Cereal production[a] Total (kg)	Net (kg)	Net fed to animals (%)	Total meat production[b] (kg)	Net fish catch[a] (kg)	Farm-animal weight–human weight[c]
Bangladesh	0.08	0	155	189	0	3.1	9.1	0.4:1
Pakistan	0.19	21	155	178	3	13.2	4.8	0.85:1
India	0.20	5	188	185	1.6	4.6	4.8	0.65:1
Nepal	0.21	38	210	233	2	8.5	0.8	0.8:1
Indonesia	0.22	27	195	225	10	10.1	18.2	0.5:1
China	0.41	80	279	289	25	39.0	15.4	1.1:1
Uganda	0.42	21	103	97	10	11.0	11.9	1.2:1
Czech Republic	0.42	21	660	664	64	87.2	2.4	2.3:1
Romania	0.65	32	796	804	49	62.2	1.6	1.7:1
Ecuador	0.72	63	142	168	2	28.1	29.3	12.5:1
Ukraine	0.81	19	632	637	60	51.4	7.0	2.6:1
Iran	0.95	71	239	311	26	19.4	5.3	1.0:1
Mexico	1.13	77	298	364	38	40.3	13.3	3.4:1
Russian Federation	1.48	40	528	643	55	45.8	29.6	2.1:1
United States	1.64	56	1 339	928	69	123.0	23.2	24.0:1
Madagascar	1.90	88	120	134	0	17.6	8.3	2.7:1
Canada	2.51	38	1 600	970	77	115.0	37.0	4.3:1
World average	0.87	69	349		33	35.4	18.4	1.7:1

Source: FAO (1997); conversion factors for production weights (carcass weights) and live weights are from USDA (1997).

[a] Net totals have been adjusted for importing and exporting.

[b] Production-weight total is based on the number of animals slaughtered annually. Actual consumption figures would be somewhat less because of losses due to the trimming of undesirable parts and wastage during final processing.

[c] This ratio is based on the combined weight of cattle, pigs, chickens, and sheep alive on any given day. The fact that average farm-animal weights differ in each country has been taken into account. For people, the average weight is assumed to be 60 kg.

conclude that even in cold climates, people should be able to live on food grown on 0.2 ha or less.

With exports taken into account, North America still uses seven times more land on a per capita basis than many countries in Asia. This is because large areas of land are used for grazing and significant amounts of domestic grain supplies are fed to farm animals (Figure 1; see also Table 1).

Farm animals are extremely inefficient converters of plants to edible flesh. To produce 31.2 million t of carcass meat in 1993, US farm animals were fed 192.7 million t of feed concentrates, mostly corn. Additional feed took the form of roughage and pasture (FAO 1997; USDA 1997). Broiler chickens are the most efficient, requiring only 3.4 kg of feed (expressed in equivalent feeding value of corn) to produce 1 kg of ready-to-cook chicken. Pigs are the least efficient. For pig meat, the feed–produce ratio is 8.4 : 1; for eggs, by weight, 3.8 : 1; and for cheese, 7.9 : 1 (USDA 1997).

In animals much of the food is converted into manure, energy for movement, and the growth of body parts not eaten by people. Very little can appear as direct edible weight gain. For example, cattle excrete 40 kg of manure for every kilogram of edible beef (Environment Canada 1995).

The meat industry makes an effort to use some of the by-products, but because of the huge numbers of animals slaughtered, this can be a challenge. Only

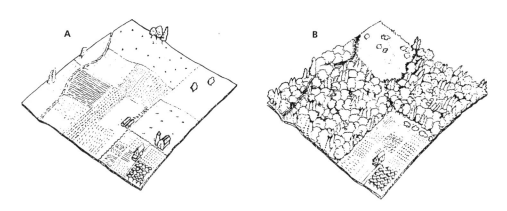

Figure I. The average area of land devoted to agriculture in North America is 1.4 ha (3.5 acres) per capita (adjusted for the exporting of grain). With a big cut in meat production, this area could be reduced to as low as 0.2 ha (0.5 acres) per capita, the rate in many Asian countries. The huge area saved could be used for reestablishing wilderness or for growing more food for people.
(A) Sketch of 1.4 ha of farm land. (B) Sketch of 0.2 ha of farm land.

about one-sixth of the manure from hog-raising operations in the United States is used (USDA 1986, cited in Durning and Brough 1991). Excess animal waste often ends up in rivers and in groundwater, where it contributes to nitrogen, phosphorus, and nitrate pollution (Durning and Brough 1991).

Livestock grazing

Roughly one-fifth of the world's land area is used for grazing, twice that for growing crops (FAO 1997). In a natural state, grasslands are healthy ecosystems supporting a diverse range of plants, birds, rodents, and wild grazing animals. Grasslands are often unsuited for cultivation, but with care they can generally be used sustainably for livestock grazing. Cattle, sheep, and goats are ruminants. They fare best on a diet of grass. In the West, cattle still spend most of their lives grazing and are only fattened on an unnatural diet of grain and soy before being slaughtered.

With most of the world's rangelands grazed at or beyond capacity, the prospects for increasing the production of grass-fed beef and mutton are unfavourable (Brown and Kane 1994). Gains are made in grazing land increasingly at the expense of wilderness areas. More than one-third of the forests of Central America have been cut since the early 1960s, but pasture land has increased by 50% (FAO 1990, cited in Durning and Brough 1991). In India, tiger reserves, national parks, and tree planting efforts are increasingly threatened by cattle and goats invading and eating young plant shoots (Gandhi 1996).

In dryland regions, cattle can overgraze perennial grasses, allowing annual weeds and scrubs to proliferate. The new weeds lack extensive root systems to guard soil against erosion. As the former diversity of plant species is lost, wildlife also declines (Durning and Brough 1991). According to a United Nations study, "The Global Assessment of Human Induced Soil Degradation" (ISRIC 1990), about 10.5% of the world's fertile land suffers from moderate to extreme degradation. Overgrazing by livestock and current farming practices are the principal causes of this degradation (ISRIC 1990).

Fish

Like meat, levels of fish consumption have also risen dramatically worldwide. The average fish harvest increased from less than 9 kg/person in 1950 to more than 19 kg by 1989, while the total global harvest more than quadrupled from 22 million t to 100 million t (Brown and Kane 1994). Since 1989 the increases in fish-harvest levels have slowed to where they are just able to keep pace with the growth in the human population (FAO 1996). Current levels are putting a strain on marine ecosystems in many areas. Of the 200 top marine fish resources in the world in 1994, about 35% were declining and 25% had been fully exploited (FAO 1996). Aquaculture, which accounted for 17% of the world's seafood harvest in 1994 (FAO 1996), has so far been making up for the decline in wild fish stocks, but a tightening world grain supply may curtail growth, as fish production requires large inputs of feed. Farmed fish yield about 1 kg of meat for every 3 kg of feed (Brown and Kane 1994).

Conclusions

Many indicators show that the world is entering an era of declining food security. Available land for agriculture has peaked and is currently declining as a result of industrial and urban expansion and losses to degradation. Freshwater supplies for irrigation are getting scarcer, and fertilizer use has just about reached its full potential (Brown and Kane 1994). Fish production per capita has reached a plateau and may start to fall, and meat production from rangelands is in decline.

Between 1950 and 1984, world cereal-crop yields increased by an average of 3% per year. Since 1984 yield increases have slowed to around 1% per year — less than the amount needed to keep pace with population growth (Brown and Kane 1994; FAO 1997). The result has been a 7% decline in world cereal production per capita — from a peak of 375 kg in 1984 to 349 kg in 1994 (FAO 1997). As the human population expands to close to 9 billion hungry people in the coming decades, it is not hard to imagine every last forest, wetland, and grassland being levelled for agriculture.

Methods to increase yields are also causing environmental problems, such as dammed rivers for irrigation; use of toxic pesticides and herbicides; erosion and salination of soil; pollution of adjacent waterways; and extensive energy use for ploughing, harvesting, pumping water, transportation, refrigeration, and fertilizer production.

A shift in society toward plant-based diets would reduce these problems simply by reducing livestock populations and their demand for land and other resources. On a per capita basis, the land requirements of plant-based agricultural economies are only a fraction of those with high rates of meat production. With fewer animals to feed, it might be possible to rebuild world grain reserves, ensuring dependable supplies for direct human consumption in countries facing food scarcity. Reducing land use by cutting meat production would also be a very effective way to ensure that wilderness areas are maintained and even expanded. Wilderness is crucial to providing biological diversity, climate control, and a store of carbon dioxide.

Getting people to change cherished eating habits will not be easy. Although it is unnecessary to reduce meat consumption to zero, significant reductions may be required. Two tools are available to reach this aim: education and price control. Education is needed to promote traditional and new plant-based cuisines as healthy alternatives to those based on meat. Numerous studies have pointed out the advantages of vegetarian foods in prevention of heart disease, cancer, and many other diet-related diseases. In addition, people need to know about how meat-centred eating habits can threaten food security and wilderness areas.

One very effective way to reduce meat consumption would be to set higher prices. Agricultural subsidies are partly responsible for the low cost of food, especially meat. Wheat and rice prices expressed in 1985 dollars have actually fallen by half since mid-century (Brown and Kane 1994). Without subsidies, even small increases in the cost of grain would make fattening animals with feed crops very expensive. People would purchase less meat, leaving more grain available for direct human consumption. Gradually increasing grain prices now may be preferable to enduring sudden price jumps resulting from climate-induced crop shortfalls or shifts in world demand. Surplus stocks of grain are now at their lowest level since the early 1970s, leaving the world particularly vulnerable (USDA 1996).

As the Earth's human population continues to expand, two things will be critical for our survival: adequate food resources and intact wilderness areas. One sure way to achieve both would be to dramatically change food choices from animal products to plant-based foods.

References

Brown, L.; Kane, H. 1994. Full house: reassessing the Earth's population carrying capacity. Norton, New York, NY, USA.

Durning, A.; Brough, H. 1991. Taking stock: animal farming and the environment. Worldwatch Institute, Washington, DC, USA.

Environment Canada. 1995. Connections: Canadian lifestyle choices and the environment. Environment Canada, Ottawa, ON, Canada. State of the Environment Fact Sheet No. 95-1.

FAO (Food and Agriculture Organization of the United Nations). 1990. Production yearbook 1989. FAO, Rome, Italy.

———— 1996. The state of world fisheries and aquaculture, 1996 summary. FAO, Rome, Italy. Internet: http://www.fao.org/waicent/faoinfo/fishery/publ/sofia/sofflye.htm

———— 1997. FAOSTAT statistical database. FAO, Rome, Italy. Internet: http://apps.fao.org/

Gandhi, M. 1996. Animal welfare is human welfare. Resurgence, 175 (Mar–Apr), 16–20.

Gardner, N. 1996. Asia is losing ground. WorldWatch, 9(6), 19–27.

ISRIC (International Soil Reference and Information Centre). 1990. The global assessment of human induced soil degradation. Commissioned by the United Nations Environment Programme, Nairobi, Kenya.

USDA (United States Department of Agriculture). 1986. Economies of size in hog production. USDA, Washington, DC, USA.

———— 1996. Global grain markets in 1996: shades of 1972–74? Economic Research Service, USDA, Washington, DC, USA. Agricultural Outlook, Sep.

———— 1997. Agricultural statistics 1997. United States Government Printing Office, Washington, DC, USA.

...ᵂᵉ ᵂᵉ ᵂᵉ...

Farming the Built Environment

Elizabeth Graham

The basic idea: the city as generator of vegetational communities

Archaeologists are well aware that the built environment is anything but permanent. Buildings, garbage, human waste, discarded furniture, hospital refuse, old houses, rusted I-beams, overgrown roads, collapsed highways, fallen bridges, cracked dishes, abandoned cars, dumped computers, headless Barbie dolls, and dead bodies influence soils and potentially their fertility as readily as anything nourished by Mother Nature or extruded by Mother Earth. We tend not to think in these terms because we are emotionally and culturally attached to the concrete world around us. But such a world decays as readily as volcanic ash or limestone bedrock. We either hide the decay or just don't live long enough in most circumstances to see it.

As an archaeologist interested in urbanism, much of my work involves ruined and decayed cities. The perspective I outline here is based on the correlation, in the area in which I work, of diverse vegetational communities and cultivable soils with the sites of ancient Mayan cities (Graham and Pendergast 1992). My idea — which is an outgrowth of my work in the tropics, specifically Belize — is that we ought to be considering soil-forming processes, or soil genesis, in urban settings, because cities provide a wide range of parent materials that have the potential to increase fertility, improve drainage, raise working surfaces, reclaim sediments, purify groundwater, and, ultimately, sustain vegetational communities more diverse than they would be outside a built environment (Graham 1999). The concomitant is that any feasible urban planning should take into account the chemical and other characters of the built environment and its potential for transformation into a cultivable landscape (Graham 1998).

Research directions

Before I describe the archaeological research that led to my interest in soils and the built environment, a brief description of my research context is in order. Twenty-five years of excavation in Belize has provided me with the opportunity to concentrate on the particularly human, or anthropogenic, contribution to soils. This work has also helped me to build my expertise in dating various periods of occupation. With a team of investigators, I have already carried out preliminary studies that isolate areas in Belize best suited for investigation of soil and environmental change (Mazzullo et al. 1994). Future research will include studies of modern waste-management and depositional practices, as well as vegetational cycling, to complement the archaeological, pedological, and geographical research. I am now at an interim stage; the preliminary work is complete, and we are planning long-term research to begin in 1999.

Research history

My dissertation research placed me in the Stann Creek District of Belize, which differs in its geological features and soils from most of the limestone-dominated Mayan low-lands (Graham 1994). Soils are highly acidic, and artifacts — including ceramics, the archaeologist's mainstay — are poorly preserved. With such poor information, it was extremely difficult to make sense of the area, and I spent weeks combing the bush, the savannas, the coastal swamps, and the foothills, looking for signs of settlement. The area had, in fact, been intensively settled from at least about 1 000 BCE, and the allu-vial soils of the major rivers had buried hundreds of Mayan buildings. But not much showed on the surface. Ultimately, I observed that the limits of soil zones and the boundaries of vegetational communities on soil and vegetation maps were in many cir-cumstances consonant, on the ground, with areas of ancient settlement. Therefore, many of the bush zones that modern scientists (geographers, botanists, geologists, etc.) take to be natural-forest communities or natural and static soil types could have drawn their character from the debris of ancient settlements beneath the surface.

At the time of my dissertation research, I published none of these thoughts. I began to touch on these issues later as I became especially intrigued by coastal areas where ancient sites in many places enabled broadleaf forest vegetation to establish in zones otherwise dominated by species such as red mangrove, white or black man-grove, and poisonwoods (Graham and Pendergast 1989). David Romney, one of the geographers in Belize responsible for the Land Use Survey (Wright et al. 1959), was supportive of my view on the human alteration of landscapes, but soil scientists strongly resisted the idea that debris from human occupation can influence long-term soil fertility. I persisted and visited Brazil and later the Netherlands to find receptive ears (for example, Smith 1980; Kern 1988; Kern and Kampf 1989; Pabst 1991). The Dutch have long recognized the importance of anthropogenic soils in agriculture — soils with a character significantly influenced by debris from human activity or by human design and manipulation. People have created soils in the Netherlands since medieval times by layering animal manure with various cut grasses in inundated areas.

Soil science and soil genesis

If research excludes the applied aspects of soil science, then the conceptual barriers that argue against considering human influences make good scientific sense in the study of soil genesis, or soil-forming processes. For example, the term *soil*, strictly speaking, refers to the products of the forces of weathering and erosion on rocks (Van Wambeke 1992) and implies no reference to organics of any kind, let alone organics generated by human occupation. Excluding human influence is appropriate if a geolo-gist is studying changes in soil-forming processes on a limestone shelf from the Creta-ceous period to the Eocene epoch. But if we are interested in the human perspective and time span, the organic contribution to soils — such as decaying vegetation or insect activity or human occupation — must be factored in, because even 100 years can make a difference between a cultivable and a noncultivable landscape. Nevertheless, organ-ics are not considered soil parent materials.

Where do organics fit in? When organisms such as plants and animals produce dead residues, they are producers of soil organic matter. While they still live, however, they are seen to "interfere with ... soil-forming processes" (Van Wambeke 1992, p. 70).

The tunnel digging of leaf-cutter ants, for example, mixes soils from surface and sub-surface soil horizons (Van Wambeke 1992). Standardized soil descriptions take organics into account (FAO 1990), and soil classification plays an important role in land-use surveys and in planning agricultural strategies. Nonetheless, human influence is categorized predominantly, although not exclusively, as a way the presumed natural environment has been disturbed, rather than as a potentially quantifiable source of minerals or nutrients (FAO 1990).

As I see it, four conceptual barriers oppose a more productive application of soil science to agriculture and land use:

- Despite the process implicit in terms such as "weatherable minerals" (FAO 1990, p. 40), soils under classification are seen as static in terms of a set of natural parameters that define them and dynamic only to the extent that these natural parameters are interfered with (farmers burning forest for swidden agriculture, for example). The result is a kind of research bind, in which those who see soils as essentially dynamic focus on huge expanses of geologic time and ignore organics, and those who include organics tend to view the soil character as a reflection of quantifiable — or at least distinguishable — natural processes that essentially do not change unless interfered with by living things, especially animals and people.

- Although organics play a significant role in the categorization of soils, the effects of human occupation are considered cultural, outside of nature, and therefore unimportant as contributors to the soil's essential (natural) character.

- The prejudice against humans as creatures outside of nature has led scientists to ignore the role of humans in altering and manipulating the inorganic, or "stone," environment (see Van Wambeke 1990, chapter 5). Termites are credited with meddling with soil parent materials (Van Wambeke 1990). Why not humans? Scientists eagerly consider the contribution of the weathering of limestone outcrops to soils but ignore Mayan ruins that blanket the landscape and weather just as effectively; indeed, these ruins have been around for almost 3 000 years. Geologically, this may be the wink of an eye, but far less than 3 000 years can make a difference in terms of land use and agriculture.

- Humans' impacts on soils are seen almost exclusively as deleterious effects — clearing trees, encouraging erosion, transforming forests to grasslands — and rarely as contributions to nutrient cycling, soil-mineral content, or soil fertility.

However, if sustainability is to be anything but a development fad, then researchers must overcome these biases and understand that the distinction of culture versus nature is inapplicable. We must give human (and animal) communities the same status as trees and plants in considerations of organic contributions to soils. We should be giving more attention to soil dynamics on a human time scale and viewing the built environment (buildings, highways, drainage pipes, junkyards) as having as much of an influence on soils and agricultural feasibility as any rock extruded or pressurized by Mother Earth.

Cities and urban farming

How does all this relate to contemporary urban situations, and what, if anything, has it got to do with urban farming? It is not so important at the level of the individual city farmer, who at most might look 30 years ahead. However, if city governments fail to take soil-forming processes and, by implication, environmental change, into account in their longer-term urban planning then we will continue to waste vast amounts of resources that could otherwise be used to enrich soil fertility.

Mayan urbanism

At another level, in addition to that of long-term environmental change, we can learn from the urban experience of the ancient Mayans and from urban experience in the tropics in general. I became interested in urbanism in the humid tropics in particular, as the result of my archaeological research in the Mayan area, where urban landscapes once dominated the Yucatan Peninsula, Belize, Guatemala, and western El Salvador and Honduras. We are now finding that the ancient Mayans incorporated agriculture, horticulture, and arboriculture into their city centres and may also have included terraces to retain and conserve soils within the urban setting (Graham 1999). I can therefore point to a conscious effort on the part of the ancient Mayans to integrate agriculture, conservation, and urban life. One of the hypotheses I plan to test is that the high population densities of the ancient Mayan cities, under certain conditions, could have had an environmental benefit. Most environmental studies of the world's civilizations emphasize degradation and erosion. The civilizations and cities of Mesopotamia, for example, constantly faced a degrading and deteriorating environment. I do not deny that these forces are at work everywhere, but I also think we should test the idea that "organic wastes and debris from the built environment contribute to soil aggradation and even the retention or recycling of nutrients, and not degradation" (Graham 1999).

An example that comes immediately to mind is the way the Mayan cities improved the growth conditions for the ramon tree. This tree produces an edible nut used by the Mayans to a varying degree (Puleston 1968). Dense clusters of ramon trees are found in two microenvironments: in areas of limestone bedrock outcrops and on and around the standing Mayan ruins (Lambert and Arnason 1982). The Mayans made no deliberate effort to create a suitable or sustainable environment for the ramon tree, which continues to be harvested today. But, through the buildings abandoned and left standing, the Mayan city life inadvertently provided an environment extremely favourable to ramon trees.

Conclusions

What is important is to be more highly attuned to the many spinoffs or incidental effects of urban life, which we can channel into productive uses if we are more aware of the city as part of nature. I gave other examples in two other articles: one of these (Graham 1998) focuses more heavily on the concept of buildings as soil parent materials; and the other (Graham 1999) is a preliminary attempt to generalize from urban developments in the humid tropics. The latter paper makes the point that most development agricultural technology in the 20th century seems to originate in temperate-climate cities of the so-called developed North and is then transferred to the South (see also Janzen 1973). I propose that it is time, now, to learn from the cities of the South, and in my case, I am particularly interested in the ecology of the cities of the humid tropics and in what the North can learn from these cities. From the Mayans, the Khmer, the Ibo, and the civilizations of Sri Lanka, we can learn not only how to manage high populations in an urban environment but also how high population densities can be turned to environmental benefit.

References

FAO (Food and Agriculture Organization of the United Nations). 1990. Guidelines for soil description (3rd ed., revised). Soil Resources, Management and Conservation Service, Land and Water Development Division, FAO, Rome, Italy. 70 pp.

Graham, E. 1994. The highlands of the lowlands: environment and archaeology in the Stann Creek District, Belize, Central America. Prehistory Press, Madison, WI, USA; Royal Ontario Museum, Toronto, ON, Canada. Monographs in World Archaeology, No. 19. 400 pp.

———— 1998. Metaphor and metamorphism — some thoughts on environmental meta-history. In Balée, W., ed., Advances in historical ecology. Columbia University Press, New York, NY, USA.

———— 1999. Maya cities and the character of a tropical urbanism. In Sinclair, P.J.J., ed., Urban origins in eastern Africa. Routledge, London, UK. (In press.)

Graham, E.; Pendergast, D.M. 1989. Excavations at the Marco Gonzalez site, Ambergris Caye, Belize. Journal of Field Archaeology, 16, 1–16.

———— 1992. Maya urbanism and ecological change. In Steen, H.K.; Tucker, R.P., ed., Changing tropical forests. Proceedings of a conference sponsored by the Forest History Society and IUFRO Forest History Group. Forest History Society, Durham, NC, USA. pp. 102–109.

Janzen, D.H. 1973. Tropical agroecosystems. Science, 182, 1212–1219.

Kern, D.C. 1988. Caracterização pedológica de solos com terra preta arqueológica região de Oriximiná, Pará. Universidade Federal do Rio Grande do Sul, Brazil. Tese de mestrado.

Kern, D.C.; Kampf, N. 1989. Antigos assentamentos Indígenas no formação de solos com terra preta arqueológica na região de Oriximiná, Pará. Revista Brasileira de Ciências do Solo, 13, 219–225.

Lambert, J.D.H.; Arnason, J.T. 1982. Ramon and Maya ruins: an ecological, not an economic, relation. Science, 216, 298–299.

Mazzullo, S.J.; Teal, C.S.; Graham, E. 1994. Mineralogic and crystallographic evidence of lime processing, Santa Cruz Maya site (Classic to Postclassic), Ambergris Caye, Belize. Journal of Archaeological Science, 21(6), 785–795.

Pabst, E. 1991 Critérios de distinção entre terra preta e latossolo na região de Belterra e os seus significados para a discussão pedogenética. Boletin do Museu Paraense Emílio Goeldi, Série Antropologia, 7(1), 5–19.

Puleston, D.E. 1968. Brosimum alicastrum as a subsistence alternative for the Classic Maya of the central southern lowlands. Department of Anthropology, University of Pennsylvania, Philadelphia, PA, USA. MA thesis.

Smith, N. 1980. Anthrosols and human carrying capacity in Amazonia. Annals of the Association of American Geographers, 70, 553–566.

Van Wambeke, A. 1992. Soils of the tropics. McGraw-Hill, Toronto, ON, Canada.

Wright, A.C.S.; Romney, D.H.; Arbuckle, R.H.; Vial, V.E. 1959. Land in British Honduras. Colonial Office, Her Majesty's Stationery Office, London, UK. Colonial Research Publications, No. 24.

PART 6

ENGENDERING THE FOOD SYSTEM

..𝜈𝜖 𝜈𝜖 𝜈𝜖..

Gender and Sustainable Food Systems: A Feminist Critique

Penny Van Esterik

Introduction

Food touches everything and is the foundation of every economy. It is a central pawn in political strategies of states and households. Eating is an endlessly evolving enactment of gender, family, and community relationships. Food sharing creates solidarity; food scarcity damages the human community and the human spirit.

Across history and cultures, women have had a special relationship between food and appetite, on the one hand, and body image, eating, and sexuality, on the other. Women, through the everyday routines of family meals, are the transmitters of cultural codes pertaining to food and eating (most of the great chefs in the commercial arena, however, have been men). Arguing for the centrality of women and food in industrialized societies sometimes poses a problem for feminist analysts who see the dangers in essentializing women and overstressing their nurturing capacities.

In this paper, I summarize some of the linkages between women and food and suggest how feminist analysis may further our understanding of the food system. In an earlier paper, I developed the idea of food praxis (Van Esterik 1991) but did not connect this with women; later, I explored the relation between women and nurture (Van Esterik 1996) without considering praxis. Here, I begin the task of integrating gender and praxis, concluding with an attempt to define a feminist food praxis as a conceptual tool to guide further research and action.

The link between food and women's identity and sense of self

Women's sense of self is often based on their ability to feed their families. As a basic part of their self-identity, this right may become even more important to women in conditions of rapid social change and food insecurity. This source of power and identity may be lost when women lack access to food, when others take over from them the right to feed their families, or when efficiency is valued more than empowerment. Women do not necessarily lose this power when others share the responsibility for household food security and contribute labour to this end. But for women who are normally responsible for providing food for their families, the experience of being unable to feed their children is tantamount to torture (and food deprivation is a form of torture). Therefore, hunger and food insecurity must be considered part of the violence that women experience and must be explored as a violation of human rights (see Waring 1996).

If culture inscribes bodies, it is food that leaves the clearest mark, and that mark is most often read on women's bodies. Of central concern in Western cultures is fat. In industrial societies, women's relation to food is problematic because of the linkage between food and body image in diet-conscious women. Anorexia and other eating disorders primarily of women are becoming more prevalent in Western societies. Even young girls are expressing dissatisfaction with their bodies. Psychological research confirms that women who eat smaller meals are commonly perceived as being more feminine, better looking, and more concerned about their appearance than those who eat larger meals (Chaiken and Pliner 1987). A study in northern England found that women viewed food as a treacherous friend: "they desired it for the pleasure it gave but denied themselves the pleasure because of the unacceptable weight gain that might result if they indulged themselves. At the same time, it was a comfort, a support in time of need" (Charles and Kerr 1988, p. 142). The complex of stress, depression, and compulsive eating among women is also well documented (Chernin 1981). Rage leaves women hungry for food and justice.

Gendered food ideologies

How do our relations with food develop? Clearly, food socialization must be strongly gendered. In a study of 10-year-old American children, Roos (1995) found that for girls, food is a symbol for friendship and connection, but for boys it is a means to express dominance and competition. In some societies, children are socialized to share food from a very early age, particularly with their younger siblings. Food socialization is critically important for understanding gendered food ideologies.

Feminist theory

Feminist theory is broadly based in the social sciences and humanities, and it informs activism in support of gender equality. Following the usage of South Asian groups, I define *feminism* as theories and actions that aim to end discrimination on the basis of gender, race, class, and ethnicity. I make use of four feminist principles:

- Theory and practice are inseparable.
- The personal is political.[1]
- Diversity and differences are resources: there is no one truth.
- Nonoppositional, nondualistic thinking is basic to theory.

Feminists, not surprisingly, have resisted making too close a link between women and food; it is a troubled relation and one that will draw feminist fire if it is not analyzed with care. Women's association with food is not a simple one — as we know from the many women suffering from eating disorders — and cannot be reduced to the notion that food work is "naturally" women's work. Fears of essentializing women and

[1] I was once told by a man that I should not take things so personally; how else is there to take anything?

of reducing them to food or to food providers have kept many feminists from delving into this relationship.

Some Western feminists see food as relevant only to the domestic sphere of social reproduction. They place a higher priority on redressing the imbalance of power in the sexual division of labour (having men take on more responsibility for cooking, feeding, and nurturing) and on more fully accounting for women's labour in food production. Latin American women's groups have successfully established collective kitchens, but "some feminists have been critical of these women's self-help organizations because they focus almost exclusively on traditional women's tasks and do not challenge the traditional division of labour" (Safa 1990).

Breaking down oppositional thinking is an important part of feminist theoretical reorientation. It opens the door to reintegrating everyday practice and objective scientific knowledge. Cooking as "thoughtful practice" blends theory and practice, body and mind; it reflects the way many women experience food — not as nutrients, but as nurture. The study of food and eating has been marginalized because of Western binary logic, which favours mind over body, theory over practice, abstract over concrete, object over subject, public over private, and reason over emotion, among others (Curtin and Heldke 1992).

Women are both vulnerable and powerful — victimized and empowered — through food. Feminist nondualistic thinking about food reminds us that ethnocentric oppositions such as production and reproduction, public and private, and self and other are a Western legacy of blinkered, binary thinking. Food practices confound the dichotomy between production and reproduction and between public and private and are part of both the formal and the informal economy ("both ... and," not "either ... or"). The special case of breast-feeding makes this clearer. Women's bodies are simultaneously a means of production and a means of reproduction — producing babies and breast milk. This is both productive and reproductive work and is both a public and a private act. Other food practices confound the dichotomies between production and reproduction and between public and private. The task of preparing meals cannot be reduced to a private act of social reproduction when the food may have involved substantial bartering and exchange in the public sector, be redistributed in community potluck dinners, and be exchanged as leftovers with neighbours. Are these public or private acts?

Eating and cooking break down these oppositions. But our disciplinary borders still keep us in separate boxes, defined by these same oppositions. The medical and the gastronomic are separated — cure and cuisine are separated — and this division further separates the professional expert from the layperson, usually the laywoman (see Curtin and Heldke 1992). Cooking and eating, feeding the self, and feeding others concern metaphor, pattern, and system and call for an epistemology of relationships between people and between people and their food, not an epistemology of cause and effect. Lineal causality is inappropriate to the world of living organisms, which adapt, relate, and learn, rather than reacting to laws. Mechanistic metaphors fail to effectively explain relationships, holism, or synergy. Cooking, feeding, and eating are metaphors for interdependence, nurture, mutual support, and pleasure in a world full of metaphors for independence, greed, ambition, and pain. Terms like *nurture*, *reciprocity*, and *intimacy* have no meaning without context, but they require a paradigm shift in thinking.

Development of a feminist food-praxis model

I call this paradigm shift the search for a model of feminist food praxis. Ironically, food praxis refers to the practical "mastery" of the routines of producing, preparing, and consuming food. Building from the basic feminist principles mentioned above and the myriad ways in which the food system is gendered, I propose the following 10 points as a place to begin:

1. Feminist food praxis builds on gender-sensitive assumptions about women as gate-keepers of the food system and mediators between food produced and food consumed. But women's association with food, feeding others, and cooking is culturally constructed and not a "natural" division of labour. Nurturing skills are acquired by those who nurture others most often, with the exception of breast-feeding, the paradigmatic act of nurture.

2. The core of a feminist food-praxis model is the need to eliminate hunger and ensure sufficient food to sustain and reproduce gendered bodies. Political forces control people's access to food by permitting corporate interests to profit from delocalization by encouraging food hegemony. Feminist food praxis thus requires an examination of women's power in relation to the food system.

3. A feminist food-praxis model is nonreductionist, combining materialist and symbolic explanations of behaviour. Components of the food system — economic conditions, ecological context, or cultural categories — are not ranked so that one has primacy over the others but are considered parts of an integrated whole within a particular social, historical, and spatial system.

4. A praxis model takes the perspective of the social actor or the social collectivity and examines the relation between agency and structure. The system acts on the individual and the individual acts on the system, providing both micro- and macro-perspectives on the food system.

5. Food praxis explains both change and continuity. Change may emerge from individuals acting out of habitual routines, producing intended and unintended results that change *habitus* (or dispositions), which in turn change material conditions and interpretations of those conditions. Continuity results from the stability of routines of food production, processing, preparation, and consumption.

6. Food praxis defines the temporal organization of these routines for food procurement or production, preparation, distribution, consumption, and waste disposal. Cooking, feeding, and eating are high-periodicity tasks that are nonpostponable and occur with a high frequency. Breast-feeding and complementary feeding of babies are significant examples of this.

7. Cooking, feeding others, and eating are simultaneously sources of pleasure and a burden, and they blur the work–leisure divide. The tasks may be carried out by people exhibiting a wide range of skills. Yet, these activities may still be nurturing, if they are performed with warmth and affection. Thus, a model of feminist food praxis considers the way an act is performed, not simply the act itself.

8. Cooking, feeding others, and eating are body-based acts that create relationships between people. Most are reciprocal, in that they benefit both the giver and the

receiver of food. Food praxis focuses on food sharing, intimacy, commensality, nurturing, and reciprocal exchange. These are, therefore, deeply implicated in cultural constructions of the body and are emotionally loaded (for example, feeding the elderly and the very young).

9. Praxis theory is broadly reflexive, encouraging critical reflection on how "our" food choices affect "other" food systems. Scientific work does not proceed independently of the subjectivity of the analyst in feminist food praxis.

10. A feminist food-praxis model assumes that knowledge can be used to improve the quality of human life, as well as human diets; it is thus a potential guide to advocacy action.

Conclusions

Bateson (1972) argued that environmental problems stem from technological progress, population increase, and errors in thinking. Errors in thinking also present challenges to global food security. Feminist food praxis is one small step to changing our mind-sets about food systems. It is up to local practitioners to determine whether viewing the food system through a feminist framework will inspire the political will to develop innovative interventions to improve food security for women and, ultimately, for children and men as well.

References

Bateson, G. 1972. Steps to an ecology of mind. Ballantine Books, New York, NY, USA.

Chaiken, S.; Pliner, P. 1987. Women, but not men, are what they eat: the effect of meal size and gender on perceived femininity and masculinity. Personality and Social Psychology Bulletin, 13(2), ·166–176.

Charles, N.; Kerr, M. 1988. Women, food and families. Manchester University Press, Manchester, UK.

Chernin, K. 1981. The obsession: reflections on the tyranny of slenderness. Harper and Row, New York, NY, USA.

Curtin, D.; Heldke, L. 1992. Introduction. In Curtin, D.; Heldke, L., ed., Cooking, eating, thinking: transformative philosophies of food. Indiana University Press, Bloomington and Indianapolis, IN, USA. pp. 3–22.

Roos, G. 1995. Relationship between food and gender among fourth-grade children. Crosscurrents, 7, 97–108.

Safa, H. 1990. Women's social movements in Latin America. Gender and Society, 4, 354–369.

Van Esterik, P. 1991. Perspectives on food systems. Reviews in Anthropology, 20, 69–78.

———— 1996. Women and nurture in industrial societies. Proceedings of the Nutrition Society, 56(1B), 335–343.

Waring, M. 1996. Three masquerades: essay on equality, work and human rights. Auckland University Press, Auckland, New Zealand.

...｜¢ ｜¢ ｜¢...

Women Workers in the NAFTA Food Chain

Deborah Barndt

Introduction

Central to a restructured global labour force are women workers — particularly young, poor, and indigenous women — who have always been engaged in food production and preparation under subsistence agriculture but are now key actors in industrialized plantations, *maquila*[1] processing plants, retail sales, food preparation, and services. Free-trade agreements, such as the North American Free Trade Agreement (NAFTA), have made it easier for multinational agribusinesses to control continental food production.

"Free trade regimes have a distinct colour as well as a gender," charged Palacios (1995), "because of the exclusionary nature of the decision-making process [in which] a small group of white males [is] determining the fate of all races in the North as well as in the South." The feminization of poverty (Tinker 1990) has continued through these latest developments. For example, in agricultural production, indigenous women who previously practiced subsistence agriculture are now migrant labourers or salaried workers for agribusinesses in Mexico. Women also make up the large majority of the work force in the burgeoning *maquila* industry, which contributes to growing internationalized and specialized production in free-trade export-processing zones, including food processing. In the Northern markets that are the destinations for these agricultural products, women also predominate in the low-paying jobs in the food-processing plants and fast-food outlets (Reiter 1991).

The Tomasita project

In a cross-border research project that began in 1995, a group of women academics and popular educators in the three NAFTA countries has been examining the impact of globalization, with a focus on food. The project has applied a variety of research methods, including corporate research, interviews with managers and workers, participatory

NB: This paper has benefited especially from the contributions of academic collaborators in Mexico, Maria Antonieta Barron and Kirsten Appendini (now with the Food and Agriculture Organization of the United Nations, in Rome); Sara San Martin and Catalina Gonzalez of the Mexican Institute for Community Development; and Lauren Baker, graduate research assistant from the Faculty of Environmental Studies, York University, who worked with me during the Mexican fieldwork. Lauren Baker and Stephanie Conway, another graduate student in the Faculty of Environmental Studies, helped design and facilitate the film workshops; Todd Southgate videotaped the responses.

[1] *Maquilas* are foreign-owned factories in Central America's free-trade zones (tax- and tariff-free enclaves); these factories use low-paid workers to manufacture cheap goods or to assemble imported parts into cheap products, almost exclusively for export to US markets.

research, and the use of photographs and videos. By following the journey and life cycle of a tomato (from a Mexican field to a McDonald's restaurant in Canada) and by calling this tomato Tomasita,[2] we are hoping to make visible the bigger picture revealed by the experiences of the women who plant, pick, sort, pack, process, sell, and prepare the tomatoes we eat.

Of particular interest is how women's work in the various stages of production in this continentalized food system gets framed, interpreted, and understood. Our research confirms that the system of globalized food production marginalizes women and that Mexican women, for example, work under even more exploitative conditions than Northern women in this system. When you listen to these women and observe how they engage with and survive in this system, however, the story becomes more complex. Many may be bound, for the sake of their survival, to this unjust system, but they also have multiple ways of resisting its effects, even as they perpetuate it. In some cases, their work in producing our food has liberating elements, so we must challenge the simplistic framing of these women as victims. The metaphor of the "chain" is useful, because it can be interpreted in multiple ways to refer to oppressive experiences, as well as to connective ones. I'd like to explore these various meanings of the chain: bound, freed, connected.

Bound by gender, race, and class

The decentralized production that characterizes these export-processing zones and the deregulation that is turning whole countries into giant *maquilas* have resulted in the feminization of labour. Appendini (1995) noted that this phenomenon has been integral to the growth of fruit and vegetable export agriculture in Mexico, which is one of the markets that has benefited from NAFTA and maintained an international competitiveness. Appendini (1995, p. 7) suggested that "firms use gender ideologies to erode stable employment and worker rights where women are concerned," and workers themselves seem to internalize the notion that women are better suited for certain jobs, such as packing, because of their accuracy, speed, compliance, sense of responsibility, and obedience. The prevailing macho view that a woman's primary role is in the home helps to maintain this "flexibilization" of women's labour.

Clear class and racial divisions separate the women who work in the fields, cultivating and picking the crops, and those who work in the packing plants. We found at least three different kinds of women workers in the tomato fields in Jalisco:

- Those from the town of Sayula who were hired year round to prepare the ground and cultivate it, as well as to pick tomatoes (though most townsfolk looked down on this work);

- Those who were brought daily by truck from surrounding villages during the harvest period; and

- The indigenous workers who came with their families from the poorer states in Mexico, again only for the peak harvest period.

---

[2] Using a Mexican name in its feminine form draws attention to the fact that the most marginalized players in this process are Mexican and women.

Although their wages were the same,[3] their living conditions were strikingly different. The indigenous workers had been recruited with great promises of good wages, benefits, and housing. They arrived to find only shells of homes in camps without running water, sewage, or electricity; disease was rampant, and no health services were provided.

Whereas indigenous women of all ages, from grandmothers to grandchildren, were relegated to the fields, young *mestizas*[4] got the jobs in the packing plants. The working days in these plants could be longer, stretching to 10 or 15 hours, but the wages were three to five times better, up to 100 MXP a day. Selectors were paid by the hour, but packers were paid by the box, which was an incentive to increase productivity. These women fell into at least two categories:

- The locals hired mainly for the harvest period; and

- The migrants who, like company girls, were transported from plant to plant, a kind of moving *maquila*.

These women were either very young, between the ages of 15 and 24, or older and single, having been "wedded" to the company for years. Their living conditions were much better than those in the indigenous camps, as they spent their (mainly sleeping) hours in company-owned houses, cooking communally and creating a woman-centred family.

The gendered nature of food production, then, is complex, integrating issues of race, class, age, and marital status. As Gabriel and Macdonald (1996, p. 167) contended, "the mobility of international capital is predicated on the politics of race and gender." Multinational corporations, as well as domestic companies competing on the international market, take advantage of deeply ingrained and institutionalized sexism and racism in their constant search for cheaper labour. And women, no matter what their ethnicity, are caught within this system and are the most exploited, whether moving from plant to plant in the packing jobs or taking their families to work in the fields and performing their double-duty household tasks before and after a grueling day under the hot sun.

Forms of resistance

Women workers resisted in a variety of ways. To break the monotony, packers in the San Isidro greenhouse played mental games and joked around with each other, especially when the foreman was out of sight. One young packer took photos inside her workplace when we were unable to do so; her act of resistance helped to make visible the experiences of women greenhouse workers.

Most tomato workers were unorganized; the official union, Confederación de Trabajadores de México (confederation of Mexican workers), operated in one plant, but workers were not even aware of it. There was greater organization around working conditions in the town of Sayula, where a group of popular-health promoters advocated for the rights (health, housing, and education) of indigenous workers living in squalor in the migrant-labour camps. Resistance was limited, of course, by the lack of other work options. Families depended on the income of several family members, and young women were expected to contribute, both through salaried work and at home.

---

[3] The average field worker earned 28 MXP a day, working from 07:00 until 14:30 (in 1998, 9.95 Mexican pesos [MXP] = 1 United States dollar [USD]).

[4] A *mestiza* is a woman of mixed European and American Indian ancestry.

Liberating elements

For young women packers who were moved by companies from plant to plant, these jobs may have represented a kind of liberation. They offered an escape from a repressive family dynamic that overprotects the daughters and gives the sons more freedom. Although the long work days left the young women with little time for a social life outside the plant, meeting young people from many different places broke the monotony of the work and of small-village life. It was especially striking to see young women all dressed up, complete with high-heeled shoes, standing up for a 10–12 hour day of packing tomatoes. Women far outnumbered men in the plants, so there was a kind of competition for potential husbands.

Connecting across borders

The Tomasita project has ultimately been a popular-education project and has attempted, even in the research stage, to engage the women involved in the food chain, both in the South and the North. One means we have used to do this is to show films or videos about food production to the women workers along this chain of producers and consumers. In 1996, we collaborated with FoodShare's Focus on Food program and 25 women who had been living on social assistance (see Barndt 1997). In a workshop series called Women to Women: Connecting Across Borders, we showed four films:

- *Dirty Business*, about the flight south of Jolly Green Giant and the subsequent environmental degradation in Mexico;

- *From the Mountains to the Maquiladores*, showing women who had lost their jobs in Tennessee visiting Mexican women workers who had gained those jobs when the plants moved to a *maquila* zone;

- *Jungle Burger*, exposing the razing of Costa Rican rainforests for beef cattle destined to become Northern hamburgers; and

- *Fast Food Women*, revealing the oppressive conditions of women working in fast-food kitchens.

These films acted as catalysts: the Focus on Food participants were inspired to tell their own stories related to food production; immigrant women remembered what they had seen and experienced in their own countries of origin. The women revealed a tremendous knowledge, both of how the global system operates (being part of cash-crop agro-export economies) and of traditional food and agricultural practices that could be more sustainable.

We eventually videotaped their responses to these films, creating a "video letter" addressed to the Mexican workers shown in the documentary films. The video letter is one way that women in the food chain can share their experiences and talk to each other. The Tomasita project has developed other popular-education visual aids on the journey of the tomato and the role of women workers, including a comic book, "Tomasita Tells All: The Story of the Abused Tomato," and a photo-testimony, "Teresa, Food Producer — At Work at Home." See also Barndt (1998).

Food has a tremendous educational potential as an entree to understanding — in a more holistic and integrated way — the massive and often overwhelming forces of globalization that seem to be engulfing us. When women break the silence, they begin to loosen the chains. And when they begin to share these stories across borders, they not only unveil the complexity and injustice of a system that binds them but also discover their own capacity to survive, to resist, and to create healthy and just alternatives.

References

Appendini, K. 1995. Re-visiting women wage-workers in Mexico's agro-industry: changes in rural labour markets. Centre for Development Research, Copenhagen, Denmark. Working Paper. 22 pp.

Barndt, D. 1997. Crafting a "glocal" education: focusing on food, women, and globalization. Atlantis Women's Journal, 22(1), 43–51.

——— 1998. Zooming out/zooming in: visualizing globalization. Visual Sociology, 12(20), 5–12.

Gabriel, C.; Macdonald, L. 1996. NAFTA and economic restructuring: some gender and race implications. In Bakker, I., ed, Rethinking restructuring: gender and change in Canada. University of Toronto Press, Toronto, ON, Canada. pp. 165–186.

Palacios, M. 1995. Globalization of capital and its impact on women. In Maria-Vigil, J., Latinoamericana 96: great homeland: global homeland. Social Justice Committee of Montreal, Montréal, PQ, Canada.

Reiter, E. 1991. Making fast food. McGill–Queen's University Press, Kingston, ON, Canada. 205 pp.

Tinker, I. 1990. Persistent inequalities: women and world development. Oxford University Press, New York, NY, USA.

...❧ ❧ ❧...

Canadian Rural Women Reconstructing Agriculture

Karen L. Krug

Introduction

If we are to develop a sustainable urban food system, we must first address the broader issues of sustainability in agriculture. Urban and rural people must work together to establish a strong enough constituency to resist the dominant system and build an alternative one. For example, local food production — which surely is a prerequisite for any sustainable urban food system — requires sufficient support from all sympathetic sectors to resist control by global conglomerates. Furthermore, structural changes are required, not just personal changes or isolated solutions to local problems. Trying to prevent short-term economic interests from influencing the consumption decisions of millions of consumers is less effective than altering the economic or agricultural system to change which kinds of products are cheapest. Urban and rural food systems must be both linked and mutually reinforcing to build a strong enough constituency to effect these structural changes.

In this paper, I examine agriculture from the vantage point of Canadian farm women seeking ways to construct a sustainable food system for the rural and urban areas of Canada. Farm and rural women have themselves documented a variety of ways in which they are less advantaged than their male counterparts. Gender stereotypes, which persist in agricultural settings, devalue farm women's work and, ironically, lead to farm women's doing a disproportionately greater amount of work. This same gender stereotyping also leads to the following structural inequalities:

- Women's unequal participation in farm organizations;

- Women's limited impact on farm policy;

- Unjust legislation;

- Restrictions on women's ownership and control of resources; and

- Farm women's lower socioeconomic status and increased vulnerability to poverty and economic insecurity (Ireland 1983; Watkins 1985; Wiebe 1987; Keet 1988; Smith 1988; Haley 1991; Miles 1991; Krug 1995).

As farm women are more vulnerable than farmers generally, they have insights that farm men may not have. Furthermore, because they are less likely to benefit from the current agricultural system, farm women have less of a stake in defending it and are therefore more likely to be critical of it (Krug 1997). Thus, farm and rural women can play a significant role in envisioning the changes required to build a sustainable food system.

Farm women face some problems that their male counterparts do not. They also suffer more acutely from many of the problems that affect both women and men. None of these problems can be adequately addressed until the system is transformed to build more feasible rural communities and secure the livelihood of family farmers. Farmers are a small minority, 4–5%, of the Canadian population, and the proportion of women farmers is even lower. On their own, farmers (especially those who benefit least from the existing system, such as small family farmers and farm women) cannot exert enough political influence to ensure change. Furthermore, the problems of rural and urban dwellers are intertwined. Thus, a secure food system that provides everyone with healthy food will only emerge with the cooperation among those aware of how the existing system is failing and how it might be restructured. Farm women's insights can contribute to the needed restructuring of the food system.

Barriers to sustainable agriculture

In discussing the problems that plague agriculture, farm women identified issues related to the economic system, declining rural communities, environmental degradation, health, and stress. In addition, they observed that some issues, such as the feminization of poverty, domestic violence, and inadequate day-care programs, affect farm women more than they do farm men. A fundamental problem in the economic system is that farmers lack control over the costs of inputs and over the prices received for their products. A few large corporations exert substantial control over what is grown, how and where it is grown, the price paid for it, and who receives it. Centralization, which is largely a result of the consolidation of power among the corporations controlling food production and distribution, contributes to the decline of rural communities. This is particularly evident in the prairies as farming there becomes less economically sustainable for small units. The style of farming supported in the highly competitive climate created by the controlling corporate interests leads to environmental degradation, primarily as a result of the use of large equipment, intensive chemical applications, and monocropping. Health problems result from stress and from the release of chemicals and other pollutants into the environment. As it becomes increasingly more difficult to earn a living from farming, the pressure to compete increases. Stress-related illnesses, heightened levels of violence, and increased suicide rates are the result. Farm and rural families feel the direct effects of these interconnected factors (Krug 1995).

Farm and rural women's alternative vision for agriculture

I want to feed people locally [grown] nutritious food. I want off this chemical fix. I want to teach my daughters how to be stewards of the land instead of how to be obedient slaves to this insane economic system.

It is time for us farm women to heal ourselves. … It is the women who will have to draw the line and say enough is enough. We will have to make our vision for self-sufficiency, of clean air and water, of nutritious food, and of healthy families and rural communities a reality for us all. We have the analysis. We have the abilities. And most importantly, we have the faith to make our vision a reality.

— Ruby Reske Naurochi[1]

[1] Ruby Reske Naurochi, a Manitoba farmer and author passionately involved in the transformation of agriculture, responding to a questionnaire sent by the author to selected Canadian farm women, 1993.

Combining the concerns raised by some farm women with the visions articulated by others points the way to effective solutions. Certain farm and rural women — among them unionists, social-change activists, critical journalists, and family farmers — articulate strong visions for sustainable rural areas, agriculture, and society.

Sandra Sorenson, who grew up in a small town in Saskatchewan and has been the director of the Canadian Centre for Policy Alternatives, insists that resistance to the dominant system and meaningful change is possible only with a clear alternative vision. Sorenson (1991) did the groundwork for this alternative vision by articulating basic principles of sustainability from the vantage point of humans. She pointed to the importance of universal access to clean water and air, nourishing food, adequate shelter, fulfilling work, good quality education and health care, and a good transportation system. In addition to these physical needs, she emphasized the need for cultural and spiritual stimulation, the right to speak and participate in society, and hope. Sorenson concluded that these standards and rights must be universal and that they must form the foundation for creative alternatives to failing systems.

In recalling the rural community of her youth, Sorenson (1991) provided a concrete picture of rural sustainability that integrates the values articulated in her vision of sustainability in general. The elements of this picture include self-reliant communities, with most services and goods provided locally; meaningful, productive work for all who can do it; local culture, with opportunities for intelligence to flourish; healthy people; a strong sense of community; willingness to share with those in need; diversity; local businesses; and a reliable transportation system. In the past, these elements were part of rural communities, and Sorenson suggests that it is necessary to recover them.

Lois Ross, a journalist in rural Saskatchewan, has also written about an alternative vision for rural and agricultural communities. Ross (1991) argued that we must link all parts of the food chain — from production to consumption — and that sustainable food production depends on sustainable rural communities. She recommended several ways to make food sustainability possible, including increasing the number of farmers on the land base, increasing the population of rural communities, decreasing farm sizes, using smaller equipment and more labour, growing food for local food consumption rather than solely for export, locally producing specialized equipment for local use, and processing crops locally. She argued that stable food systems can be maintained, for example, by planting a variety of crops, preserving the soil and habitat, and decentralizing the food industry. Ross's vision for agricultural communities incorporates and expands on elements of Sorenson's (1991) vision of sustainability.

Betty Kehler, a farm woman who married late in life and recognizes that she has more choices than many farm women, as she has no children, explains how she seeks to live out her vision of sustainability for agriculture:[2]

> We decided right from the start that we wanted to farm as sustainably as possible, so our use of artificial inputs has been limited to soaps and other biological control methods and we spend considerable time and energy educating the people that visit our farm on how it is possible and preferable to grow food that is healthy by "treading lightly on the earth."
>
> We concentrate on creating our farm in the vision we have for agriculture and whoever comes by, whether they're a strawberry picker, an El Salvador refugee, an agriculture diploma student or a busload of elementary school kids on a school trip, we try to explain how we "actualize" the dream and challenge them to find what is

[2] Response to a questionnaire sent by the author to selected Canadian farm women, 1993.

inside them that they can "realize" so we can live in a world where we can drink the water, breathe the air and live off the land together with all of God's creatures. My hope is that if enough of us start acting like we really make a difference, we will.

Although she attributed her personal understanding of sustainability to her experience as a farmer, Kehler optimistically affirmed that everyone can and should contribute to the well-being of the planet.

Several solutions to the problems faced by farmers and rural communities revolve around the theme of living personally responsible lives. For Shirley Sarvas and her farm family, this involves a holistic lifestyle, taking responsibility for education, the soil, the quality of products they sell, and their own health (Ross 1984). In modeling and providing these alternatives, the Sarvas family has, as a social unit, tried to have an impact on the broader culture. According to organic farmer Arlette Gaudet, part of the solution to the problem of the environmental degradation resulting from current agricultural practices lies with education. She believes that if children are taught to respect the basic elements of life as they grow up, they learn to respect all of life; thus, she chooses to raise her children on a farm so that she can model healthy ways of relating to the Earth (Ross 1984). Harkin (1987) urged farmers to use caution in their handling of farm chemicals. She also encouraged farmers to consider the negative health and environmental effects of pesticides and to question the profit-motivated propaganda of chemical companies when making decisions about their own farm practices. Miller (1990) pointed to the importance of shopping locally. Giangrande (1985) recommended that people grow as much of their own food as possible and be socially responsible, rather than passive, consumers. She pointed to the ways individuals' lifestyle decisions influence the lives of others. For example, buying locally produced food supports local producers and short-circuits the loop of exploitation of labourers by multinationals. Although personal-lifestyle choices can contribute to resolving some of the problems Canadian farmers face, in isolation from concerted political action, such choices are bound to remain ineffective.

Several other solutions proposed by farm and rural women revolve around the theme of cooperation. Miller (1990) advocated "letter-writing bees to government agencies, requesting continued or developing services" in rural areas. Giangrande (1985) argued that through alliances with the labour movement and organizations such as the Nutrition Policy Institute in Nova Scotia, the United Church of Canada's Committee on Agriculture and Food Resources, and the Saskatchewan Women's Agricultural Network, Canadian farmers can "build a national constituency of concerned citizens whom they see as political allies and not just as consumers of the products they sell." In this way, rural–urban dialogue can be encouraged. Such cooperative efforts can begin to address some of the major difficulties faced by farmers.

Clearly, such initiatives are necessary to bring about the radical changes that rural and farm women envisage making to the food system, as these changes would require sustained cooperation among various sectors of the food system. For example, Wiebe (1991) recommended removing food from the realm of global commodities. An interviewee in Ross (1984) called for an end to the speculation on land prices that makes them escalate to a point at which they no longer reflect the productive value of land. The interviewee maintained that regaining security of land tenure is needed to give control to agricultural producers over what and how they produce. She added that Canadian farmers should concentrate on meeting our domestic needs, rather than export quotas, seeking to produce only what is good for the land and for people.

Giangrande (1985) advocated increasing urban agriculture as a way to "exercise control over a food supply normally run by multinational corporations," enable hungry people to feed themselves, interest urban people in agriculture, and provide a practical education program for youth. Giangrande argued that to support such activities it would be necessary to create an alternative agricultural system, with increased demand for locally grown food and the development of regional markets and distribution systems. All these suggestions involve radical changes to the current food system and require support from a wide cross-section of society.

Farm and rural women have suggested numerous ways for individuals and groups to implement changes to contribute to a more sustainable food system. Not only must the proposed changes be linked together, if they are to contribute to system-wide change, but they must be supported by both urban and rural people. As a farmer active in the National Farmers Union, Wiebe (1991) acknowledged that significant change must happen at the community level:

> The problems in agriculture are global in nature, but we do not have to turn around the global situation. How change will happen in terms of both cultural and agricultural sustainability will be at the local community level. That's where it has to start and where we as local farming people are the experts. …
>
> We won't be able to make change as individuals, but change can happen with groups of people who are committed to a healthier, more sustainable way of living together and of using the land.

Similarly, Ross (1991) maintained that transforming agriculture into a sustainable system requires "the participation of rural people and the implementation of programs to ease the transition toward ecological labour and lifestyles." Although she was convinced that the initial focus must be on rural people, she was also clear that "if we make the country a better place to work and live, then people in urban areas will benefit as well" (Ross 1991). Building a sustainable food system ultimately requires urban–rural cooperation at the individual and community levels.

Urban–rural cooperation

Many of the solutions proposed by farm and rural women to the problems affecting agriculture point to the importance of connecting rural and urban initiatives to build a strong food system. Ultimately, the success of the urban food system depends on the health of the rural food system, as the latter will always have the greatest potential to provide food security to Canadians. However, the two are interdependent: the success of urban agriculture contributes to that of rural agriculture; and the well-being of rural communities contributes to that of urban communities.

Urban agriculture, as a food-system initiative, is designed to benefit urbanites directly, but it has a positive impact on rural people as well. If urban people grow their own food, they are more likely to appreciate what rural farmers do for them. If they become used to the taste and quality of homegrown, organic foods, their expectations of purchased foods are likely to rise, and they are therefore more likely to demand more locally grown, pesticide-free food and be willing to pay more for such products. By taking food production and distribution out of the hands of large corporations, urban agriculture directly subverts the control wielded by transnationals. Indirectly, urban agriculture is likely to sensitize consumers to the value of food security and to create a broader base of support for local control over food production and distribution in rural areas.

Initiatives to address rural and farm problems likewise benefit urban dwellers. For example, stable, revitalized rural communities require broad-based support for smaller farm sizes, as well as incomes that cover farmers' costs of production while providing reasonable wages. Such support for rural communities can result in lower unemployment in cities and a healthier economy overall. Curbing the negative effect of speculation can also stabilize agricultural economies. Speculation in urban contexts, which is not beneficial to the average citizen, has led to speculation in rural areas. As a result, the prices of farm land, especially of that immediately surrounding cities, exceeds the productive value of the land, and this makes farming an unfeasible enterprise. Introducing legislation to reduce or halt speculation, like other initiatives noted above, would benefit both urban and rural citizens. Such initiatives require a national constituency that is committed to solidarity between rural and urban people and recognizes that their needs are connected in ways that go beyond consumer–producer relations. A sustainable food system can only emerge with strong bridges between urban and rural settings, thereby connecting the people who live in those settings.

Conclusion

Farm women in Canada have been involved in clarifying the problems in agriculture and identifying solutions aimed at transforming the system. They have advocated growing as much food as possible on one's own and have sought increased demand for locally grown and distributed food, rather than food produced primarily for export — both are initiatives that directly support urban agriculture. They have called for an end to speculation on land prices and emphasized the importance of secure land tenure. They have supported fostering alliances between labour, church, and food and agriculture groups to build a national constituency that improves rural–urban relations. They have advocated locally supported, smaller scale, labour-intensive styles of agriculture to increase rural populations, and they have requested government support to help rebuild programs and infrastructure to re-create strong rural communities. Each of these strategies is imperative if a sustainable food system is to emerge, and they each require increased cooperation between rural and urban people. Farm women's own analyses confirm that the well-being of Canadian rural and farm women is closely tied to the welfare of people in both urban and rural settings and that a sustainable urban food system requires a sustainable rural one.

References

Giangrande, C. 1985. Down to Earth: the crisis in Canadian farming. Anansi, Toronto, ON, Canada.
Haley, E. 1991. Getting our act together: the Ontario farm women's movement. In Wine, J.D.; Ristock, J.L., ed., Women and social change: feminist activism in Canada. James Lorimer, Toronto, ON, Canada. pp. 169–183.
Harkin, D. 1987. Agriculture chemicals poisoning our soil, and human water supply. The Farmgate, ON, Canada.
Ireland, G. 1983. The farmer takes a wife: a study by Concerned Farm Women. Concerned Farm Women, ON, Canada.

Keet, J.E. 1988. Matrimonial property legislation: are farm women equal partners? *In* Basran, G.S.; Hay, D.A., ed., The political economy of agriculture in western Canada. Garamond Press, Toronto, ON, Canada. pp. 175–184.

Krug, K. 1995. Farm women's perspectives on the agricultural crisis, ecological issues, and United Church of Canada social teaching. Emmanuel College of Victoria University and the University of Toronto, Toronto, ON, Canada. PhD thesis. 298 pp.

——— 1997. Farm women and the ecosystem: allies in agriculture. *In* Wellington, A., et al., ed., Canadian issues in applied environmental ethics. Broadview Press, Peterborough, ON, Canada. pp. 352–362.

Miles, A. 1991. Reflections on integrative feminism and rural women: the case of Antigonish town and country. *In* Wine, J.D.; Ristock, J.L., ed., Women and social change: feminist activism in Canada. James Lorimer, Toronto, ON, Canada. pp. 57–74.

Miller, O. 1990. Sowing circles of hope: support groups for older farm women in Saskatchewan. Women's Inter-Church Council of Canada, Toronto. ON, Canada.

Ross, L. 1984. Prairie lives: the changing face of farming. Between the Lines, Toronto, ON, Canada.

——— 1991. Rural development. Briarpatch, 20(2), 22–23.

Smith, P. 1988. Murdock, Becker's and Sorochan's challenge: thinking again about the roles of women in primary agriculture. *In* Basran, G.S.; Hay, D.A., ed., The political economy of agriculture in western Canada. Garamond Press, Toronto, ON, Canada.

Sorenson, S. 1991. Creating alternatives. Briarpatch, 20(8), 19–21.

Watkins, S. 1985. What are you worth? A study of the economic contribution of eastern Ontario farm women to the family farm enterprise. Women for the Survival of Agriculture, ON, Canada.

Wiebe, N. 1987. Weaving new ways: farm women organizing. National Farmers Union, Saskatoon, SK, Canada.

——— 1991. Cultivating hope. Briarpatch, 20(2), 20–21.

PART 7

THE POLITICS OF FOOD AND FOOD POLICY

Contemporary Food and Farm Policy in the United States

Patricia Allen

Food security in the United States

Food security eludes the estimated 30 million Americans who suffer chronic undercon-sumption of adequate nutrients (Cook and Brown 1992). Even before the recent welfare cuts, food security for many Americans was eroding. Hunger in the United States has increased by 50% since 1985 (CHPNP 1993). Lack of access to food is, of course, closely linked to poverty. Wages have declined steadily since the 1970s for production and non-supervisory workers, with average weekly earnings in 1993 being lower than those in 1960 (USDL 1994). Between 1989 and 1993, a 26% increase occurred in the number of children living in families with incomes below 75% of the poverty line (FRAC 1995).

Despite poor people's worsening economic conditions, policymakers began cutting food programs in the 1980s. The *Personal Responsibility and Work Opportunity Reconciliation Act* of 1996 (welfare reform) made substantial cuts to the three largest social-welfare programs in the United States: Aid to Families with Dependent Children, Supplemental Security Income, and the Food Stamp Program. Fully half of the projected budget savings from the 1996 welfare bill was expected to come from reduced expen-ditures for the Food Stamp Program (CBPP 1996), which has been the primary source of food assistance for the poor. Another $2.9 billion (US dollars throughout) in savings has been realized by cuts to child-nutrition programs. Although policymakers say that pri-vate charity can be expected to mitigate these cuts, this is unrealistic. A recent study estimated that even if the nation's largest emergency-food network continues to expand at its average 1991–95 rate, it would only cover less than 25% of the food short-fall projected to result over the next 6 years from food-stamp cutbacks (Cook and Brown 1997). This is particularly disturbing in light of the fact that 17% of requests for emergency food already go unmet (USCM 1991). By instituting the largest cutbacks since food programs were first established in the United States, policymakers have clearly rejected the notion that federal policy should provide a safety net against hunger.

Ending welfare for whom?

Policymakers explain cuts to food programs for the poor in terms of federal-budgetary exigencies. Yet, the federal government spends only 7% of its budget on programs to enhance the income security of low-income families (Zedlewski et al. 1996). Policy-makers have chosen to further reduce this cost by making cuts that will affect the nation's poorest children and adults. Only poor people receive food stamps in the first place. To be eligible, someone's net monthly income must be at or below 100% of the poverty-line income stipulated in the Federal Poverty Guidelines. Fifty percent of food-stamp cuts will be absorbed by people with household incomes less than 50% of the federal poverty-line income; 66% will affect families with children; 20%, the working poor; and 7%, the elderly (CBPP 1996). Those with incomes below half of the federal poverty-line income will lose an average of $650 a year in food-stamp benefits. With half of the poverty-line income for a family of three set at $6 250, this 10% cut can only come from the most essential household maintenance, such as in food, shelter, and utilities. The food-stamp provision also limits food stamps to unemployed people who are not raising minor children, even if actively seeking work. Trying to "take responsibility for yourself" does not protect you against going hungry. Current estimates indicate that 1 million people (40% of them women) who are willing to work but are unable to find a job will be denied food stamps every month under this provision (Super et al. 1996). Most of these people are the very poor (with only 28% of the poverty-line income) and rely on food stamps as their main source of food because they qualify for no other income-security program (Super 1997). The loss of food-stamp benefits is especially troubling in light of estimates that show that only about half of those eligible to receive food stamps did so even before these cuts (Lipsky and Thibodeau 1990).

In contrast to food programs, which benefit the poor, farm programs such as payments to commodity producers have tended to benefit the economically better off. The average food-stamp benefit for each recipient in March 1997 was $72 (USDA 1997), which works out to $864 per year. By contrast, under the provisions of the 1996 Farm Bill, annual payment limitations per farm range from $80 000 (or $40 000 per person) to $230 000. Farmers of certain commodities (more than half of the payments will go to producers of feed grains) will receive fixed annual payments through 2002. Payments of $45.3 billion will be made, regardless of commodity prices; in fact, the Bill provides for additional payments to farmers of $5 billion in 1996/97, even though farm prices are expected to be high during this period (Hosansky 1996). Another $4.7 billion is authorized by the Farm Bill to be spent to promote and subsidize sales of US agricultural products overseas, which benefits commodity producers and merchants.

Farm programs can be seen as income transfers from consumers to producers. One reason farm programs were originally instituted was to transfer income from the more affluent nonfarm citizens to lower income farmers, but this objective has long since been met, thanks at least in part to US farm programs. In 1990, for example, compared with the average US household, farm households had $1 604 higher annual incomes, $13 320 less in expenditures, and $319 664 more in net worth (Ahearn et al. 1993). The vast majority of US farm operators (93%) were found to be financially stable (USDA 1990). Luttrell (1989) estimated that farm subsidies cost the average taxpaying family $400 per year, but the number of families that benefit from these programs is probably no more than 500 000. In contrast, the Food Stamp Program served about 27 million poor people a month in 1995, more than half of whom were children (Kuhn et al. 1996). Farm programs have also been promoted to support small and medium-sized farms, but this has not been their effect. In 1992, 68% of US-government farm payments went to the wealthiest 19% of agricultural producers (USDA 1994).

Another long-standing justification for farm programs has been to keep food costs low for consumers — a cheap-food policy (Browne et al. 1992). Yet studies by agricultural economists and the President's Council of Economic Advisers have demonstrated that farm-program costs to consumers and taxpayers exceed producer benefits by several billion dollars per year (Luttrell 1989). For example, in the 1991 US sugar program, 58% of benefits went to 1% of sugarcane growers. This program costs American consumers $1.4 billion per year; and taxpayers, $90 million per year (Hamel 1995). Between 1982 and 1988, higher food prices resulting from restricted supplies generated by farm programs cost US consumers between $5 billion and $10 billion in indirect costs (Faeth et al. 1991). Ironically, falling commodity demand resulting from food-stamp cuts are expected to result in increased farm-program costs of $187–420 million for the first 5 years in which the cuts take effect (Kuhn et al. 1996). Although this increase in farm-program payments may seem to be dwarfed by the savings in food stamps, it will privilege relatively affluent producers at the expense of poor consumers.

The political challenge

Agricultural policies create significant benefits for certain groups of individuals, who therefore organize politically to maximize these benefits. One measure of the influence of the food and agricultural industry is its financial prominence in Congress. Agricultural interests contributed $24.9 million to presidential and congressional candidates in the 1991/92 elections, resulting in an average of $76 000 for each member of the House agricultural committee and $123 000 for each member of the Senate agricultural committee (Makinson and Goldstein 1994). These contributions were 50 times greater than those from groups promoting either health and welfare or children's rights. Nearly all food and agriculture committee contributions come from producers, business, and industry, with a very small amount coming from consumer or labour groups. As agricultural firms are dependent financially on federal agricultural policies, they allocate time and money for lobbying efforts as a cost of doing business. The hungry, who are by definition poor, cannot generate vast sums of money to lobby or make contributions. As a result, groups representing their interests tend to be few, small, poorly funded, and unable to lobby on behalf of more than a few policies per year — no match for entrenched agricultural interests.

    In addition, the demography of US policymakers is completely different from that of the hungry, who tend to be the least powerful in our society. Many of the hungry are children, and 76% of the hungry are people of colour (Hoehn 1991). US food and agricultural policy, on the other hand, has been made by a relatively small group of predominantly affluent European–American men. No other federal agency ranks lower in hiring and promoting minorities than the United States Department of Agriculture (USDA) (Kansas City Star 1991), and in 1992, 89% of senior-level USDA employees were white and 82% were male (USOPM 1992). The priorities of such groups have been represented as being in the general interest of society but have tended to eclipse the priorities of the hungry. For example, in April 1997, the House Agricultural Appropriations Committee voted not to fully fund the Special Supplemental Food Program for Women, Infants, and Children (WIC), despite the fact that WIC demonstrably reduces health problems and improves cognitive development in children (CBPP 1997). In 1997, WIC was expected to serve 150 000 fewer women and children who are poor and at nutritional risk than it did in 1996. Welfare cuts were expected to reduce the incomes of families in the lowest income group and to add another 2.6 million people (1.1 million of them children) to those living in poverty in the United States (Zedlewski et al. 1996). Poor children will become poorer, even though most of them live in families with a working parent, and most if not all of these families will go hungry for at least part of every month.

To achieve food security, it is necessary to completely change the terms of the policy debate and to engage basic questions about how the state has and should intervene in the food and agricultural system. Recent changes in US welfare and food assistance represent a sea change in 60 years of commitment to providing some form of safety net for the poor. The scope of these policy changes provides us with an opening to simultaneously reveal and work to change agricultural and other corporate-welfare programs. At the same time, the struggle to end hunger must continue. Nine out of 10 voters were found to consider hunger to be a serious issue for the United States, and the same proportion believed that hunger problems can be solved, unlike other problems for which they found ready solutions less apparent (US Congress 1992). These voters believed that the principal responsibility for ending hunger belongs to the government and indicated that they would be willing to accept a tax increase for food-assistance programs, even in these tax-phobic times. Experience in other food-policy arenas provides some essential guideposts for taking action. For example, the Toronto Food Policy Council (TFPC), in Canada, has developed a food policy that supports the right of all residents of Toronto to adequate, nutritious food and promotes equitable, nutritionally excellent, and environmentally sound food production and distribution systems. TFPC frames food security as a health issue, in which it views hunger and poverty as part of the larger health issue; in this perspective, access to food is not only equitable but also economical. Although food-policy councils have worked at the local or regional levels, their priorities and organizational strategies have also been relevant to federal policy-making. The European Parliament, for example, recognizing the lack of attention to consumers' needs in European Community agricultural policy, has called for the creation of a European food agency to balance consumers' needs with those of the agricultural industry (Rogers 1992). Working toward innovative food policies will be challenging at a time when advocates and providers must devote themselves to managing escalating emergencies and garnering all-too-scarce resources. Still, nothing less than instituting a comprehensive, need-based food policy can prevent increasing hunger in the midst of staggering agricultural abundance.

References

Ahearn, M.C.; Perry, J.E.; El-Osta, H.S. 1993. The economic well-being of farm operator households, 1988–90. United States Department of Agriculture Economic Research Service, Herndon, VA, USA.

Browne, W.P.; Skees, J.R.; Swanson, L.E.; Thompson, P.B.; Unnevehr, L.J. 1992. Sacred cows and hot potatoes: agrarian myths in agricultural policy. Westview Press, Boulder, CO, USA.

CBPP (Center on Budget and Policy Priorities). 1996. The depth of the food stamp cuts in the final Welfare Bill. CPBB, Washington, DC, USA.

———— 1997. WIC program faces caseload reductions in coming months unless supplemental funding is provided. CPBB, Washington, DC, USA.

CHPNP (Center on Hunger, Poverty and Nutrition Policy). 1993. CHPNP, Tufts University, Medford, MA, USA.

Cook, J.; Brown, J.L. 1992. 30 million hungry Americans. Center on Hunger, Poverty and Nutrition Policy, Tufts University, Medford, MA, USA.

———— 1997. Analysis of the capacity of the Second Harvest Network to cover the federal food stamp shortfall from 1997 to 2002. Center on Hunger, Poverty and Nutrition Policy, Tufts University, Medford, MA, USA.

Faeth, P.; Repetto, R.; Kroll, K.; Dai, Q.; Helmers, G. 1991. Paying the farm bill: US agricultural policy and the transition to sustainable agriculture. World Resources Institute, Washington, DC, USA.

FRAC (Food Research and Action Center). 1995. A survey of childhood hunger in the United States. Community Childhood Hunger Identification Project, FRAC, Washington, DC, USA.

Hamel, K. 1995. Harvesting handouts I: The federal farm price support scandal. Public Voice for Food and Health Policy, Washington, DC, USA.

Hoehn, R.A. 1991. Hunger, 1992: second annual report on the state of world hunger. Bread for the World Institute on Hunger and Development, Washington, DC, USA.

Hosansky, D. 1996. Details of 1996 Farm Bill. Congressional Quarterly, 4 May, 1243–1252.

Kansas City Star. 1991. Inside the USDA, it's a white male bastion. Kansas City Star, 8–14 Dec.

Kuhn, B.A.; Dunn, P.A.; Smallwood, D.; Hanson, K.; Blaylock, J.; Vogel, S. 1996. The Food Stamp Program and welfare reform. Journal of Economic Perspectives, 10(2), 189–198.

Lipsky, M.; Thibodeau, M.A. 1990. Domestic food policy in the United States. Journal of Health Politics, 15(2), 319–339.

Luttrell, C.B. 1989. The high cost of farm welfare. Cato Institute, Washington, DC, USA.

Makinson, L.; Goldstein, J., ed. 1994. The cash constituents of Congress. Congressional Quarterly.

Rogers, A. 1992. Europe: Parliament vs Commission on Food. Lancet, 339(8796), 799.

Super, D. 1997. Overview of the food stamp time limits for people between ages 18 and 50. Center on Budget and Policy Priorities, Washington, DC, USA.

Super, D.A.; Parrott, S.; Steinmetz, S.; Mann, C. 1996. The new welfare law. Center on Budget and Policy Priorities, Washington, DC, USA.

USCM (United States Conference of Mayors). 1991. Report on hunger and homelessness in America's cities. USCM, Washington, DC, USA.

US Congress. 1992. Hunger in America: who cares? Hearing before the Select Committee on Hunger, House of Representatives, 102nd Congress, 2nd session, Apr 30. House Select Committee on Hunger, US Congress, Washington, DC, USA.

USDA (United States Department of Agriculture). 1990. 1990 agricultural chartbook. USDA Economic Research Service, Washington, DC, USA.

———— 1994. Economic indicators of the farm sector: national financial summary 1992. Agriculture and Rural Economy Division, USDA Economic Research Service, Herndon, VA, USA.

———— 1997. Preliminary summary of food assistance program results for March 1997. USDA Food and Consumer Service, Washington, DC, USA.

USDL (United States Department of Labor). 1994. Employment, hours, and earnings, United States, 1909–1994. Bureau of Labor Statistics, Washington, DC, USA.

USOPM (United States Office of Personnel Management). 1992. Federal civilian workforce statistics: demographic profile of the federal workforce. Statistical Analysis and Services Division, USOPM, Washington, DC, USA.

Zedlewski, S.; Clark, S.; Meier, E.; Watson, K. 1996. Potential effects of Congressional welfare reform legislation on family incomes. Urban Institute, Washington, DC, USA.

...✻ ✻ ✻...

Policy Failure in the Canadian Food System

Rod MacRae

Introduction

We can choose, you know we ain't no amoebas ... .
— American songwriter John Hyatt
("Thing Called Love")

Although Hyatt was writing about love, about how humans should have the capacity to consciously choose loving relationships, instead of drifting unconsciously into them, his words are equally applicable to what passes in Canada as food policy. We do have this thing that some regard as being collectively a food policy — many odd bits of policy, programing, and regulations — but it's something policymakers drifted into, not something people consciously and intelligently chose. Certainly, Canada has nothing specifically labeled a food policy. In Hyatt's terms, that might make us amoebas.

One might argue that Canadian agribusiness has intentionally acted, in collusion with government, to ensure that Canada has no coherent food policy. To determine whether this is so is beyond the scope of this paper, but even a cursory review of policy statements and government practice shows that governments' view of food and food policy is mechanistic, technocratic, incomplete, fragmentary, and contradictory — sufficiently so that it may not be accurate to refer to what Canada has as food policy. In my view a coherent food policy has optimal nourishment of the population as its highest purpose, makes agricultural production and distribution a servant of that purpose, and ensures that the food system is financially and environmentally sustainable (see below).

Canada has agricultural policy ...

Agriculture has been the primary driver of food-related policy in Canada since it became a nation. Canada's agricultural policy in the 19th century dealt primarily with colonial obligations (fueling the Industrial Revolution in the United Kingdom) and efforts to secure national boundaries (for example, settlement of the prairies) (Skogstad 1987).

Health concerns achieved some policy status in the early part of the 20th century. Early food regulatory efforts focused on sanitation and prevention of adulteration (Macdougall 1990) — important work, but not indicative of a strong sense of the critical link of nourishment to health. One can find little indication that, for example, the work of such pioneers as Picton (1946) and McCarrison (1943) on the relationship between food-production systems, food quality, and health status had any impact on

Canadian policymakers. Unfortunately, most Canadian food regulations remain rooted in a traditional food-safety and fraud-prevention framework (TFPC 1997).

As industrial approaches to agriculture took hold after World War II and the number of diversified farms declined, farmers increasingly organized around the dominant crops and animals they produced. Divisions along commodity lines were created and solidified. Farm organizations evolved to dominate farm-level input into the policy system (Forbes 1985; Skogstad 1987). Consequently, few voices have spoken of the need for a systems approach to policy development, with even fewer people in policy circles to hear the message.

The message in more recent government documents is consistent: we do not have a food system but an agriculture and agrifood industry. Its purpose is not to nourish the population but to be

> *a growing, competitive, market oriented agriculture and agri-food industry that is profitable and responds to the changing food and non-food needs of domestic and international customers; is less dependent on government support; and contributes to the well-being of all Canadians and the quality of life of rural communities, while achieving farm financial security, environmental sustainability and a safe, high quality food supply.*
>
> (AAFC 1994)

And something that passes as nutrition policy ...

The roles of Health Canada revolve around improving the nutritional quality of the food supply, defined primarily through nutrition labeling and meeting the *Food and Drug Act* regulations. This department also sets dietary guidelines. The weaknesses of these activities call into question any claims that they are components of a nutrition policy.

Nutrition labeling in Canada is inadequate. It is optional unless a producer is making a specific nutritional claim, in which case, only the amount of nutrient for which the claim is made must be disclosed.[1] Where labeling is provided, it is often incomplete or difficult for the consumer to read and interpret. Nutrition labels appear on only about 20% of packaged foods in Canada (Grier 1990). Nutrition information is not usually provided for fresh meat, poultry, seafood, fruits, or vegetables. Companies may voluntarily list nutrients, which must include energy, protein, fat, and carbohydrates. Other listings are at the discretion of the company. Regulations also make it difficult for consumers to understand the significance of any particular nutrient content, because the labels make no reference to what levels are optimal for human consumption.

The *Food and Drug Act* regulations are inconsistent with nutrition objectives (TFPC 1997). For example, the regulations contribute to excess fat consumption. The regulations permit on the market many high-fat products, which tends to confuse consumers about how much fat they are consuming, in part because of the way foods are defined, in part because of different ways of measuring fat. For example, several prepared meats can be very high in fat, and the fat in dairy products is labeled differently than fat is described in the Healthy Eating Guidelines (HWC 1990). Manufacturers now

---

[1] A few minor exceptions can be cited to this rule. When a claim is made for a fatty acid or cholesterol, the label must also list total fat plus polyunsaturates, monounsaturates, saturates, and cholesterol. For potassium or sodium claims, both must be listed. Labels carrying the expressions "special dietary use," "carbohydrate reduced," "sugar-free," "low sodium," or their synonyms must also list the energy, protein, fat, and carbohydrate contents.

have a much greater variety of low-fat items on the market, but these changes have resulted largely from consumer and regulatory pressures. Further changes to the marketplace will likely result from government policy initiatives to shape market behaviour.

The Healthy Eating Guidelines are just that — guidelines. They cannot be enforced, and as shown in the above examples they have not been integrated into other policy arenas. Most Canadians have little comprehension of how to implement them in their daily dietary practices.

And we almost had a food policy, sort of ...

For a brief period, the federal government considered food policy and the language of food systems. In the late 1970s, Canada was influenced by the work Norway had done on food-policy development (NMA 1975), the National Nutrition Survey of 1973 (Sabry 1975), the Lalonde report on health promotion (Lalonde 1974), and the Mustard report on diet and cardiovascular disease (CDCD 1976). Financial problems for farmers and dramatic food-price increases also brought pressure to bear. In particular, the Food Prices Review Board, functioning in the mid-1970s, revealed these problems.

The federal government developed its food strategy in 1977/78. Two departments — Agriculture Canada and Consumer and Corporate Affairs — had the leadership role; the Deputy Ministers' Committee on Food Policy and the Interdepartmental Steering Group on Food Policy (ISGFP) developed the strategy, but their work was confined to six major policy areas:

- Income stabilization and support;

- Trade policy and safeguards;

- Research, information, and education;

- Marketing and food aid;

- The processing, distribution, and retail sectors; and

- Consumer concerns — price stability, nutrition, and food safety.

Their philosophy did not depart significantly from that of earlier approaches to agricultural policy. For example, according to ISGFP (1978),

> Government policies must continue to develop and expand Canada's production and export strengths to ensure the adequacy of safe and nutritious food supplies for the domestic and export markets at reasonable prices which are responsive to competitive forces over time.

To their credit, these policymakers were concerned that the economics of agriculture should not override national nutritional priorities. They asked that nutrition-impact statements be prepared for policy initiatives related to food (only one ever was). Still, they believed that the efficient operation of the marketplace was the best way to meet policy objectives.

Aside from the limitations and contradictions inherent in this emerging policy and the struggles of interdepartmental collaboration, what really killed this approach was the Ministry of Agriculture's unwillingness to support it. This was rooted in the changes this approach would impose on the food production, processing, and distribution sectors. Also, the Ministry of Agriculture had long been described as one of the most captive of ministries.

Agriculture Canada did, some years later, adopt a policy statement in support of Health Canada's work on nutrition, but again one that reflects the primacy of production over nourishment: "In order to support the Canadian agri-food industry, Agriculture Canada has a major responsibility with respect to nutrient composition and nutritional value of agri-food products" (Agriculture Canada 1988).

Further fragmentation and contradiction of current policy approaches

Further indicators of Canada's failure to consciously chose a food policy are apparent in three significant themes in Agriculture and Agri-Food Canada (AAFC) policy documents that stand in stark contrast to the stated (at least rhetorically) objectives of improving health and ensuring environmental sustainability.

You aren't what you eat

It's hard to find substantial references to consumers and health in AAFC documents. It's as if they don't believe food production, diet, and health are intimately related.

Yet, diet is a significant risk factor in 70% of diseases (USSG 1988). Many chronic diseases and poor-health conditions, including cardiovascular disease, hypertension, stress, cancer, diabetes, low-birth-weight infants, anemia, and some infections in children now pose major public-health challenges. All of these chronic diseases and poor-health conditions are related to nutrition.

They affect both the food rich (those with sufficient income to acquire whatever foods they desire) and the food poor (the hungry and food insecure). A high percentage of the Canadian population is at risk of disease because most people do not eat in a manner optimal for health. For example, according to the 1992 Ontario Health Survey, 75% of the population eats more than the recommended dietary intake of fat. More than 50% of the population fails to consume recommended levels of vegetables, and more than 66% fails to consume recommended levels of grain. About 15% of the Ontario population does not have sufficient income to afford a nourishing diet.

In Canada, we all pay, through publicly funded health insurance, for the costs of individual poor food choices or hunger. In AAFC's view, the food system, through which most people acquire food, bears no responsibility for the consequences of what it produces for the consuming public. Except in some cases, food companies are not obligated to provide consumers with substantial information about the health-related dimensions of their products. The efforts of health agencies to promote healthy eating are ultimately overwhelmed by agribusiness advertising of unhealthy eating patterns.

AAFC and the food industry seem to believe that the individual is responsible for sorting out what is nourishing and how to fit various food products into a healthy diet. That might make sense if we each paid our own health-care bills, but because we all pay for each other's health care through the tax system, it makes sense to encourage some collective responsibility for diets, including making the food system act as if it believes "we are what we eat."

Trade globally to sustain locally

According to AAFC, expansion of trade in agricultural products is entirely consistent with efforts to ensure environmental sustainability in Canada. This position shows a lack of understanding of the ecological principles underlying sustainability (TFPC 1994). Current Canadian agricultural trade policy and practice contravene most of these ecological principles. In part, this is because trade theory evolved at a time when people gave no consideration to finite resources and ecological limits. As a result, they took no account of the costs of possible future resource depletion. Although this may have been understandable in the early 19th century when the basic assumptions about trade benefits were adopted, it is inexcusable that present-day trade theorists and policymakers continue to use 200-year-old assumptions to guide policy-making.

A key ecological principle is that nutrient and energy flows are cyclical, rather than linear, and thus the practice of consuming resources close to where they are produced sustains ecosystem integrity. Cyclical relations cannot be respected in a global trading environment because of the great distances goods travel. In North America alone, the average food molecule travels 2 100 km (Cornucopia Project 1981).

Present trade practice constantly exceeds environmental limits because Canada depends so heavily on agricultural (particularly grain) exports to preserve a positive balance of trade. This pressure to produce for the export market results in a continuous overharvest. Similarly, trade pressures reinforce monocultural or simplified agroecosystem designs, and this reduces functional diversity and limits the producers' ability to design self-maintaining and self-regulating systems.

In practice, all this encourages farmers to pursue fundamentally contradictory objectives. They are expected to invest in environmental stewardship, yet also produce for the global marketplace, driven largely by cost-efficiency considerations. The global market implicitly encourages producers to externalize their environmental costs, but domestic policy encourages them to internalize these costs. AAFC documents suggest that policymakers are either unaware of these contradictions or deliberately avoid addressing them.

Knowledge is too much power

Although health and sustainability are (at least rhetorically) stated agricultural public-policy objectives, our food-information rules and practices stand in the way of achieving these objectives. No one has responsibility for determining the overall coherence of consumer food messages. As a result, consumers get information that is often incomplete, contradictory, and misleading (TFPC 1998).

Individual consumers do not have the resources to determine, with any ease, the accuracy or completeness of any firm's messages. Government rules confound this problem because of a lack of consistency among the efforts of the parts and levels of government that have responsibility for advertising rules, labeling, and grading systems.

The healthy-eating messages from federal, provincial, and municipal health departments are often contradictory, as a result of differences in the regulatory framework of diverse arms of government. Investments in programs to promote environmental stewardship in agriculture are undercut in the market because without the right information consumers cannot support these efforts with their dollars. It seems to me that government and business are unwilling to unleash the power of consumers to create a new food system.

Contradictions among the messages from within federal, provincial, and municipal health departments result in wasted public dollars and continued health and environmental problems. Government policies and programs fail to give consumers a real opportunity to support them when they shop.

So the end result of all these intersecting factors is that departments of agriculture do not have a comprehensive, overarching policy framework to evaluate specific proposals. Instead, departments generally allow the marketplace to determine the overall direction of agricultural production and define what is valuable and desirable for society; they only intervene to attempt to mitigate the negative impacts of the market. This approach might be theoretically rational if Canada had a fully functional food marketplace. It does not. For example, there is exceedingly imperfect competition in the Canadian food marketplace because Canada has the most oligopolistic food system in the Western world. Powerful food-system players have excessive influence over policy. In fact, federal and provincial departments of agriculture in Canada are widely viewed as captives of farm and food-industry interests (Winson 1992).

A consequence of this policy void is the absence of mechanisms to bring large issues to the debate on agricultural development. The governments' review frameworks focus on the specific dimensions of a technology or process, and no units take responsibility for the macropolicy questions that might confront the traditional reliance on the market to solve problems. Pragmatically, this means that discussions often take place at the level of regulation and program implementation, but without a comprehensive framework for guidance.

How would we know if we had an effective food policy?

Even without a thorough review, it's clear that Canada is meeting few of these conditions to any significant degree.

In my view, a comprehensive food policy would create a food system in which

- Everyone has enough food (quality and quantity) to be healthy;

- Food production, processing, and consumption are suited to the environmental, economic, technological, and cultural needs, potentials, and limits of the various regions of Canada;

- The food system is seen as providing an essential service, food supply and quality are dependable, and they are not threatened by social, political, economic, or environmental changes;

- Food is safe for those who produce, work with, and eat it, and it's safe for the environment;

- Resources (energy, water, soil, genetic resources, forests, fish, wildlife) are used efficiently (in an ecological sense) and without waste;

- The resources of the food system are distributed in a way that ensures that those who perform the most essential tasks have a decent income (in particular, people in rural communities have enough work and income to maintain or improve their life and to care for the rural environment);

- The system is flexible enough to allow people to improve and adapt it to changing conditions;

- Everyone who wants to be involved in determining how the food system works has a chance to participate;

- Opportunities are available in the food system for creative and fulfilling work and social interaction; and

- Our food system allows other countries to develop food systems that express similar values.

Key food-policy principles

The following are some key principles with which to build a food policy:

- *Integrated responsibilities and activities* — Systems should be designed to acknowledge the interconnectedness of activities in agriculture, food, and health. Professionals should have expertise across these three domains and work collaboratively with people who are knowledgeable within these spheres.

- *An emphasis on macropolicy* — The policy-making process should start with an examination of global questions and options and then, as appropriate, the development of more specific policy tools and interventions consistent with macropolicy. This approach would recognize that policy-making involves identifying what is societally desirable.

- *Transdisciplinary policy development* — Because food is a multidimensional endeavour, policy sections must include professionals from a diverse range of disciplines, only one of which should be economics. The recommended system would properly define economics and science as tools to help society achieve identified goals.

- *Collaboration with the diverse groups affected by problems in need of resolution* — A more diverse group of people should participate in policy-development work; community-development principles should be employed in developing policy; and policymakers should work with a very diverse group of people, as everyone is affected by the way the food system operates.

- *Food-systems policy* — The policy system should be designed to work with systems and subsystems, and policymakers should apply systems thinking in their analysis of problems and design of solutions.

Anything promising on the horizon?

Some initiatives recently completed or in progress provide hope for those in Canada who are interested in having a coherent national food policy. For example,

- AAFC does have a sustainable-agriculture statement (AAFC 1996). Unfortunately, the document falls victim to the major contradictions outlined above and makes only small progress over similar documents at the beginning of the decade (EAP 1997).

- Canada released a federal Plan of Action on Nutrition (JSC 1996) in response to the International Conference on Nutrition, held in Rome in 1992. In many ways, this is the closest the federal government has come to developing an integrated food and nutrition policy. However, it shies away from addressing the substantial problems in the agriculture sector.

- Canada's Minister of Agriculture in 1992 was a star at the World Food Summit (WFS) meetings in Rome. Canada has felt some compulsion to respond to the WFS call for action and has been consulting people across the country to develop a response.

Provinces and municipalities have also made some attempts to create food policy:

- In 1995, British Columbia produced a food-policy document (MAFF 1995). It was largely about agricultural-production issues, but the ministry has at times showed interest in creating a new vision for the food and agriculture sector.

- The City of Toronto adopted what is arguably Canada's most definitive food and nutrition policy, the Toronto Declaration on Food and Nutrition (TCC 1992).

- The Ontario Ministry of Health has planned for several years to release an Ontario food and nutrition policy. As yet, none has appeared; however, the Ontario Public Health Association has produced a very comprehensive report that, if adopted by the provincial government, may create one of the most progressive policies in the world (OPHA 1996).

- Nova Scotia produced a response to the International Conference on Nutrition (NSNC 1997) that is strong on concept, even if it is still weak on strategies for implementation.

New organizations

Theory

In this paper, I am concerned particularly with policy-making institutions. Few positive developments have occurred at the level of institutional structures. Although the new ecological organization theory is relevant to how institutions need to behave to create a new kind of food policy, the practice of institutional policy-making remains rooted in old ways.

Increasingly, organizational-design theorists are recognizing the need for institutional forms and processes that match or mimic the diversity and complexity of the ecosystem problems (including those related to humans) they are attempting to solve (Walters and Holling 1984). Theorists now recognize that organizations have their own ecology (Plumptre 1988; Morley and Wright 1989), an ecology that can potentially mimic that of the systems and processes with which the organization is concerned.

Although business management theory has been moving in this direction for some time, management in government has been slower to adapt (Plumptre 1988).

In this emerging organizational paradigm, particularly as it relates to diversity, a key concept is that of "fit" — an organization's ability to fit into the environment in which it works. The language of fit is ecological. People speak of an organization as a miniature ecosystem; of its uniqueness; of its symbiotic relationships, internal consistency, and integrity; and of complex webs of relationships, processes, systems, and structures. Morgan (1989, pp. 55–56) wrote that "the internal diversity of any self-regulating system must match the complexity of its environment if it is to deal with the challenges posed by that environment."

An organization attempting to mimic this diversity should adopt (TFPC 1995) the following principles:

1. The organization should have well-established intelligence networks that focus on key indicators of activity and change. Decisions have to be based on both technical and qualitative information from these key indicators, before all the information is available. Such a system can be effective if the intelligence networks are extensive and include many kinds of actors.

2. The organization should consist of open-ended networks of interdependent allies, inside and outside the organization, to build collaborative solutions.

3. Decision-making should be shifted to the people closest to the environment.

4. Lines of communication should be more horizontal, as opposed to vertical.

5. The organization should spread risk by investing in more than one approach to solving a problem. Structures should be disaggregated so that more operating units are created, each with a low cost associated with failure.

6. Teams should be created, disassembled, and reassembled for different tasks to respond quickly to changing conditions. Generalists of different backgrounds who can work in different teams should be hired. Problems should be approached by different teams, from different angles. This approach, known as redundancy of function, spreads risk and produces greater diversity of thought and action.

These principles ultimately produce an organization that is less expensive to operate and produces results in a timely and efficient manner.

The challenge is to apply these emerging ecological organizational-design principles to the agricultural policy-making system. No Canadian department of agriculture has embraced these ideas and redesigned its form and process consistent with these principles. I propose such a redesign in the next section.

A department of food and food security

Given the ecological organizational-design principles described above, what kinds of new intergovernmental arrangements and organizational forms might be appropriate for developing food and agricultural policy?

The Toronto Food Policy Council (TFPC) has proposed the creation of new units at the municipal level and of departments of food and food security at the provincial and federal levels. The missions of all these units and departments would be the creation of food security and sustainability. For this proposal, the TFPC assumed that no significant changes to constitutional divisions of responsibility would be needed.

The provincial and federal departments would be organized according to food subsystems (Table 1): Consumption, Nourishment, and Health; Distribution and Storage; Processing; Production; and Export and Import. Consequently, certain

Table 1. Organization of a Department of Food and Food Security.

	Division					
	Consumption, Nourishment, and Health	Distribution and Storage	Processing	Production	Export and Import	Administrative Services
Functions						
Monitoring and evaluation	•	•	•	•	•	
Administration	•	•	•	•	•	
Research and development	•	•	•	•	•	
Food regulations and standards	•	•	•	•	•	
Policy development and planning	•	•	•	•	•	
Technology approvals	•	•	•	•	•	
Education and training	•	•	•	•	•	
Financial services						•
Development and training						•
Computer systems						•
Personnel						•
Issue area						
Consumer information systems	•					
Cooperative systems		•	•			
Corporate accountability and monitoring		•	•		•	
Demand management	•					
Dispute resolution					•	
Farmer–consumer linkages	•					
Food access	•	•				
Pricing	•					
Proximity	•					
Cultural suitability	•					
Health promotion	•					
Import standards adherence and control					•	
Import substitution		•	•	•		
Integrated production systems[a]				•		
Intergenerational transfer and training				•		
Land use				•		
Marketing		•	•		•	
Micro and mobile processing		•	•			
Nutrition	•					
Self-reliance monitoring					•	
Special products				•		
Supply coordination		•	•	•		
Interdivisional committees	Demand and Supply Management; Economic Development and Strategic Procurement; Environmental Sustainability; Equity and Social Justice; Food Quality; Monitoring and Evaluation; Public Participation and Community Development; Sectorial, Incomes, and Employment					

[a] Includes transition systems and supports, genetic resources and biodiversity, and natural-habitat integration.

functions would be taken from other departments (particularly the current ministries of Health, Economic Development and Trade, and Community and Social Services).

Similar functions would be carried out in many of these divisions. This arrangement would address the application of principles 4, 5, and 6, presented in the previous section. Cross-cutting interdivisional committees would provide coordination for issue areas common to all divisions (for example, food quality, environmental sustainability). Each division would contain a mix of professionals, who would have sufficient general training to accommodate flexible inter- and intradivisional movement. Management structures would be much less hierarchical in this system. The divisional design by food subsystems would accommodate much more diverse interactions with stakeholders. Each division would have knowledge of community-development principles and practice.

The federal department would differ from the provincial ones in that it would perform more significant functions in the areas of export and import, interprovincial trade and demand-and-supply coordination, technology approvals, national-standard setting for research and development, and nutrition and consumer information systems. I suggest, however, that research programs devolve to lower levels in the system, consistent with the need for more location-specific research. As well, additional responsibility for financial support to various sectors of the food and agriculture system would be transferred to the provincial governments, for similar reasons. Responsibility for education and training would remain primarily a provincial function.

These changes would be enhanced if relations with the municipal governments were also altered. The existence of municipal or regional food-policy councils (FPCs), patterned on the existing Ontario models, would facilitate the work of the provincial department. Proponents of FPCs feel strongly that existing institutional responses at the federal, provincial, and municipal levels are inadequate to address fundamental food-security problems at the local level and that municipalities, which in many provinces have responsibility for public health, need to take a new approach if long-lasting solutions are to be found. The FPC model is consistent with the organizational theory provided above (MacRae et al. 1992).

Concluding remarks

Some argue that the development of a sustainable food policy (and associated institutions) will be a lengthy process. Here's hoping it's a bit faster than our evolution from amoeba to *Homo sapiens*.

References

AAFC (Agriculture and Agri-Food Canada). 1994. Future directions for Canadian agriculture and agri-food: a vision of growth through security, security through growth, creating the balance. AAFC, Ottawa, ON, Canada.
———— 1996. Strategy for environmentally sustainable agriculture and agri-food development in Canada. AAFC, Ottawa, ON, Canada.
Agriculture Canada. 1988. Nutrition policy statement. Rapport, 4(1), 7.
CDCD (Committee on Diet and Cardiovascular Disease). 1976. Report of the Committee on Diet and Cardiovascular Disease. Ministry of Supply and Services Canada, Ottawa, ON, Canada.

Cornucopia Project. 1981. Empty breadbasket: the coming challenge to America's food supply and what we can do about it. Rodale Press, Emmaus, PA, USA.

EAP (Ecological Agriculture Projects). 1997. Agriculture and Agrifood Canada's strategy for environmental sustainability. EAP Comment, 1(1), Feb.

Forbes, J.D. 1985. Institutions and influence groups in Canadian farm and food policy. Institute of Public Administration of Canada, Toronto. ON, Canada. Canadian Public Administration Monograph No. 6, Institute of Public Administration Monograph No. 10.

Grier, K. 1990. Canada's new nutrition labelling recommendations. PDR Notes, 64, 1–2.

HWC (Health and Welfare Canada). 1990. Nutrition recommendations: the report of the Scientific Review Committee. Ministry of Supply and Services, Ottawa, ON, Canada.

ISGFP (Interdepartmental Steering Group on Food Policy). 1978. Recent developments in food strategy. Government of Canada, Ottawa, ON, Canada, 13 Dec.

JSC (Joint Steering Committee). 1996. Nutrition for health: an agenda for action. Health Canada, Ottawa, ON, Canada.

Lalonde, M. 1974. A new perspective on the health of Canadians. Ministry of Supply and Services Canada, Ottawa, ON, Canada.

Macdougall, H. 1990. Activists and advocates: Toronto's Health Department 1883–1983. Dundurn Press, Toronto, ON, Canada.

MacRae, R.J.; Welsh, J.; Kneen, B.; Friedmann, H. 1992. Municipal food policy councils: diversifying institutional form and process to support the transition to just, healthy and sustainable food and agricultural systems. Paper presented at the Diversity in Food, Agriculture, Nutrition and Environment Conference, 6 Jun 1992, Lansing, MI, USA. Agriculture, Food and Human Values Society, Gainesville, FL, USA.

MAFF (Ministry of Agriculture, Fisheries and Food). 1995. Securing our food future: an agri-food policy for British Columbia. MAFF, Victoria, BC, Canada.

McCarrison, R. 1943. Nutrition and natural health. Faber and Faber, London, UK.

Morgan, G. 1989. Organizational choice and the new technology. In Wright, S.; Morley, D., ed., Learning works: searching for organizational futures. Faculty of Environmental Studies, York University, Toronto, ON, Canada. pp. 47–62.

Morley, D.; Wright, S. 1989. Epilogue: organizational and contextual change. In Wright, S.; Morley, D., ed., Learning works: searching for organizational futures. Faculty of Environmental Studies, York University, Toronto, ON, Canada. pp. 256–278.

NMA (Norwegian Ministry of Agriculture). 1975. On Norwegian nutrition and food policy. NMA, Oslo, Norway. Report 32 to the Storting.

NSNC (Nova Scotia Nutrition Council). 1997. Nutrition for health: the Nova Scotia agenda for action. Nova Scotia Dietetic Association and Nova Scotia Department of Health, Halifax, NS, Canada.

OPHA (Ontario Public Health Association). 1996. Food for now and the future. OPHA Food Security Group, Toronto, ON, Canada.

Picton, L.J. 1946. Thoughts on feeding. Faber and Faber, London, UK.

Plumptre, T.W. 1988. Beyond the bottom line: management in government. Institute for Research in Public Policy, Halifax, NS, Canada.

Sabry, Z.I. 1975. The cost of malnutrition in Canada. Canadian Journal of Public Health, 66, 291–293.

Skogstad, G. 1987. The politics of agricultural policy-making in Canada. University of Toronto Press, Toronto, ON, Canada.

TCC (Toronto City Council). 1992. Declaration on food and nutrition. TCC, Toronto, ON, Canada.

TFPC (Toronto Food Policy Council). 1994. Health, wealth and the environment: the impacts of the CUSTA, GATT and NAFTA on Canadian food security. TFPC, Toronto, ON, Canada. TFPC Paper No. 2.

——— 1995. Setting a new direction: changing Canada's agricultural policy making system. TFPC, Toronto, ON, Canada. TFPC Paper No. 4.

——— 1997. Cutting out the fat: food and agricultural policies, programs, regulations and pricing mechanisms that promote the production and distribution of fat in our food system. TFPC, Toronto, ON, Canada. TFPC Paper No. 6.

——— 1998. Consumers are sovereign: how to change food information systems so food shoppers are the informed consumers governments and businesses say they should be. TFPC, Toronto, ON, Canada. TFPC Paper No. 10.

USSG (United States Surgeon General). 1988. Report on nutrition and health. United States Department of Health and Human Services, Public Health Service, Washington, DC, USA.

Walters, C.J.; Holling, C.S. 1984. Resilience and adaptability in ecological management systems: why do policy models fail? *In* Conway, G.R., ed., Pest and pathogen control: strategic, tactical, and policy models. John Wiley, Chichester, UK. pp. 470–479.

Winson, A. 1992. The intimate commodity. Garamond Press, Toronto, ON, Canada.

...ﷺ ﷺ ﷺ...

Urban Agriculture as
Food-access Policy

Desmond Jolly

Introduction

Policy development and implementation fail more often than not to allow for irony or for dialectical thinking. To make an impression on policymakers, so that policy outcomes are as intended, policy advocates typically feel compelled to emphasize the potential positive impacts of a proposed intervention. Uncertainties, complexities, and possible adverse outcomes are often glossed over or simply ignored. In some sense, policy advocates must present themselves as — to use a term of Hoffer's (1951) — true believers. Movements that reshape economic and social landscapes, such as revolutions, are typically driven by such true believers. But we often miss the fact that less grandiose schemes for social reform are also proposed, adopted, and implemented in the context of the true-believer syndrome. The social psychology, therefore, that informs expectations of policy interventions is typically overly simplistic, with linear perceptions of cause and effect. Goodwill is conflated with good sense.

One observes examples of this syndrome in a series of policy prescriptions and their ultimate outcomes, as well as in the responses to these outcomes, in social and economic programs adopted in the United States over the last half century. Similar observations can be made about global interventions. Examples include the War on Poverty and associated "great-society" interventions, which were premised on the notion of the potential abolition of poverty or, at the least, the construction of a platform of opportunity from which individuals could launch themselves out of the gravitational orbit of poverty. The fact that poverty has not disappeared from the social and economic landscape of the United States is used as a rationale for dismantling antipoverty or equal-opportunity programs. Now the market is deemed to be more intelligent than social engineers. Apparently, at least some policymakers, as well as lay advocates, seemed to have expected that civil-rights laws and affirmative action would, in three decades, produce racial equality and banish racial distinctions and discrimination from US society (Hacker 1995). Opinion surveys and everyday incidents indicate how illusive and intractable these outcomes are. But again, civil rights and affirmative action are now not only perceived to have been ineffective in eradicating the problems that they ostensibly aimed to address but are also stigmatized as the cause of, not remedy for, the problems of racial discord and inequality. Various "wars" on drugs, crime, and other social pathologies may have attenuated, but have not removed, these problems, and they remain serious social maladies.

What can policy analysts, if not lay advocates, learn from these experiences and from the backlash engendered by the perception of failed social programs? Policy analysts must question whether the presentation of cause–effect intervention relationships in a simplistic, linear framework, without reference to the associated ironies and dialectics, does justice to the cause and to the assorted stakeholders and intended beneficiaries. I am currently planning a reform of the welfare apparatus in a county of California to comply with the "welfare to work" policies that the California legislature implemented in 1997. Happily, there does appear to be some regard for the multiple factors that put households at risk of social dependency. Thus, at least in this instance, apparently some application is made of lessons learned from failed interventions. But welfare reform as national policy does not appear to have escaped the syndrome of true believer, oversimplification, a short time horizon, an underappreciation of the complexity of the issues of social dependence, and the fragility of the web of social communities, including the family structure. Changes in food-stamp eligibility, for example, have merely relocated the recipients of food aid from public to private agencies, with little regard, excluding faith, for the ability of private charitable organizations to meet the increased demand.

This paper examines the dialectics of urban agriculture as an intervention process to meet the food needs of urban populations. As a general discussion of the philosophical approach to urban agriculture as a policy intervention, it does not draw extensively on data related to populations at risk, their food demands, the availability and quality of land and other resources to produce this food, and questions about the logistics of food distribution. The empirics are drawn from my own observations and experience in the United States and in several lower income nations and from some published and unpublished studies on the sustainability of urban agriculture projects in the United States.

Towards a dialectical understanding of social change

I do not subscribe to the Malthusian postulates regarding the relationship between food sustenance, population growth, and the quality of life. But Malthus did recognize that social change is often not linear. As he proposed, an improvement in food availability and in the nutrition of peasant or worker households would engender an increase in population, either through increased fertility or decreased mortality rates. Assuming that agricultural productivity is limited, he postulated that the ensuing population growth would lead to a subsequent decline in per capita food consumption. Thus, as he saw it, we can do harm by doing good. To reiterate, I do not agree with the Malthusian syllogism. But I believe that the articulation, analysis, and implementation of social policies and programs would be better served if we recognize the potential ironies and contradictions inherent in technological or social change.

Application of dialectical understanding to the urban agricultural movement

Urban agriculture is not a novel phenomenon. It is likely as old as the earliest urban settlement. Indeed, *economics* is derived from *oikonomia*, which referred to the affairs of household production and management in ancient Greece, when nearly all households in Athens had gardens that contributed substantially to household food consumption. In contemporary China, I observed significant food production in what the

Chinese refer to as "the suburbs." And few cities, even in the more industrialized nations, are devoid of agriculture. In Havana, Hong Kong, and Singapore, people even use rooftops in food production. What is new is the movement advocating urban agriculture as social policy. The community food-security movement in the United States has its counterparts in other advanced nations. Urban agriculture is also being advocated at international levels. This articulate, organized advocacy can have salutary impacts. But it can have, as well, not-so-salubrious outcomes.

Urban agriculture presents opportunities, but it also faces substantial constraints. In the industrialized nations, the success of urban agriculture depends on the demographic characteristics of the community; the local structure of support; the availability, quality, and permanence of land; access to, and cost of, water; leadership; and local organization. If urban agriculture is entrepreneurially driven, its potential success hinges on access to capital, risk-management instruments, cost and quality of labour, and a complex array of other factors. Generally, a similar set of factors would determine outcomes in Third World nations. Even on the edges of US cities, the proximity of urban householders to agricultural production raises concerns about noise, dust, odours, and other hazards. Thus, urban agriculture must also deal with zoning constraints.

The California experience illustrates the challenges posed to urban agriculture projects. Within the past decade, a number of urban agriculture projects have been implemented in the United States, including California. Some attempts have been made to research the experiences of these projects. In particular, a number of studies have looked specifically at their sustainability. The results raise serious questions about the extent to which urban agriculture can feasibly meet the food, employment, and entrepreneurial needs of participants, let alone neighbourhoods and entire cities.

Suzanne Monroe-Santos presented data from a survey of community gardens carried out in 1992 and 1996 under the aegis of the American Community Gardening Association (Monroe-Santos 1998). She received responses from 38 cities, covering 6 018 gardens. She studied the sustainability of community gardens: whereas 1 851 new gardens had been created over the period, these cities reported losing 542 gardens (9%) between 1992 and 1996. She also studied land tenure, a key factor in sustainability: a mere 1.5% of the gardens were sited on owned land; 32% of the gardens reported had been in existence for more than 10 years, although they were perennially at risk of takeover by their private lessors or public and municipal agencies. Most were threatened by "economic development." Community gardens do not figure importantly in current conceptions of urban planning and development. Additionally, according to the study, the primary reason reported for loss of gardens was the gardeners' reduced interest, which again raises questions about the dependability and stability of community gardens and their ability to consistently provide a meaningful contribution to the food security of urban residents.

The Monroe-Santos study noted the rise of interest in entrepreneurial gardens — gardens that operate to generate profit, develop human capital, or spawn economic enterprises. According to Monroe-Santos (1998), these gardens

> include training at risk youth and adults about horticulture and landscaping, marketing to exclusive restaurants or farmers markets, and making byproducts such as vinegars and jellies. Other economic endeavors may include greenhouse operations, raising cut flowers, and herb production.

Only 36 of these operations were reported in the study, representing a mere 0.6% of the total gardens reported. Feenstra et al. (1999) studied the performance of these entrepreneurial gardens and concluded as follows:

> Preliminary evidence suggests that most entrepreneurial gardens that also do job training and employ local residents are not able to completely cover the costs of their program through the sales of their products. This "economic self-sufficiency" standard, however, is not the only or even the best standard to use in measuring the "success" of these gardens in the community. The real "payoff" from these gardens comes in creating neighborhood-based job training and employment opportunities, educating youth and adults about maintaining a more sustainable environment, and building individual self-esteem and community pride that allows low-income populations to realize their leadership capacities in the midst of difficult economic and social circumstances.

Feenstra et al. found that these projects injected significant amounts of money into their host communities: 24 out of 27 projects surveyed generated 605 000 United States dollars in wages over a 3-month production season and employed 348 individuals. External grants from foundations covered more than two-thirds of total expenses. The study observed that these programs were unable to cover their costs from sales of food products, but their ancillary benefits might justify the social investment. Nonetheless, the sustainability of these local urban farming projects is in question.

We need to further concern ourselves with whether the role of urban agriculture and local food systems in overall food-access matrices can be politically manipulated to mask a net decline in food access brought about by changes in public policies. Those of us who are concerned with food access in a broad sense — that is, with the food consumption and nutritional status of at-risk populations — need to keep focused on the myriad ways in which people gain access to food through alternatives, such as purchase on the open market, purchase at subsidized price, gleanings and home production, donations, and community feeding programs. If supplies fail to expand to meet increased potential demand, the result will be food-price inflation and a diminution in the quality of life. Thus, we need to question the motive and method of the United Nations Development Programme, which, in its book *Urban Agriculture — Food, Jobs and Sustainable Cities* (UNDP 1996), made the following comments:

> Many developing countries face the late 1990s deeply in debt and with a poor foreign trade balance. For some of them, it is possible and appropriate to put their good rural agricultural land into export crops and to let the cities provide for their food and fuel needs as much as possible through urban agriculture. Self-reliant cities thus advance rural agriculture's export goals. Nicaragua's government, for example, has made a decision to earn foreign exchange in the next few years through agricultural exports.

But the notion that large Third World cities can feed themselves may be chimerical, potentially as successful or unsuccessful as previous development fads. Mexico City, for example, has 20 million inhabitants and is growing at an alarming rate. What is the prognosis that Mexico City can achieve self-sufficiency in food production or even produce 20% of the food it needs?

The case of Havana is cited to show the potential for urban agriculture. But because of the US embargo, the critical scarcity of foreign exchange, the availability of land and vacant lots, and strong, organized support from the Cuban University of Agriculture, the Havana case may be more unique than general. Reportedly, 26 000 gardens grown for the gardeners' own needs contribute to Havana's food security. Moskow (1997), reporting on her 1994 survey of 42 gardeners in Havana, found that an average of 5.83 persons ate from garden production in each gardener's household and that 9.52 persons in extended families received produce from the garden. The gardens made a significant impact on household food budgets and allowed for contributions of food to schools, nursery schools, and nursing homes. Noting the "enormous contributions the gardens make to the gardeners' households and surrounding communities," Moskow (1997) cited the important constraints faced by gardeners, including constraints on access to water, information, and training, as well as to material inputs. Thus, even in Havana, with support from the authorities, gardens face serious limiting factors, as a result of material conditions.

Conclusions

Clearly, urban agriculture, as one component in a complex food-security system, has an important role to play. But we must be careful not to oversell its potential. To do so may ultimately constitute a betrayal of the urban poor and middle class. Self-sufficiency is a worthwhile goal, but is it attainable for large metropolitan areas? Or shall we develop a two-tiered food system — a market-based system for the upper-middle and upper classes and a subsistence, self-sufficiency-based system for the poor and the lower-middle class? Should Third World nations be allocating their prime agricultural land to crops destined for the tables of rich consumers in metropolitan areas while leaving their poorer citizens to feed themselves from marginal lands in the countryside and in the cities so that these nations can import nonessentials — VCRs, luxury automobiles, and Barbie dolls — for their upper-middle-class cosmopolites?

The new world order has witnessed the corporatization of public policy and the privatization of poverty. In this context, urban agriculture is not just necessary, it's essential. For the poor, it's a defensive option. The Cubans, for example, have experienced a 20% decline in caloric intake and a 27% drop in protein consumption. For the powerful, it might be a way to devolve social responsibility. This is the essential dialectic of urban agriculture in the evolving new world order. Advocates of urban agriculture need also to be mindful and supportive of all other avenues to food security, if their objective is the mitigation of poverty, hunger, and malnutrition. To do less is to be mindlessly myopic and to court another failed experiment.

References

Feenstra, G.; McGrew, S.; Campbell, D. 1998. Entrepreneurial community gardens; growing food, jobs and communities. Sustainable Agriculture Research and Education Program, University of California, Davis, CA, USA.

Hacker, A. 1995. Two nations: black and white, separate, hostile and unequal. Ballantine Books, New York, NY, USA.

Hoffer, E. 1951. The true believer: thoughts on the nature of mass movements. Harper, New York. NY, USA.

Monroe-Santos, S. 1998. Longevity of urban community gardens. University of California, Davis, CA, USA. PhD dissertation.

Moskow, A. 1997. Havana's self-provision gardens. Community Greening Review, 7, 17–19.

UNDP (United Nations Development Programme). 1996. Urban agriculture — food, jobs and sustainable cities. UNDP, New York, NY, USA.

PART 8

TOWARD FOOD DEMOCRACY

...❦ ❦ ❦...

Reaffirming the Right to Food in Canada: The Role of Community-based Food Security

Graham Riches

Introduction

This paper considers the question of whether people enjoy the right to food in Canada, addresses the causes of hunger in First World societies, examines the responses of the state and civil society to food insecurity in terms of the depoliticization of hunger, and argues that collaborative and adversarial actions at the community level are essential to eradicating hunger.

Reaffirming the right to food is not simply a matter of technical feasibility (for example, growing more food, teaching better nutrition, developing national action plans), it is a profoundly political matter, raising significant questions about distributional justice. Achieving food security means creating a food system that is sustainable, secure, safe, sufficient, nutritious, and equitable (Tansey and Worsley 1995). This involves issues of ecological, economic, and social justice and forging alliances between sectors such as agriculture, the environment, food policy, and health and social welfare and between various levels of the state and civil society.

Two questions are posed. How are we to move from the declarations and rhetoric of world summits, international conventions, and federal and provincial governments and their assertions of a right to food, when the evidence suggests that governments and to some extent civil society have in recent years sought to depoliticize the issue of hunger, making it no longer the responsibility of the state? How also do we ensure that the complex and interrelated issues of hunger and food security become the subject of informed democratic debate and are thereby publicly understood to be critical not only to the interests of the poor and vulnerable but also to society's interest in long-term ecological and societal well-being?

The right to food: do people enjoy this right in Canada?

Although the right to food is not entrenched in the Canadian *Charter of Rights and Freedoms* (Canada 1982) and is therefore not justiciable, the Government of Canada has historically acknowledged a right to food in a number of international conventions, including the 1948 International Bill of Human Rights (United Nations 1985), the International Covenant on Economic, Social and Cultural Rights (United Nations 1966), and the Convention on the Rights of the Child (United Nations 1989). In recent years, Canada has also committed itself to supporting a number of international declarations with immediate and practical implications for the implementation of the right to food: the World Declaration on Nutrition (adopted in Rome in 1992), the Declaration on Social Development (adopted at the World Social Summit in 1995), and the recent Rome Declaration on World Food Security (FAO 1996), which affirmed "the right of everyone to have access to safe and nutritious food, consistent with the right to adequate food and the fundamental right of everyone to be free from hunger." This right is also expressed at the federal level in the actions of Agriculture and Agri-Food Canada (AAFC) — along with the Global Network on Food Security — to shape the Canadian commitments and follow-up to the World Food Summit.

Yet, from a social-rights perspective the situation is dismal. In April 1996, Canada repealed the federal–provincial cost-shared Canada Assistance Plan, which for a generation had sought to guarantee national standards in the provision of social assistance and meet basic requirements, including food adequacy. Provincial governments have also engaged in massive restructuring of their welfare programs and undermined the right to food. Welfare benefits have been denied or cut, and food allowances have been rendered inadequate. In 1995, AAFC eliminated its nutritious-food-basket costings, thereby removing the one relatively objective way of measuring national nutritional adequacy.

Clearly, the domestic commitment to the right to food has been abandoned, though Canada's international human-rights commitments and federal initiatives suggest a degree of official ambivalence. However, the growth of hunger means that entrenching the right to food in the Charter and establishing it in domestic legislation should be a prime policy objective.

Hunger and its causes in First World societies

Since the early 1980s evidence has been mounting that hunger and food insecurity remain critical global issues, not just in the countries of the South but also in the advanced welfare states of the North, such as Australia, Canada, New Zealand, the United Kingdom, and the United States (see Riches 1997). Estimates based on a variety of studies in Canada and the United States (Poppendieck 1997; Riches 1997) conservatively suggested that at least 8–10% of the population is hungry or at risk of hunger. In Canada, 456 food banks provide food to 2.5 million Canadians a year (CAFB 1995). More than 49% of those who use these food banks are children and women. First Nations people, immigrants, the unemployed, and people with disabilities are overrepresented in food-bank lineups. Public begging is now seemingly accepted as part of the new economic order and serves, along with food banks, as a visible indicator of growing food poverty and inequality. What is perhaps most remarkable is that since 1994 Canada has been ranked first in the world on the United Nations Human Development Index.

Three factors explain the increase in hunger and food insecurity in Canada. First, global economic restructuring, mass unemployment and underemployment, work and income polarization, and the decline of household purchasing power have demonstrated the inadequacy of residual safety nets. In all the countries studied — Australia, Canada, New Zealand, the United Kingdom, and the United States — social-assistance benefits (based on the poor-law principle of less eligibility) have proven inadequate to guarantee affordable nutritious diets (Riches 1997).

Second, the responses of the state and civil society to hunger have encouraged its growth. Promarket governments, committed to structural-adjustment policies, which treat welfare as a direct function of labour-market policy, have undermined any previous commitments to food security. In fact, welfare-reform policies have reinforced the commodification of welfare (the idea that the receipt of public benefits should be directly linked to labour-force participation) by promoting the Organisation for Economic Co-operation and Development's idea of the "active society" (less eligibility, reciprocal obligations, training, and workfare). As a result, benefits have been cut or eliminated, and participation in low-wage work has been required as a condition for the receipt of benefits. Such policies create conditions for the growth of hunger and are antagonistic to the idea of a right to food.

Third, in line with global structural-adjustment policies, new international trade agreements have fostered increasingly unregulated markets and granted more powers to transnational corporations, thereby undermining Canada's sovereignty over its social programs. More profoundly, this globalization (marketization) of the food system erodes the capacity of nation-states and local communities to feed themselves and increases food inequality within and between countries of the South and North, including Canada.

The depoliticization of hunger

If the right to food is to be established, it is essential to understand the ways the state and, to a certain extent, the organizations of civil society have effectively depoliticized the issue of hunger. The depoliticization of hunger is a process that undermines the right to food and allows governments, business, and charity to erode food sovereignty. It also brings with it the erosion of state power to intervene in favour of hungry people and secure their rights.

Since the early 1980s considerable international evidence from Australia, Canada, New Zealand, the United Kingdom, and the United States has shown that governments have denied the existence of food poverty, neglected their international and domestic human-rights obligations to provide food security, refused to acknowledge the inadequacy of welfare benefits, framed issues of welfare costs in terms of fraud and abuse, implemented punitive systems of welfare reform, transferred national responsibilities to lower levels of government and to charity, and consistently blamed the victims.

Food banks in these countries now form one of the major responses of civil society to the hunger issue, and food banks have, as charitable institutions, become institutionalized extensions of the public-welfare system. Although they provide immediate assistance to hungry people, they have enabled governments to look the other way and avoid their political responsibilities (Riches 1986, 1997).

The increasing marketization and commodification of food have actively promoted the depoliticization of hunger. Progressive food-policy experts have been arguing that too many people are no longer in control of what they eat, whether or not they have sufficient income. The giants of the transnational corporate agriculture and food industry have taken over local control of the production and distribution of nutritious food, and their bottom line is food for profit, not nutritional value or the health of the community. Food is understood less and less as a social and cultural good. Kneen (1993) referred to the development of this global food system as a process of distancing, separating people from the sources of their food and nutrition with as many interventions as possible. As a result, individuals, families, and communities have become disempowered and deskilled in their capacity to produce their own food, make sound choices when they purchase food, and feed themselves nutritional and well-balanced diets. These are significant issues, which we ignore at our peril, because, as Winson (1993, p. 2) wrote, "the rituals of food preparation and communal food consumption have played a central, integrative role in human society. They have formed an essential means of bringing people together — of establishing human existence as a social existence."

Community food security: the key to a new politics of hunger

How then do we ensure that the complex and interrelated issues of hunger and food security become the subject of informed democratic debate and that the right to food finds expression not only in international declarations and domestic legislation but also, and meaningfully, at the level of the household and the local community? A key priority is to reengage the politics of hunger and food security at the local level, as well as continuing to work nationally and globally. Without such action, efforts to entrench the right to food in domestic legislation will have little prospect of having any measurable effect.

In the follow-up to the World Food Summit, Canada has engaged in considerable activity internationally and at the national level. It is considering a national action plan and a Food for All campaign, with attention focused on the next World Food Day. Yet, to what extent will this officially organized response promote the ideas expressed by the NGO Forum (1996) at the World Food Summit in Rome? This global community consultation, attended by 200 representatives of civil-society organizations around the world, produced an alternative document and agenda. In essence, the NGO Forum (1996) document challenged the present development paradigm and growth model that informs the Rome Declaration on World Food Security and advocated, instead, "food sovereignty," which is "the freedom of states and communities to decide production, marketing and consumption strategies and policies." Food sovereignty, as the NGO Forum (1996) document pointed out, must assume political and economic autonomy. This document also referred to the growth model's potential to increase poverty, inequality, the marginalization of the poor and landless (farmers, farm workers, women, youth, children, marginalized rural and urban groups, etc.), and their exclusion from decision-making. It clearly stated that "the World Food Summit needs to focus on development, support and propagation of current locally practiced alternative models and further exploration in other new paradigms promoting people's participation and empowerment for all" (NGO Forum 1996, p. 1).

One critical task, therefore, is to build community coalitions of individuals and organizations with food-security interests. This is not always easy to accomplish because, as Carson (1962) remarked in *The Silent Spring*, we live in an era of specialists. The problem with specialism is that it is a recipe for learning more and more about less and less, and it is always easier to more intensely cultivate one's own plot than to share one's knowledge and commitments across the broader field.

Certainly, at the community level, people need to build on the efforts some are making in Kamloops, Prince George, Toronto, Vancouver, and Victoria, where they are working collaboratively on a range of food-security initiatives (Houghton and Riches 1997). In the short term, public action should focus on developing, with the people who are hungry, new forms of service (community gardens, collective kitchens, etc.), seek to educate the public about the reasons for the problem, and work with government at all levels to promote food policy. Municipal governments, regional health and school boards, agriculture and fisheries organizations, and band and tribal councils are all key players at the local level.

Adversarial work is also necessary (Dreze and Sen 1989) to monitor and, when necessary, contest federal and provincial actions (and inaction). In an era of downloading, it is essential that local food-security organizations recognize the significant constitutional powers of provincial governments in many aspects of food security and ensure that their policies comply with international conventions and declarations regarding the right to food.

In conclusion, if Canada is to reaffirm the right to food, it will require active community action and democratic debate. Policy-making simply at the level of the federal government, which remains ambivalent about the right to food, is not enough. As the NGO Forum (1996) statement on food security made clear, nations need to engage in fulfilling a huge and comprehensive agenda for change. It also rightly asserted that their efforts will only be effective if local communities and marginalized peoples are allowed to play full roles in regaining the right to food.

References

CAFB (Canadian Association of Food Banks). 1995. Annual data. CAFB, Toronto, ON, Canada.

Canada. 1982. The Charter of Rights and Freedoms. Ministry of Supply and Services, Ottawa, ON, Canada.

Carson, R. 1962. The silent spring. Houghton Mifflin, New York, NY, USA.

Dreze, J.; Sen, A. 1989. Hunger and public action. Clarendon Press, Oxford, UK.

FAO (Food and Agricultural Organization of the United Nations). 1996. Rome Declaration on World Food Security and World Food Summit plan of action. World Food Summit, Rome, Italy. FAO, Rome, Italy.

Houghton, J.; Riches, G. 1997. Food security in Prince George. *In* Michalos, A., ed., Report on the quality of life in Prince George. University of Northern British Columbia, Prince George, BC, Canada.

Kneen, B. 1993. From land to mouth: understanding the food system (2nd ed.). NC Press Ltd, Toronto, ON, Canada.

NGO Forum. 1996. Statement by the NGO Forum to the World Food Summit. *In* Report of the World Food Summit. Food and Agricultural Organization of the United Nations, Rome, Italy. Annex III.

Poppendieck, J. 1997. The USA: hunger in the land of plenty. *In* Riches, G., ed., First World hunger: food security and welfare politics. Garamond Press, Toronto, ON, Canada. Chapter 6.

Riches, G. 1986. Food banks and the welfare crisis. Canadian Council on Social Development, Ottawa, ON, Canada.

——— ed. 1997. First World hunger: food security and welfare politics. Garamond Press, Toronto, ON, Canada.

Tansey, G.; Worsley, T. 1995. The food system: a guide. Earthscan, London, UK.

United Nations. 1966. International Covenant on Economic, Social and Cultural Rights. United Nations, New York, NY, USA. General Assembly Resolution 2200A (XX1). 16 Dec.

——— 1985. The International Bill of Human Rights. United Nations, New York, NY, USA. DPI/797-40669-June 1985-30M.

——— 1989. Convention on the Rights of the Child. United Nations, New York, NY, USA.

Winson, A. 1993. The intimate commodity. Garamond Press, Toronto, ON, Canada.

Youth, Urban Governance, and Sustainable Food Systems: The Cases of Hamilton and Victoria, Canada

Zita Botelho

Introduction

A common theme in many of the sessions at the Conference on Sustainable Urban Food Systems was "the larger picture," or the international political economy in which we operate and in which our food systems function. Cities are increasingly important actors in the world system (Knox 1995). An analysis of decision-making in urban areas requires a discussion of governance to determine its role in this process. This discussion will focus specifically on the place of youth in this decision-making context, the barriers they face, and the action they take. Youth face many challenges in their efforts to contribute to environmentally sustainable food systems. They are important stakeholders embedded in an unsustainable food system, and many are trying to make their voices heard and contribute to solutions. By 2000, half the world's population will be under 25 years old (CWY 1996).

Political economic structures have been identified as major obstacles to food security in urban environments. For the first time in history, urban areas are home to most of the world's population, making urban environmental and food issues more urgent. Citizens seem to have lost control of the food system, and this threatens the availability of locally grown organic foods produced using environmentally sensitive practices. Similarly, citizens have lost control of the uses of urban space, which now is often determined by a constituency of business interests and global economic factors (Logan and Molotch 1987). The decision-making process in urban areas often excludes citizens. Citizens are invited to participate in public forums or meetings, but these are often unsatisfying to participants because they fail to see how their input is implemented (Pateman 1970; Sewell and Phillips 1979; Warriner et al. 1996). Urban governance, then, becomes an important factor in the struggle to create sustainable urban food systems.

Governance is the broad process of public decision-making, as influenced by a complex set of formal and informal factors. Governance is not synonymous with government, as it refers to an institution and its practices, whether public or private. Rather than focusing on the structure of the institution (council, executive arrangements, departments), governance comprises policies, operational characteristics, mandates, norms, roles, relationships, and operating practices and processes that are so stable, structured, and accepted that they can be said to have been institutionalized (Wolman 1995). Governance includes relationships between organizations, including nongovernmental organizations, economic pressure groups, and other interest groups. These institutionalized relationships are critical to any discussion of the public's potential participation in making decisions regarding local resources.

Pervasive characteristics of social organizations in modern capitalist society include efficiency and profit. These are reflected in the bureaucratic organizations of the public and private sectors, which privilege efficiency, calculability, and profit maximization (Weber 1946). Government institutions have a hierarchical power structure, which often lacks accountability, transparency, and legitimacy. The hierarchy tends to concentrate power in a centralized authority, far from the areas over which power is exercised.

In this model of governance, people are perceived as actors in the market and state, thereby divorcing people from place and their food and divorcing areas of food production from those of food consumption. Current governance creates systemic obstacles to efforts to preserve ecological integrity and break down the unnatural food system that the state and market sustain. Who has access to decision-makers? Although many groups are marginalized by this system, one segment of the population, excluded from even the democratic process of voting, is youth. Youth are defined nebulously as individuals anywhere from 15 to 29 years old. This definition often depends on country and culture.

Youth have a unique concern for ecological integrity and food security, as they will inherit the systemic problems of environmental degradation and food insecurity. Many young people recognize the ramifications of unsustainable agricultural practices. In decision-making processes, youth find themselves with less access than most citizens to urban decisions, although the future holds devastating ecological problems for their generation.

Exclusion from the political process forces youth to move outside of traditional political space and institutions. As citizens of the state, youth often find the institutional framework for public participation, communication, and decision-making inadequate, unwelcoming, and unsatisfying. Participation in social movements can provide youth with a means to express themselves and their ideas that is unconstrained by institutional conventions. Social movements are a form of collective action motivated by a desire to alter particular conditions in society. Magnusson (1996), a political scientist, calls social movements "new ways of being, thinking and acting." As these movements attempt to present alternatives to address current political, cultural, or social issues, they are often classified in negative terms as "collective manifestations of irrational or deviant behavior" (Fainstein and Hirst 1995). These negative connotations are often also associated with youth. This perception and this negation of initiative serve to further alienate youth from political institutions and processes.

Social movements seek to politicize civil society without the constraints of representative–bureaucratic political institutions (Offe 1987). They are emergent forms of practice, with the potential to transform everyday life and larger institutional practices. This is evident in two case studies of youth action on food production. Youth activity in urban food systems calls on us to rethink our attitudes toward nature and the community, both spatially and temporally. Such activity can and does reshape the terrain of politics in distinctive and potentially radical ways, through personal and cultural transformations that refuse accommodation within existing institutions (Carroll 1992). The role of youth in social movements is not without challenge. Youth are subject to discrimination in social movements as well, because older activists do not always recognize the oppression of youth. Similarly, older activists may not welcome the unique contribution of younger members. Examples of youth social movements are actions against racial segregation and the Viet Nam war in the United States in the late 1950s and the 1960s; the antinuclear movement in Germany; and the peace, environmental, human-rights, and woman's-rights movements around the world.

The following two case studies demonstrate the struggle youth groups face when trying to promote sustainable, healthy, local food systems; they represent attempts by youth to access power over urban space via state structures. The information in the following came from informal interviews with project members.

Case studies

Case 1: The Hamilton Organic Mentorship Experience

The Hamilton Organic Mentorship Experience (HOME) project is a youth-based community gardening project in Hamilton, Ontario, Canada. The objectives of the organization include skills development for youth, education, and the establishment of community gardens.

The founder and creator of the HOME initiative, Ryan Kraftcheck, encountered many challenges during his attempts to establish this organization. The main obstacle was a lack of cooperation from local government. Procuring municipal land for the project was a difficult task. The group received no initial political support from the municipality. Several key factors influencing municipal actors were identified: lack of resources, preconceptions about youth projects, land-use issues, lack of trust, and local–regional-government relations.

When the initial proposal for HOME went to the municipality, little enthusiasm was shown. At this time, HOME did not have financial resources, and this was a concern for the municipality. It was uninterested in supporting a project without a strong resource base. When HOME received a substantial federal grant, the attitude of municipal actors changed notably, and the municipality presented the youth organization with more options. Local government reluctantly supported HOME with a land allotment. When the task of land acquisition arose, however, the HOME coordinator was sent from department to department of the municipality. Finally, it was determined that Parks and Recreation was appropriate to deal with HOME's needs for a land allotment. The municipality did not provide for other important project needs, such as liability insurance or access to water. Local government made no effort to participate in HOME activities. It also showed a lack of interest in special events. The HOME team planned a public community event, Garden Sculpture Day, but no government official showed up. HOME participants said that the bureaucrats had negative preconceptions about youth-based projects. The municipality's past experience with unsuccessful youth initiatives had made it sceptical, and this attitude influenced its treatment of HOME project workers. The group gained more legitimacy and credibility in the eyes of the municipality when it allied with an established community group called FoodShare.

Parks and Recreation had very specific notions about appropriate land use in municipal parks. Departmental land-use priorities included baseball diamonds and swimming pools. Bureaucratic attitudes about land use stemmed from a very narrow and unholistic view of the possible uses of urban park space. The land granted to HOME was known to be in a problematic area, as this was in neighbourhoods where people were uninterested in, or even against, the project. The government agencies did not participate in or have an interest in ensuring the sustainability of the project, nor did they show any interest in the creativity expressed in the community gardens.

The HOME coordinator liaised with regional government officials. The regional government's influence in municipal planning worked in HOME's favour. The region of Hamilton–Wentworth had developed a regional plan called Vision 2020, modeled on the principles of Local Agenda 21. Agenda 21 was ratified at the 1992 Earth Summit in Rio and outlines the need for sustainable development in urban planning (UNCED 1992). There is still much scepticism about the implementation of this document, but some officials at the regional level in Hamilton–Wentworth supported it and recognized the significance of HOME's efforts from the point of view of the objectives of Agenda 21.

The regional government held a meeting for the annual Vision 2020 Day, a day celebrating the region's move toward a more sustainable future. At this meeting, it was suggested that the HOME community gardens provide food for the event. The regional government's enthusiasm for the HOME project influenced the attitude of city officials. The city is currently pursuing land acquisition to support HOME participation in the Vision 2020 community event. This clearly reflects the impact of regional government planning on municipal land use.

HOME's participation in Local Agenda 21 is politically significant. Participation in the Vision 2020 initiative provides an opportunity for youth to actively engage in political life at the local level and to have input in decisions concerning living conditions, access to resources, and decision-making structures. Agenda 21 is innovative in its approach to creating more sustainable communities through holistic regional-planning methods. This very public event has given HOME a higher profile in the community and given its participants an opportunity to provide public education about youth activities and community gardening.

The youth in the HOME project did attempt to work with their local government, but because they received little cooperation, they decided to try to influence urban decision-makers in other ways. The HOME strategy tended to focus on leading by example and making links with community groups. As municipal support was negligible, the youth had to be innovative. They were determined to have their case heard and demonstrate the worth of their vision by example, against all odds. HOME's networking in the community involved alliances with Hamilton Community Garden Network, the Urban Core Health Centre for the Homeless, the local Conservation Authority, the Bruce Trail Association, and the Bay Area Restoration Council. HOME participants also hosted coffeehouses in an attempt to share their message about the need for sustainable food systems and spread the awareness of food issues. This work with the community has given the HOME project a higher profile and has also contributed to citizen awareness of land-use issues and the need for a more holistic approach to urban food systems. HOME participants' community involvement also gives the project a different political profile, as it is difficult for local officials to ignore a group that has alliances with many other interest groups in the city. With the HOME project, the youth created their own political space, in their gardens and in their community (Kraftcheck, personal communication, 1997[1])

The HOME project is in its second year and is growing with greater municipal support.

---

[1] Ryan Kraftcheck, HOME, personal communication, May 1997.

Case 2: LifeCycles

LifeCycles is a youth group in Victoria, British Columbia, Canada. It initiates action on issues of food, health, and urban sustainability. The group promotes and creates personal, shared, and community gardens, youth skills and development programs, and educational activities. It was founded in 1992.

LifeCycles has encountered significant challenges from local decision-making bodies in Victoria. When LifeCycles attempted to establish a community-garden project in Victoria, it had to lobby to change local bylaws. Park policy prohibited gardening in parks, as it was deemed to be an inappropriate use of public land. In fact, City Council stated that, in effect, community gardens privatized the land. LifeCycles staff began looking for land and conducted a study to determine areas of high-density population with low access to land by residents. They were approached by people who wanted access to land in a neighbourhood called Fairfield. As a result, LifeCycles started working with a subcommittee of the Environment Committee of the Fairfield Neighbourhood Association, called the Community Gardens Subcommittee. Together, LifeCycles and the community group identified potential sites, most of which were municipal lands.

LifeCycles approached City Council and had its item placed on the agenda of a meeting of the Committee of the Whole.[2] LifeCycles representatives made a presentation on community gardens, their benefits, and the need for Council support to make community gardening possible in Victoria. City Council had the power to direct the city manager to free up land for community gardens, but its response was unfavourable. It decided not to give up municipal lands because it was under pressure to sell those lands for revenue.

City Council then directed LifeCycles to approach the Parks Department. Once again, LifeCycles made a presentation to the Parks Department steering committee, including information on the positive benefits of community gardens and citing examples in the United States. and Canada. The steering committee did not think community gardens were an appropriate way to use park lands. This sent LifeCycles back to City Council, where they articulated the decision of the Parks Department, who had recommended that LifeCycles look to municipal lands for its project. As a result, City Council issued a directive to Parks to change the departmental policy. The Parks Department refused. Finally, the decision went back to City Council, and Council changed the policy.

Once it had approval, LifeCycles completed surveys with the local community to determine the need for access to land. It identified three sites for consideration. Once a site was chosen, LifeCycles encountered another barrier: a councillor, who lived in the neighbourhood where the garden was to be located, exerted his influence and worked to overturn the decision. He maintained that he had received complaints from local residents. He also went to the Fairfield Neighbourhood Association and had a meeting, not with the appropriate subcommittees, but with general members and convinced them it was a hot issue and should not be dealt with by the Fairfield Community Association. The association wrote a letter about its concerns to City Council. Council then overturned the decision. The youth expressed to City Council that the dealings with this issue clearly demonstrated little respect for the process LifeCycles used and for the amount of work they had put into their proposals. LifeCycles then approached the Community Gardens Subcommittee and stated that the community needed to

---

[2] In British Columbia's *Municipal Act*, this refers to a meeting where public or broader interests are allowed to participate in decision-making or debate.

provide stronger support before LifeCycles would dedicate more energy to this project. To make City Council recognize LifeCycles' credibility, it needed very strong community backing. LifeCycles' staff have expressed frustration with the system, feeling that municipalities are not youth friendly and do not promote youth involvement. They also expressed that they are often not taken seriously and not perceived to be legitimate actors in the political forum.

Finally, LifeCycles successfully lobbied to have the bylaw concerning the use of park land changed. The City of Victoria now has several community gardens, thanks to LifeCycles' perseverance. LifeCycles' success in projects such as the community-gardening initiative has helped the organization increase its resource base. Initially, funding came from provincial and federal agencies. As its work in the community gained a higher profile, LifeCycles sought local funding and partnerships. It currently receives funding from, and works with, the Ministry of Small Business, Tourism and Culture, Ministry of the Environment, and Pacific Coast Savings on Community Economic Development. LifeCycles has received Victoria Foundation, Vancouver Foundation, and intermunicipal grants.

LifeCycles spearheaded the creation of the Capital Region Food Roundtable. Its purpose is to provide a multistakeholder organization to meet every 3 or 4 months to discuss food issues in the region of Victoria. It was born out of a World Food Day discussion, sponsored by the Oxford Committee for Famine Relief and the Victoria International Development and Environment Association. As the coordinating body, LifeCycles brings its holistic philosophy to the roundtable and ensures that all interested sectors are involved in dialogue and action. A youth member has a leadership role in each working group and acts as a facilitator for each committee. LifeCycles has been the lead organization in the implementation of this initiative.

Currently, LifeCycles is lobbying the federal government's representatives on the Multilateral Agreement on Investment, regarding the implications of the agreement for Canadian agriculture. Additionally, it is lobbying to have the provincial Ministry of Agriculture and Foods establish a food policy for the future (Gegie and Prouse, personal communications, 1997[3]). The youth in this organization serve as a catalyst for change and as lobbyists, organizers, planners, instigators of practical projects, activists, and educators.

A role for youth

Because local government is often unreceptive to youth as stakeholders, they must be strategic in their attempts to influence decision-making. Youth can be leaders through their implementation of environmentally sustainable alternatives. Many youth projects in urban food production help to reshape conventional views of appropriate land use, thereby providing a different perception of the appropriate use of urban space. This can move society toward a change in consciousness and make people aware of food systems and our relationship to urban ecosystems. These projects also serve to bring communities together.

Successful youth projects and public acknowledgment give credibility to youth as significant stakeholders. This provides youth with a more powerful voice in the

[3] Linda Gegie, Program Coordinator, LifeCycles, and Lonnie Prouse, LifeCycles, personal communications, May 1997.

public process and grants legitimacy to youth within this process. Additionally, youth can create alliances and partnerships with other community groups, neighbourhood associations, or other levels of government to gain greater credibility as a voice in the community. Gaining political and bureaucratic support, through the assistance of those sympathetic to the need for environmental sustainability, can help to pressure unsupportive actors. Youth networking can build a united voice, help in sharing resources (financial resources and information), and ensure that all interested groups are aware of land-use decisions in their region, as information is often difficult to acquire. Many groups also have difficulty accessing the institutions and processes that affect decisions about where and how we get our food. All concerned citizens must demand public processes that give them a legitimate and equal voice in urban decision-making.

What needs to happen in urban governance to ensure adequate youth participation? How can changes in urban governance help achieve ecologically sustainable food-production systems? We need to move away from centralized authority and start having an input into local political decisions that affect our daily lives. To ensure that better decision-making occurs at the local level, municipal governments need to adopt policies to emphasize public input (ICLEI 1996). Current governance does not promote local decision-making on issues of food sustainability. Local government needs to evaluate the public processes it uses and ensure that substantive public input is part of its decision-making process. The public must help to facilitate the development of policies that look beyond short-term economic gain and development; instead, we must emphasize the need for local stewardship and empowerment to aid in securing a healthy local food supply.

Similarly, institutions must develop flexible designs to accommodate more environmentally sustainable practices that include a growing role for youth. Youth are pushing the envelope in many areas of sustainability. Youth demonstrate excellent leadership, skills, dedication, innovation, commitment, and vision. The success of their projects demonstrates their potential to succeed, despite heavy opposition. Youth bear the greatest risk from the environmentally unsustainable practices that characterize our state and market structures. They recognize the peril of our mega food system and offer leadership in promoting sustainable urban food systems.

References

Carroll, W., ed. 1992. Organizing dissent. Garamond Press, Toronto, ON, Canada.

CWY (Canada World Youth). 1996. Today's leaders. CWY, Montréal, PQ, Canada.

Fainstein, S.; Hirst, C. 1995. Urban social movements. *In* Judge, D.; Stoker, G.; Wolman, H., ed., Theories of urban politics. Sage Publications, London, UK.

ICLEI (International Council for Local Environmental Initiatives). 1996. The local Agenda 21 planning guide: an introduction to sustainable development planning. ICLEI, Toronto, ON, Canada.

Knox, P.L. 1995. World cities in a world-system. *In* Knox, P.L.; Taylor, P.J., ed., World cities in a world system. Cambridge University Press, Cambridge, UK.

Logan, J; Molotch, H. 1987. Urban fortunes: the political economy of place. University of California Press, Berkeley; Los Angeles, CA, USA.

Magnusson, W. 1996. The search for political space. University of Toronto Press, Toronto, ON, Canada.

Offe, C. 1987. Challenging the boundaries of institutional politics: social movements since the 1960s. *In* Maier, C., ed., Changing the boundaries of the political: essays on the evolving balance between the state, society, public and private in Europe. Cambridge University Press, Cambridge, UK. pp. 63–105.

Pateman, C. 1970. Participation and democratic theory. Cambridge University Press, Cambridge, UK.

Sewell, W.R.D.; Philips, S.D. 1979. Model for the evaluation of public participation program. Natural Resources Journal, 19, 337–358.

UNCED (United Nations Conference on Environment and Development). 1992. Agenda 21: programme of action for sustainable development. United Nations, New York, NY, USA.

Warriner, G.K.; Madden, J.J.; Lukasik; L.; McSpurren, K. 1996. Public participation in watershed management: a comparative analysis. Canadian Water Resources Journal, 21(3), 253–274.

Weber, M. 1946. Bureaucracy. *In* Gerth, H.H.; Mills, C.W., ed., From Max Weber: essays in sociology. Oxford University Press, New York, NY, USA.

Wolman, H. 1995. Local government institutions and democratic governance. *In* Judge, D.; Stoker, G.; Wolman, H., ed., Theories of urban politics. Sage Publications, London, UK. pp. 135–159.

Food Policy for the 21st Century: Can It Be Both Radical and Reasonable?

Tim Lang

Introduction

To understand the complexities of the food system, we must understand the drivers that shape the food economy and create the territory on which food policy operates. We need to map the features of that territory closely. This paper highlights 10 features that seem particularly important today. Some are drivers, some are trends, some are contradictions, but all are key features.

Ten key features of the food-policy landscape

The food-policy crisis

The first feature of food policy to recognize is that it is in some turmoil, almost everywhere. Over the last 200 years, changes in the nature of production have heavily influenced food policy in the developed world. Over the last 20 years, there has been a rising awareness that the nature of food production has been profoundly altered from the field, in factories, on the shelves, and in kitchens. The resulting food-policy crisis is not surprising, and we can detect four areas in which policy and practice are in a particular ferment:

- *Public health* — Even in rich countries, the quality of diet has a direct impact on people's health (Cannon 1992). However, degenerative diseases, notably heart disease, associated with affluent overconsuming parts of the globe are on the rise in the South. The rate of the occurrence of food poisoning is rising as food systems become more complex. With bovine spongiform encephalopathy (BSE), the possibility of contagious diseases spread through food has reared its head once more (Lang 1998).

- *The nature of supply* — What I call the new adulteration thesis is that changes in production and distribution, even cooking, have altered the nature of food. Additives, pesticide residues, and genetically engineered foods all testify to changes resulting from the use of science and technology to make food production more "efficient" and profitable. Awareness is now growing that this adulteration of food is associated with, and may even cause, ecological problems.

- *Social justice* — Mass inequity appears in all aspects of the food system, both between and within countries, globally, nationally, and regionally.

- *Consumer demand* — Overconsumption occurs alongside underconsumption; distorted demand, alongside real need; and the rhetoric of consumer sovereignty, alongside consumer confusion and anxiety. Companies that have invested billions are bemused at consumer reactions. This interests me. In most countries of the world, not just the rich ones like Canada, the United Kingdom, or the United States, something very positive is emerging out of the demand for better labeling, information, and knowledge. A shift from consumerism to citizenship is discernible.

Conflicts in food policy

A second feature we have to recognize is that food policy cannot be understood as an issue of consensus. It is, and almost always has been, a battleground of competing interests. The well-intentioned model is promoted, for instance, by John Boyd Orr, the Scottish nutritionist who became the first director of the Food and Agriculture Organization (FAO); under this model, food policy seeks to transfer the fruits of overproduction in one area to alleviate underconsumption elsewhere. This model of justice through global food trade is, I believe, now inappropriate ecologically, socially, and culturally.

However, I detect the beginnings of a reaction, a search to relocalize food production. The trade model is, of course, triumphant economically and ideologically and is promoted through the world food system under the General Agreement on Tariffs and Trade (GATT), but conflict is building. What underlies this conflict? We need to recognize that the central driving force in the food economy is the desire to make money out of food. As humans, we may think of food as an issue of need; economically it is a commodity for greed. Those of us who observe and research this process need to build into our analyses the complexity of competing sectoral interests.

In most countries, the food system can only be understood if the different power relations between the various sectors — farmers, processors, traders, retailers, caterers, etc. — are sketched. In most countries, power in agricultural production has shifted from farmers to the agricultural-input industry, from food processors to distributors and food retailers, and from domestic to commercial cooks. Within these shifts, the general rule in post-Fordist economies is that power resides with the sector that mediates between production and consumption. It is a trader's world. The trader is sovereign, although according to the ideology the consumer is in command. However, on some issues, such as safety and ethics, the new citizenship movements referred to earlier are now challenging the power of the trader. Public-health interests are also becoming more active in food policy.

Implicit and explicit policy

The third key feature of the food-policy landscape is the difference between implicit and explicit food policies. In wartime, governments almost always have explicit policies. They say, "We want to protect everyone; we want every woman to have her child well fed." Security of supply is a national responsibility. In peacetime, suddenly it becomes a familial responsibility. A general assumption is that markets will provide. Implicit food-policy outcomes can be, for example, the growth of ill health or the creation of the new food poor. No one explicitly says they intend the poor to starve. Yet, implicitly, this is the inevitable outcome. The point to note is that explicitly the state takes responsibility under certain circumstances and not under others. The challenge to food activists is to make those explicit benefits available in peacetime. Food policy has consequences, and it is important to draw a distinction between intended policies, such as deregulation and support for industry, and unintended consequences, such as BSE or wildlife damage.

The dynamic of food control versus food democracy

The fourth feature concerns what I call food democracy. I use the expression *food democracy* to refer to the demand for greater access and collective benefit from the food system. Support for this approach continues to bubble in most parts of the globe, even in rich areas. They too are socially divided. Ultimately, food is both a symptom and a symbol of how we organize ourselves and our societies. It is both a vignette and a microcosm of wider social realities. From the political perspective, it makes sense to see the dynamics of the food system as a titanic struggle between the forces of control and the pressure to democratize. To characterize one set of forces as driven by greed, and the other by need is probably too crude, but it certainly contains an element of truth.

Studying food policy over the years, I have been impressed by how often one can map motivations for sectional interest by whether they promote individualism or collectivism, private or public interest. If the control approach to food policy is associated with pressure from above, in societal terms, food democracy is a set of demands from below. Food democracy, as a force in food policy, is significant because for two centuries, since industrialization and the modern globalization experiment unfolded, there has been counterpressure to provide the means to eat adequately, affordably, safely, humanely, and in ways one considers civil and culturally appropriate.

In every country, the struggle for food democracy appears to ebb and flow. In the United Kingdom, this can be mapped out absolutely clearly. In the mid-19th century (1820–75), the central demand was for quality and affordability, confronting adulteration of food. A struggle also raged over whether farmers should be supported to grow food. By the turn of the century, the food struggle was for food welfare. From the 1890s to the 1950s, services such as school meals and meals-on-wheels were won, which gave a big boost to the social wage. Today, after two decades of retreat and restructuring of welfare (cutbacks, removing nutrition standards from school meals, tightening up on eligibility for welfare, etc.), pressure is once more building up from below to ensure that food is fit to eat, that the poor are not disenfranchised by the rise of supermarkets and the destruction of locally accessible stores, that food is affordable, etc. The point is that we can only make sense of what happens in food policy if we see it as the result of social forces competing for influence and power. Food policy, like all public policy, has to be situated historically.

Uncertainty in the food system

The fifth feature, one that is particularly interesting at present, is the uncertainty of the food economy. Although powerful forces seek to control the food system, key uncertainties loom ahead. These uncertainties include issues such as climate change, population pressures, consumerism, the internal conflicts of market forces, and inequalities driven by globalization and the restructuring of welfare. Rising population is a subject much researched and now used by genetic engineers to rationalize their developments. Population is an issue, but what this means and how it is interpreted varies enormously. When analyzing countries such as China, we note that its rapid rise in disposable income is allowing rising aspirations (why not?) and increased meat eating. This is going to transform China's and possibly the world's agriculture. Some US farmers see the future of intensive (Western) agriculture as providing feedstuffs to fuel China's animal production. This may be good news for North American grain producers, but is it ecologically sound? Climate change is another threat to food systems. What if the sea rises? What cropping changes will happen? Another uncertainty is in business. An extraordinary wave of mergers and acquisitions has emerged globally. Sometimes I think that large companies seem more concerned to eat each other than to feed the world. The merging of large companies that dominate the marketplace threatens to saturate national as well as international markets. Competition policy, which currently exists in some countries at the national level, is powerless or nonexistent internationally.

The limits of consumer sovereignty

The sixth feature concerns consumer sovereignty. As I have already hinted, I think this is one of the great myths of food policy in the late-20th century, indeed, of neoliberal ideology. Consumers are far from sovereign. If they were, why is there hunger or food poisoning? In *The Unmanageable Consumer* (Gabriel and Lang 1995), Yiannis Gabriel and I argued that it is misleading to talk of "the consumer." Consumers come in millions of forms, broken down and divided by class, income, family, gender, taste, lifestyle, sexual orientation, aspirations, etc. Consumers are highly diverse, even though the consumer movement would like them not to be. In food tastes, rich consumers in diverse countries may be more similar than consumers within the same country. In our book, we tried to tease out various core models of what it is to consume according to Western ideology. We found that, far from being homogeneous, they are collectively confused and often contradictory. Nongovernmental organizations, for instance, tend to appeal to consumers as victims, activists, citizens, or possibly identity seekers. "Look at the latest scam being foisted on you," they say; or "Consume wisely, using our notion of value for money, and you will be better off and more contented."

The food industry approaches consumers as choosers, communicators, explorers, and hedonists. It appeals to a positive notion of ourselves, the people we would like to be. Environmentalists, health educators, etc., too often appeal to us in negative terms. "Don't do this or that." "Be fearful." The complex set of meanings of consumption is not just a feature of the modern world. It has been recognized, for instance, in the cooperative movement, from the mid-19th century on. The proponents of the cooperative movement argued that only by controlling the system of food production can consumers have confidence in both quality and price. This movement was a powerful corrective on the worst excesses of the food sector of the day, and its impact rolls on still, having inspired many consumer organizations over the years. (We forget our food-policy history at our intellectual peril. We are constantly reinventing the wheel, when in fact others have dealt with a problem very elegantly before us.)

The nature of production and distribution

The seventh feature has, again, already surfaced but has to be restated as a key feature of contemporary food policy in its own right. Food policy is increasingly concerned not just about what we eat or whether we eat but also about how food is produced. Arguments about food's impact on health, the environment, social justice, or welfare all lead us to the conclusion that the nature of production and consumption, even how we cook, has altered. We will have difficulty understanding the failure of attempts to achieve food security and food democracy or to appreciate how intensive food production has an impact on health and the environment if we don't recognize that the challenge is about the nature of production. In food policy, too often progressive social forces, such as the proponents of ecological agriculture or the new public-health movements, fail to see that their concerns have a common theme — the need to change methods of production and control throughout the food chain. Failure to see this weakens the impact that they could, if allied, have on food policy. An illustration of the impact a common cause can have is the debate over the introduction of genetically engineered products.

Rethinking the role of the state

The eighth key feature of the food-policy landscape is that (although it is unfashionable to stress this) a central role is needed for state action in food policy. A limit attaches to how much improvement ("food democracy" in my terms) can come from individual action. Although the rhetoric of late capitalism focuses on individual consumer action and responsibility, in practice the food system is so concentrated that individuals are relatively powerless. A rethinking of the state's role in food is long overdue. The Americanization of public policy tends to celebrate the virtues of the hands-off state. The European tradition is worth noting. In Europe, citizens, from the French Revolution to the present, have argued that the state has to express the collective will. In food, the state regulated production, set standards for food adulteration and contamination, and intervened in the workings of the marketplace. This state role has been whittled away in recent decades to such a point that the notion of "reinventing" the state is a misnomer for its privatization and evisceration.

Looking ahead at food-policy challenges, I see no alternative to a thoughtful role for a state that can mediate between individual and collective wills. Only a benign state, democratically accountable, can tame the worst excesses of increasingly powerful corporations in the food sector. In fact, by accepting the argument that we should not turn to the state for the general good, but seek it in markets, we actually allow corporate interests to penetrate and dominate what the state does. We see this most blatantly in the regulatory process in which corporate interests have infused the supposedly neutral state discourse in setting standards. This is now happening at the global level through bodies such as Codex Alimentarius Commission, which the representatives of big companies excessively influence. In short, as researchers and involved people, we need to get more sophisticated about the state.

The United Kingdom's experience of evolving notions of the role of the state in food might be illuminating. In UK food policy, three phases of state involvement have occurred or will occur in the post-war period:

- The first was interventionism: Boyd Orr was an interventionist in food policy. He saw a benign global state in the FAO; its role was to get surpluses to places where people suffer deficiency. He left the FAO before long, we should note, discontented about its direction. In the post-war period, a benign Keynesian corporatism introduced regulations and intervened in markets.

- The second phase was the neoliberal counterrevolution, which we have experienced these last two decades. Anti-interventionism, associated with Thatcherism and Reaganism, promoted self-regulation and deregulation. This phase still unfolds. GATT almost makes this mandatory.

- But waiting in the wings is a third phase of state involvement. This heralds a proactive partnership, with the state playing the roles of facilitator, educator, and promoter of efficiencies. It is unclear where this model will go. It could fuse into neoliberalism, or it could signal a new collectivism.

Centralization

The ninth feature is centralization, with the policy tensions that follow from it. I have been heavily involved in the UK debate about our government institutions, for reasons suggested just above. Specifically, my colleagues and I have argued for a reform of food governance. Our ministries and committees are out of date, in need of overhaul. Happily, after the 1997 election, we are promised one aspect of what we want, a reform of the Ministry of Agriculture, Fisheries and Food, long associated with unnecessarily rigid support for production interests. Involved in this unfolding saga, we conducted a study of seven countries' systems of food governance, in particular their food-control systems. This revealed that the mechanism for food governance, in all of these countries, was in flux. Everywhere food governance was creaking. Agencies were being overhauled, and new ones were being set up. Existing institutions have been losing their public trust. Why? Partly, this is because they have lost sight of the public interest and confused it with corporate efficiency. Partly, government institutions no longer have sufficient control to address the issues raised by globalized corporations or the new, more complex chains of production and distribution. The capacity of government to govern is itself in some doubt. For example, Norway has probably the most progressive food policy anywhere in the developed world. In 1975, it made a proactive policy commitment to keep small-scale farmers on the land and it banned Azo dyes and all food colours — in other words, no adulteration. The argument was partly health, partly environment, and partly small-business-support driven. Norway argued against joining the European Union because of the Common Agricultural Policy. Yet, in 1994, it signed the new GATT. Its government has been under pressure to protect and promote Norwegian agriculture and food; the reality has been that Norway's food policy is hitched to a globalized system. Its food-colouring rules, for example, and its additives policy have been brought into line with the more permissive regime of Codex Alimentarius.

Everywhere, the food economy is centralizing. The top five companies in the world control 77% of the world market in cereals (Cargill more than 60%); in tea the top three control 85% of the world market; the top three in cocoa have 84%; in agrochemicals, the top 10 have 90% of the market. Everywhere, small-scale farmers are being driven off the land, and retailing is dominated by fewer and larger companies. Concentration is occurring not just within countries but across borders, either through takeovers or through strategic alliances.

The environmental challenge

The tenth key feature of the food-policy landscape is the potential threat and, in some areas, the already real threat to sustainability — how to make the food system ecologically feasible. This is the great environmental challenge, in which I see the need for public and environmental analyses to coalesce. The model of production, developed over the last 30–40 years, has had a deeper and deeper ecological footprint; its impact increases by the day. The world now emerging is divided into a variety of consuming classes, and this raises important environmental-health issues and has important public-health implications. In the United Kingdom, my colleagues and I have been conducting research on the impact of shopping. People now travel 50% farther to get their food than they did 15 years ago. Few do their food shopping on foot. They get into a car to go to the supermarket. This has enormous implications. The amount of time people spend shopping has, in fact, gone up, rather than down, over the last 30 years. Shoppers' time comes free, enabling the distribution sector to take greater control over the post-Fordist food economy. Or, to put this notion differently, the cost of consumers' time and their use of cars is not reflected in the price of the food they purchase. The health implication of this change from local to more distant shopping is that people are becoming more obese while making greater use of nonrenewable fossil fuel. Consumers use nonrenewable fossil fuel, instead of using food. The restructuring of the food economy is thus playing its part in the alarming rise of obesity in most developed — that is, car-based — economies. We are not burning off the foods, yet we are obsessed about being thin. A mass psychological schizophrenia is entrenched within and by food culture.

The supposedly efficient globalizing food system is posing an immense ecological challenge. The rich consumers of the world are increasingly using the world as their larder. Green beans are being flown to UK dinner tables in the middle of winter from Zambia, and this sets Zambia against Tanzania and Tanzania against Kenya to decide which is to have the privilege of feeding us. This is creating a neocolonial relationship. This also leads to the ecological absurdity I have called the "food–miles (or food–kilometres) problem." By food–miles, I refer to the physical distance that foods travel between grower and consumer. It is easier in UK supermarkets to get Spanish asparagus that has come 1 000 km than it is to get asparagus from the Midlands or Worcestershire, in the heart of the United Kingdom. Long-distance food is cheaper, but the energy and environmental costs are externalized: that is, they are not reflected in the retail price. Cheap energy (oil) underpins "cheap" food. The investment plans of the European Union will accelerate this process. Jacques Delors' legacy includes the pan-European Union motorway system, now being put in place (as well as high-speed trains). This is a mixed blessing. For present purposes, I merely suggest how the state investment in transport infrastructure heightens the food–miles problem.

At the same time, European Union governments have signed the European Convention on Biodiversity, to protect biodiversity. This is excellent, but the problem is that the words of biodiversity are not being put into practice in the field, because it is easier and more economical to buy distant food from monocropped lands — where labour, land, and water are cheap — than to support diverse local production. Rich, consuming regions are sucking in foods from other regions. This is grossly unequal. Massive imports come into the European Union, for instance, just to feed animals. This is surely madness.

The ecological footprint of the supposedly efficient West is deeper and wider than it ought to be, because of the power of the trader. The downside of this efficiency is immense. Gradually, a difference between the consumerism of food and the citizenship of food is emerging. We are being encouraged to think of ourselves as consumers (power at the point of sale or purchase), rather than as citizens who have some leverage in the food economy. In this process, I see new opportunities for food's democratic struggle. The issue of skills, for instance, is becoming very important. Is the future one in which people feed themselves or are fed? In the United Kingdom, for instance, a culture of noncooking is emerging. Even if people have cooking skills, are they using them? Food processors are delighted to see a growth in the number of homes in which people have never really cooked, with the result that children's role models don't teach their children to cook. If you think of the evolution of cooking skills over 10 000 years, an immense culinary shift is taking place in mere decades. Schools and the state are colluding in this process, encouraging computer skills but not life skills. This should not be an either–or public policy. The United Kingdom's national curriculum, for instance, removed cooking skills from the classroom. We no longer teach cooking skills to our children. They are taught a theoretical exercise of designing a snack bar, with the emphasis on packaging; thus a practical issue becomes a matter of theoretical culture.

Summary of features of the food-policy landscape

To sum up these 10 features, I see the landscape of food as dominated by contradictory pulls. Two overreaching tendencies are discernible — two policy packages:

- On the one hand, globalization; on the other, pressures for localization;

- On the one hand, long trade routes; on the other, pressures for local, sustainable food systems;

- On the one hand, intensification; on the other, calls for extensification and biodiversity; and

- On the one hand, deskilling; on the other, new skills (managing a microwave!).

But for me, the heart of the policy choice is the issue of consumerism versus citizenship. Unchecked consumerism heralds a diminution of food culture, an erosion of many of the gains in the struggle for social improvement over the last two centuries. Consumerism implies a relationship in the market; citizenship implies a permanent struggle to control markets. One is food control from above and beyond; the other is the constant search for food democracy from below. I identify with the latter, even though my observation and studies lead me to conclude that, at present, we are drifting to the former. My heart and brain are in conflict! Where a few hundred corporations and two regional trading blocks — North America and Europe — dominate food policy, what other intellectual conclusion can be drawn? I'm hopeful, however, that change is coming.

The need for new goals

If we are to achieve food citizenship, I believe we must find new goals. We need to open up the process of setting food policies, globally, regionally, nationally, and locally. If we don't, we will be allowing other corporate identities to dominate and determine the shape of food policy.

In particular, I think we can share the following 10 goals:

- Security of supply for an increasingly urban population;

- Expansion of environmentally sound production methods;

- Access for all to a good-quality, health-enhancing diet;

- Stable employment in the food sectors;

- A reduction of the dietary gap between rich and poor (by giving policy priority to low-income consumers);

- A reduction of national import–export imbalances (what we call, in the United Kingdom, the food "trade gap") (we should support local food and reduce long-distance trade);

- Support for biodiversity (by encouraging variety in production in the field and transferring this biodiversity from field to the plate);

- The creation of explicit comprehensive food policies, globally, nationally, and locally;

- An emphasis on rebuilding the local food economy, celebrating and enhancing diversity of taste, cuisine, and culture; and

- The creation of strategic alliances and much more international sharing of experiences, not just among academics or within the voluntary sector, but between and across the sectors.

Conclusions

The task ahead is awesome — intellectually, politically, and culturally — but these are exciting times. Unparalleled interest is shown in food issues in both the North and the South. Also, exciting new issues face us from biotechnology to competition policy. For food policy, as ever, the challenge is to move it from a position in which it reacts to events and is driven by the powerful to one in which democratic debate clarifies long-term goals. Our horizons need to be 30–50 years hence. Corporate giants plan this way; we should too.

References

Cannon, G. 1992. Food and health: the experts agree. Consumers' Association Ltd, London, UK.

Gabriel, Y.; Lang, T. 1995. The unmanageable consumer: contemporary consumption and its fragmentations. Sage Publications, London, UK. 214 pp.

Lang, T. 1998. BSE and CJD: recent developments. In Ratzan, S.C., ed., The mad cow crisis: health and the public good. UCL Press, London, UK.

Abstracts

PART 1. THE CONCEPT OF URBAN FOOD SECURITY

For Self-reliant Cities: Urban Food Production in a Globalizing South

— Luc J.A. Mougeot

In this chapter, the problem of food security is examined in the context of globalization and the opposing forces of interdependence and self-reliance. While disparities between haves and have-nots continue, people have learned to cope using ingenious ways to feed themselves, urban farming being one. The food they produce is consumed by their families or sold to provide income for other basic needs. The author outlines the characteristics of urban food systems in the South and the factors that determine the ability of formal food markets to provide for city dwellers. As poverty rises in urban centres and some people spend as much as 50–80% of their income on food, access to food has become an important issue. Most developing countries are net importers of food, and it is predicted that the fastest urban growth will occur in the countries least equipped to feed the people in their cities.

As a response to food insecurity, urban food production is not new, and today millions of people are producing and distributing food via intricate social systems. The paper discusses the major issues surrounding urban agriculture and the need to study its management — particularly land use, environmental impact, and municipal policy — as not all city officials accept or endorse urban agriculture. Joint initiatives among international and bilateral development agencies have emerged during the 1990s, resulting in the formation of a Support Group for Urban Agriculture that sets priorities for research, training, and information. Options for the future must include strategies for self-reliance and an acknowledgment of the contribution urban agriculture can make to intensive and efficient local production, waste reuse, and the involvement of women.

Urban Food Security in Sub-Saharan Africa

— Daniel Maxwell

Cities in Africa face numerous problems, including alarming increases in the levels of urban poverty. The urban poor devote large proportions of their total incomes to procurement of food, meaning that, to a large extent, the poverty problem manifests itself as a food-security problem. However, the problems faced in the area of urban food security, particularly giving the urban poor access to sufficient food, are scarcely recognized in policy arenas or contemporary political debates. This paper traces the reasons for the "disappearance" of urban food security from the political agenda, noting that urban food security classically meant ensuring the food supply for a city. More recently, the problem has become one of access to sufficient food, as a result of rapidly growing urban poverty, and the urban poor have relatively little political voice. The paper goes on to suggest a series of questions to guide policy research and action to alleviate urban food insecurity in sub-Saharan Africa.

Combining Social Justice and Sustainability for Food Security

— Elaine M. Power

There are two broad, fairly distinct approaches to the promotion of domestic food security in contemporary Canada: one seeks to establish a sustainable food system and the other aims to eliminate poverty. These approaches correspond to the two main dimensions of food security, both of which are currently under threat in Canada. In this paper, I briefly describe these two approaches and the attempt to bring them together in the community-development approach. Community-development food projects emphasize making the food system local to minimize environmental impacts and fostering the development of community to make links among people who are isolated from each other. It is neither a simple nor self-evident task to use community-development food projects to address the needs of those who are poor. Some of the issues neglected to date include the hidden aspects of the rhetoric of community, reinforcement of individualistic ideology, limitations of coverage, and increased burdens on women. I call for clarity in framing food-security problems because this determines what solutions are proposed; I also call for reflexivity on the part of academics and activists because our positions in the social and economic structure affect how we understand the problems.

PART 2. LOCAL FOOD SYSTEMS

Promoting Sustainable Local Food Systems in the United States
— *Kenneth A. Dahlberg*

This paper draws on the experience of the Local Food Systems Project, a 3-year effort by a team of four people to assist six communities in the United States in strengthening their local food-policy capabilities. The six sites were Los Angeles, CA; Berkshire County, MA; a nine-county planning region around Rochester, NY; Pittsburgh, PA.; Austin, TX; and Moyers, WV. Underlying the effort was a broad food-systems approach that stresses not only production aspects but also processing, distribution, access, use, recycling, and waste issues. The paper outlines the next steps needed to promote more sustainable local food systems. In the short term, "practical theories" are needed to assist local communities in their organizing and planning efforts. This involves examining the interactions of key contextual variables, such as scale and patterns in landscape, population, socio-economic characteristics, and food organization. In the longer term, both capacity- and infrastructure-building are needed to strengthen the emerging community of local, regional, and national groups working to build more sustainable and localized food systems. Here, one needs to facilitate leadership training and development while establishing national and regional structures to provide better networking, technical assistance, strategic evaluation, and longer term research on practical theory.

Community Agriculture Initiatives in the Metropolitan Borough of Sandwell, United Kingdom
— *Laura Davis, John Middleton, and Sue Simpson*

This paper explores the issues raised in a 1996 study of the practical, legislative, and economic feasibility of community agriculture in Sandwell. The Metropolitan Borough of Sandwell, in the West Midlands of England, has a history that dates back to the beginnings of the Industrial Revolution. Sandwell's people have experienced at first hand the economic, social, and health effects of the processes of industrialization and its decline. Local regeneration policy will affect health, and health services can improve regeneration. A coordinated approach to developing a community agriculture program in Sandwell may make an important contribution to the realization that environmental regeneration and the regeneration of the health of Sandwell's people are inextricably linked.

The paper focuses in particular on general issues of health and sustainability and health and economic inequality, how these may be tackled at a local level, why Sandwell is the kind of place where one should try to tackle them, and the potential role of community agriculture and direct food link schemes if they are integrated with existing initiatives in community development. Finally, problems and ways forward are considered.

Developing an Integrated, Sustainable Urban Food System: The Case of New Jersey, United States
— *Michael W. Hamm and Monique Baron*

The establishment of more localized food systems that achieve social-justice goals is an important strategy for developing sustainable urban food systems. The discussion in this paper begins with several concepts: (1) an exclusively local food supply would be isolating, necessitate cultural denial, and be potentially unstable; (2) sustainable food systems will develop within the current social, political, and economic framework; (3) development of sustainable communities with sustainable food systems begins with the idea that people have value and that the production of life's necessities has value; and (4) people have an inherent interest in connecting with the food they consume. We use New Jersey, United States, as a case study to explore avenues for impacting various components of the food system in ways that (1) incorporate social-justice issues into a more localized system; (2) alleviate constraints on access to adequate, nutritious food; (3) develop the economic capacity of residents to purchase food; (4) develop people to grow, process, and distribute this food; (5) maintain adequate land to produce a high percentage of the locale's food needs; (6) educate a population increasingly removed from food production to participate in, and respect, its generation; and (7) integrate environmental stewardship into this process.

Public Policy and the Transition to Locally Based Food Networks

— *Ellie Perkins*

Food networks play an important role in local economies because of their many forward and backward linkages, their employment requirements, and the ties among food, culture, health, and well-being. From an ecological standpoint, producing food close to where it is consumed saves fossil fuels, strengthens local environmental awareness, creates green jobs, and provides strong incentives for forms of agriculture that are less polluting, energy-intensive, and damaging, that use available infrastructure efficiently (thus reducing throughput), and that have many other positive multiplier effects.

This paper explains the social, economic, and ecological importance of locally based food production and distribution systems, giving examples of policies and institutions that communities and governments can use to help develop them. It provides examples of such measures in action from Toronto and other places. The paper also discusses the relationship between public policy and grass-roots community initiatives as part of the local institutional structures surrounding food. Finally, the paper sets out several criteria for assessing the ecological implications of public-policy measures and discusses the political and cultural conditions that favour development of locally based economies and food systems.

PART 3. URBAN AND COMMUNITY AGRICULTURE

Urban Agriculture in the Seasonal Tropics: The Case of Lusaka, Zambia

— *A.W. Drescher*

This paper focuses on different components of urban agriculture in Lusaka, Zambia. Both of the major agricultural activities — the dry-season gardening and rainy-season production of staple food crops — largely depend on access to resources like water and land. It was found that dry-season cultivation is not practiced by the most vulnerable households but by those with access to the resources essential to this activity. This access is lowest in the high-density, low-income compounds in Lusaka. There are significant differences between the roles of women and men in urban household food security. Women are the major actors in urban agriculture, but they are disadvantaged with respect to income generation and access to resources and markets. Women's agricultural activities differ from those of men. Therefore, special attention is given to the cultivation of indigenous vegetables ("locals") and ongoing vegetable-gathering activities, which each play an important role in nutrition and are mainly undertaken by women.

A household-gardening model that is also applicable to other household activities was developed to come to a better understanding of household activities in their social, economical, and environmental contexts. Urban agriculture obviously contributes to household food security directly by providing food and indirectly by creating income through avoiding some expenditures in the urban environment.

The Contribution of Urban Agriculture to Gardeners, Their Households, and Surrounding Communities: The Case of Havana, Cuba

— *Angela Moskow*

Urban agriculture is promoted in Havana, Cuba, as a means of addressing the acute food-scarcity problems that developed when Soviet aid and trade were drastically curtailed in 1989. A number of urban agricultural activities are under way, including the more than 26 000 gardens in Havana grown to provide for the gardeners' own needs. Research was conducted in 1995 to determine the ways these gardens contributed to the gardeners' sense of control over their lives and the role of the gardens in enhancing the surrounding communities. Results indicate that the gardens significantly incremented the quantity and quality of the food available to the gardeners' households and neighbourhoods; improved the financial welfare of the gardeners' households through reduction in weekly food bills and through money earned from sales of garden products; and made aesthetic, environmental, and other contributions to the community.

Agriculture in the Metropolitan Park of Havana, Cuba
— *Harahi Gamez Rodriguez*

The Metropolitan Park of Havana (PMH) is an urban, social, and ecological project being developed around the final 7 km of the Almendares River, the most important river of the Cuban capital. It overlaps four of the capital's municipalities — Playa, Plaza, Marianao, and Cerro — an area of great cultural, racial, and social diversity. As an urban project, the PMH will retain a dense urban network of industries, military entities, and population centres that today occupy the territory. As an ecological park, the PMH will provide a solution to the problems of deforestation in the zone, the uncontrolled social and industrial waste, and the general lack of care for the region that threatens the area's flora and fauna and the Almendares River itself. As a social project, the PMH will provide a space for a population of nearly 9 000 inhabitants, who will be an integral part of the development planning of the park. The PMH is committed to integrating development, environmental recovery, education, and participation — concepts that are frequently addressed independently in large urban-development projects. This paper outlines the fundamental mission, objectives, goals, and strategic planning of the PMH, which is still in the planning phase.

People at the Centre of Urban Livestock Projects
— *Alison Meares*

Promoting urban agriculture is an important means of ensuring sustainability of regional community food security and human settlements. However, too often the focus is exclusively on technology and agricultural-production methods. For urban agriculture to be sustainable, projects must incorporate both the agricultural setting (the landscape) and the people who live in, and benefit from, that setting (the lifescape). In its urban animal-agriculture initiative in Chicago, Heifer Project International promotes a method of participatory development that enables low-income neighbourhood groups to reach beyond the goals of beautification and environmental improvement and become a vehicle for social and economic development in their communities. The elements of that model include the interdependence of the landscape and lifescape, full participation of intended beneficiaries, values-based planning, and "passing on the gift." When approached as a vehicle for community development, urban agriculture can bring multiple benefits: economic benefits, by providing opportunities to earn income; educational benefits, by teaching technical and job skills; environmental benefits, such as land reclamation; and, finally, empowerment, by enabling communities to take control of family food security. It is at the crossroads of these goals that urban agriculture projects can thrive and influence the character of human settlements.

Measuring the Sustainability of Urban Agriculture
— *Rachel A. Nugent*

Urban agriculture provides economic, social, and environmental benefits to local communities. These include food production, paid labour, community and psychological well-being, and improved functioning of ecological systems. It also imposes risks and consumes resources. When improperly managed, urban food production can pose risks to human health. Scarce land and water resources are diverted from other uses. The paper defines economically relevant benefits and costs of urban agriculture to evaluate conditions needed for sustainable urban agriculture. Urban agriculture is sustainable if the benefits exceed the costs over a relevant period and the impacts are equally distributed. This study presents a cost–benefit framework for measuring whether the benefits of urban agriculture outweigh the costs in a particular locale. Urban agriculture is defined, and comparison of a sustainable local food system and the traditional import–export local food-system model is discussed. Sustainable urban food systems can form a closed loop if they reduce the need for cities to import resources to satisfy their production and consumption needs and reduce the amount of waste leaving the city for disposal elsewhere. A theoretical model for measuring the sustainability of urban agriculture in a community is presented.

PART 4. ACCESSIBILITY AND URBAN FOOD DISTRIBUTION

Food Banks as Antihunger Organizations
— *Winston Husbands*

The Daily Bread Food Bank (DBFB) was established in Toronto in the early 1980s in an environment of high unemployment. It was established to provide emergency food assistance to people in need. The organization's founders claimed that DBFB would work to put itself out of business. Since that time, however, the demand for emergency food assistance has grown enormously, as a result mainly of lingering unemployment and cuts to social assistance. In other words, the food-security situation of low-income households in Toronto has worsened. In hindsight, DBFB's original focus on more or less traditional food banking undermined its intention to work to put itself out of business. Traditional food banking, though important, is of limited value in securing reasonable alternatives to the current situation. Consequently, over the past 2 years, DBFB has been transforming itself to operate more explicitly as an antihunger organization, without abandoning or compromising its commitment to providing emergency food assistance. Food banks need to organize their resources to focus considerably more on research, public education, public-policy advocacy, and community mobilization. Food banks, but not traditional food banking, have a role to play in the struggle for food security.

Bottlenecks in the Informal Food-transportation Network of Harare, Zimbabwe
— *Shona L. Leybourne and Miriam Grant*

People in the informal sector are often food insecure because their jobs are not legally protected by the state. In the context of the bottlenecks that pervade the internal informal food-distribution flows of Harare, urban dwellers who work in the informal food-distribution network or live in the poorer areas of the city, or both, are facing food insecurity. The ways policy writers' attitudes are framed differently from those of the people for whom they script policies are underscored by an examination of (1) consumers' impecunious realities and (2) impediments to their entrepreneurial networks. Gender, class, and race are axes of perceptual difference between policy writers, policy enforcers (who favour formal, tax-generating activities), and the recipients of these policies, and these axes affect how individual transporters, food retailers, and consumers choose to manoeuvre in the grid of authority's domination. It is suggested that the state should recognize the contribution that the informal food-distribution network is making to the food security of the city. A strategically oriented dialogue that seeks to ensure the security of these people's basic food requirements would protect the local structures that have been created by the people for the people. Such discussion might include the formalization, hence protection, of the actors within the informal food-distribution system, including the intraurban transportation of food, thus cushioning a large proportion of the urban poor from immediate food insecurity.

From Staple Store to Supermarket: The Case of TANSAS in Izmir, Turkey
— *Mustafa Koc and Hulya Koc*

This paper examines a successful staple-store project operated by the municipal government of Izmir, Turkey. Whereas its immediate success offered relatively affordable food to urban poor and middle-class consumers and helped to curb inflationary tendencies to a certain extent, the project later extended beyond its original goals and turned into one of the two biggest supermarket chains in Turkey. The paper suggests that staple stores can be effective tools for food access if they can be kept as small operations, and the paper offers some insights on the impacts of supermarketing on food access, pricing, and consumption. Yet, the paper also points out that there are no easy solutions that improve access to food. Often, the cure becomes a problem. Although TANSAS protected consumers from high inflation and speculation in the 1970s, it inadvertently played a role in introducing and spreading supermarket chains in Turkey, altering food-consumption and food-distribution patterns irreversibly. The paper also warns of the impacts of global economic pressures and neoliberal restructuring schemes on the future of public enterprise and public policy at the local level. Steps need to be taken to ensure that public agencies will be at least within arm's length of governments.

A Nonprofit System for Fresh-produce Distribution: The Case of Toronto, Canada
— *Kathryn Scharf*

The Good Food Box (GFB) project of FoodShare Toronto is a nonprofit fresh-food-distribution system that operates like a large buying cooperative: 4 000 boxes of fresh fruit and vegetables are delivered through 200 volunteer-run neighbourhood dropoffs each month. This paper provides a case study of the development, operation, and principles of the program. The GFB is a successful community-based and market-driven food-distribution alternative. The ways that the program resembles traditional community-development or nonprofit-sector projects are explored, as well as the ways it departs from this model by incorporating "business principles" needed to ensure its success in the marketplace. Stimulating community self-organization, improving food access for low-income people, promoting healthy food choices, and avoiding the stigmatization involved in charity-based models of food distribution are all important goals of the GFB. As a fee-based service, the GFB must also compete effectively with other food-purchasing options, meaning that it must maintain a high level of customer service, a high level of sales, a fairly low level of mandatory time investment from participants, and attractive advertising — characteristics that are not often seen in nonprofit community-development projects.

PART 5. ECOLOGICAL AND HEALTH CONCERNS

Urban Food, Health, and the Environment: The Case of Upper Silesia, Poland
— *Anne C. Bellows*

In 1997, Poland celebrated 100 years of urban allotment agriculture, which has buffered local publics from alternating problems with food supply and food costs. Typically conducted by women, retirees, and other reserve labour, this local food production has provided a measure of autonomy or shelter from the vagaries of inefficient production and food distribution (typical of centralized socialist states) and from inaccessibly high food prices, compounded by unemployment (typical of market systems). However, the yields and safety of local food labour are sometimes sabotaged in regions burdened with severe pollution, most characteristically in household food production from contaminated landscapes in and near urban and industrialized areas. Urban food sustainability ultimately must reflect a local determination of food needs, which, among other things, reflects experience with local complications of environmental health. In such cases, the goal of local food security may incorporate nonlocal strategies. The case study from Gliwice in the Upper Silesia region of southwest Poland discusses (1) organizing an acquisition, labeling, and distribution system for retailing chemically tested organic products, linking farmers to consumers; (2) distributing chemically tested produce directly to schools and hospitals and creating subsidies for their purchase; and (3) educating community groups about food contamination and the benefits of organic foods and farming.

Reuse of Waste for Food Production in Asian Cities: Health and Economic Perspectives
— *Christine Furedy, Virginia Maclaren, and Joseph Whitney*

Asian communities have many practices involving the reuse of organic wastes in agriculture and aquaculture, even in urban areas. These practices contribute to sustainable development by using resources that are otherwise a burden on the waste-management system. Improvements in organic waste reuse in the context of modern urbanization require attention to health and economic considerations. This paper discusses these aspects of the reuse of organics from municipal wastes in South and Southeast Asia. Recent research in this region is used to suggest the potential for wise exploitation of links between waste reuse and urban agri–aquaculture, including work in Bangkok, Bandung, Bangalore, Hanoi, Ho Chi Minh City, Jakarta, and Manila. Important constraints on the reuse of organic wastes are contamination (which has both health and economic impacts) and the greater cost of making compost than of buying chemical fertilizers. The paper suggests strategies for minimizing these constraints and improving the marketability of organic wastes. Contamination can be reduced by collecting waste separately from certain generation points and by separating organics at source. Market research is needed to promote the use of compost. Health risks can be reduced through education and the amendment of agricultural practices.

How Meat-centred Eating Patterns Affect Food Security and the Environment
— *Stephen Leckie*

As the Earth's population continues to increase, our ability to adequately feed everyone will face growing challenges. Scaling back on resource-intensive meat production may be the best way to ensure food security for all into the next century. Essentially, the world is experiencing an over-population of farm animals. The combined weight of the world's 15 billion farm animals now surpasses that of the human population by more than one and a half times. Since 1950 global meat production has jumped from 18 kg/person to more than 35 kg/person. Grain yields have also increased, but much of the gain has gone to fattening farm animals that are very inefficient at converting grain to meat. Per capita land use in countries with plant-based agricultural economies stands at only a fraction of the levels seen in countries with high meat-production rates. With exports taken into account, North America still uses seven times more land on a per capita basis than many countries in Asia. Having fewer animals to feed might lead to a rebuilding of world grain reserves, ensuring dependable supplies for direct human consumption. Furthermore, a reduction in land use by cutting meat production would be an effective way to ensure that wilderness areas are maintained and even expanded.

Farming the Built Environment
— *Elizabeth Graham*

New interest is now being generated in cities as sites for food production. In this context, people are focusing on what the soils in and around urban centres can produce. Over the longer term, however, the sustainability of cities will not be improved by urban agriculture alone. The fertility of urban soils and their relationship to the built environment must be viewed as a dynamic regime in which building breakdown, drainage patterns, burials, industrial debris, garbage dumping, and human and animal waste disposal are acknowledged and analyzed for their positive as well as negative effects on soil-formation processes and long-term cultivability. In this article I introduce the idea that urban decay and the destructive processes of cities can be harnessed productively. I also make the argument that archaeology can play a role in planning for sustainable cities, because the results of research on the physical and chemical transformation of urban environments through time, such as my own research in the Mayan area, can provide guidelines for highly effective recycling, not only of organic waste, but also of the built environment itself.

PART 6. ENGENDERING THE FOOD SYSTEM

Gender and Sustainable Food Systems: A Feminist Critique
— *Penny Van Esterik*

This paper explores conceptual and practical linkages between women and food and suggests how feminist analysis may further our understanding of food security. Women's special relationship with food is culturally constructed and not a product of a natural division of labour. Women's identity and sense of self are often based on their ability to feed their families and others; food insecurity denies them this right. Food socialization and body image are also strongly gendered. The paper concludes with a working definition of feminist principles and a call for a paradigm shift, the development of a model of feminist food praxis. Food praxis refers to the practical "mastery" of routines of producing, preparing, and consuming food. Considering how the food system is gendered, the paper proposes 10 points to guide further research and action. These include acknowledging women as gatekeepers of the food system, placing priority on the elimination of hunger, using multiple research methods, recognizing how political forces control people's access to food, emphasizing the temporal complexity of food routines, and providing a critically reflexive guide to advocacy action.

Women Workers in the NAFTA Food Chain

— *Deborah Barndt*

Efforts to develop sustainable urban food systems must take into account the role of women workers in the various stages of production, preparation, and consumption of the food we eat. The Tomasita project explores women's shifting roles in the restructured global labour force, tracing the journey of a tomato from a Mexican field to a Canadian table. This essay focuses particularly on salaried workers in Mexican agribusiness, which has exploited institutionalized sexism and racism, perpetuating a "feminization of poverty" that is also racialized. Yet, on closer examination, the story is more complex. Young women packers moved by companies from plant to plant may simultaneously be freed from restrictive family contexts in a macho culture while being bound to monotonous work routines, long working hours, and unhealthy working and living conditions. The Tomasita project also aims to connect women food workers in Mexico and Canada, in both dominant and alternative food systems, through photo-stories, films, and video letters. Sharing these stories across borders helps women understand how they are part of a broader global process while they learn from each others' tales of local survival and resistance.

Canadian Rural Women Reconstructing Agriculture

— *Karen L. Krug*

A fundamental premise of this paper is that if a sustainable urban food system is to develop, broader issues of sustainability in agriculture will have to be addressed. The paper considers Canadian farm women's perceptions of the barriers to sustainable agriculture in relation to the general categories of the economic system, declining rural communities, environmental degradation, health issues, and stress. It then examines Canadian farm women's visions of how agriculture ought to be and their general perspectives on how the desirable alternatives might be achieved. The focus then shifts from the alternative visions for agriculture embraced by farm and rural women to a discussion of how and why urban and rural people must cooperate to achieve a sustainable food system built on a foundation of sustainable agriculture. The paper concludes with a summary of the suggestions made by Canadian farm women for agricultural reforms to strengthen both rural and urban sustainable agricultural systems. These solutions include emphasizing local food production and distribution over export and import systems, ensuring security of land tenure, reducing or eliminating land speculation, building national constituencies to foster urban–rural connections, and increasing rural populations through smaller scale local production and strong government support.

PART 7. THE POLITICS OF FOOD AND FOOD POLICY

Contemporary Food and Farm Policy in the United States

— *Patricia Allen*

Two movements affecting the food security of Americans have emerged in recent years. One is the community food-security movement, dedicated to ensuring that everyone has the ability to obtain a nutritionally adequate diet. The other is the movement to dismantle social-welfare programs — to "end welfare as we know it." While interest in domestic food security is increasing in some areas the food-security safety net is unraveling in others. Cuts in food programs for the needy have been justified in terms of balancing the budget and getting people to take responsibility for themselves. Yet, these notions are distinctly at odds with expectations for commercial agriculture, which has a long tradition of significant financial support from the US government. This brief paper explores the character of this disjuncture between governmental farm and food programs in the United States. It examines the demographic characteristics of those who benefit from food programs (usually low-income people) and of those who benefit from farm programs (rarely low-income people). The privileging of agricultural producers over poor consumers is framed in its political and ideological context. Ensuring food security for the poor will require innovative food policies capable of operating effectively in this political and ideological environment.

Policy Failure in the Canadian Food System
— *Rod MacRae*

Canada has flirted with the idea of creating a national food policy, but for a number of reasons described in this paper, it has failed to do so. Instead of a national food policy, we have an agricultural policy with significant contradictions and a very weak nutrition policy. A coherent food policy should have the optimal nourishment of the population as its highest purpose, make agricultural production and distribution servants of that purpose, and ensure the long-term financial and environmental sustainability of the food system. The absence of a comprehensive food policy has resulted in health and environmental-sustainability problems that the current policy apparatus is inadequately equipped to address. A national food policy should be designed with an emphasis on integrated responsibilities and activities, transdisciplinary development and implementation, food-systems thinking, and a focus on macropolicy. New policies and policy-making structures are proposed, based on the emerging theory of ecological organizational design. An outline for a new Department of Food and Food Security, with health and sustainability as its central thrust, is presented.

Urban Agriculture as Food-access Policy
— *Desmond Jolly*

Hunger, malnutrition, and suboptimal access to food have resulted from a number of political, economic, and demographic forces. Among these are urbanization, unemployment and underemployment, food-marketing systems, and welfare policies. Urban agriculture can enhance access to food and thus enhance the welfare of low-income urban residents. However, the net outcome may be negative if urban agriculture is seen as a substitute for, rather than an addition to, food and agricultural policies designed to improve rural conditions and provide affordable access to food for the full spectrum of residents in urban systems. Hence, the benefits of urban agriculture may depend integrally on an overall context of food and agricultural policies designed to meet the food needs of the entire population.

PART 8. TOWARD FOOD DEMOCRACY

Reaffirming the Right to Food in Canada: The Role of Community-based Food Security
— *Graham Riches*

Hunger and food insecurity are critical issues in Canadian society. This paper explores two questions: How is it possible to move from the declarations and rhetoric of world summits, international conventions, and federal and provincial governments and their assertions of a right to food when evidence suggests that governments and to some extent civil society have in recent years sought to depoliticize the issue of domestic hunger and make it no longer a responsibility of the state? How is it possible to ensure that the complex and interrelated issues of hunger and food security become the subject of informed democratic debate and thereby publicly understood as being critical not only to the poor and vulnerable but also to long-term ecological and social well-being? The paper examines these questions by asking whether the right to food in Canada exists, addressing the causes of First World hunger, and analyzing the responses of federal and provincial governments, businesses, and charities (food banks) to food poverty in terms of the depoliticization of hunger. It argues that collaborative and adversarial actions at the community level are essential if the right to food is to be established and food security for all is to be achieved.

Youth, Urban Governance, and Sustainable Food Systems: The Cases of Hamilton and Victoria, Canada
— *Zita Botelho*

This paper examines the challenges that youth groups encounter in their attempts to participate in urban decision-making related to developing sustainable food systems. The background for this discussion includes a brief examination of several very important concepts. The first is that of urban governance. Governance often frustrates marginalized political actors, and thus the relationship between youth and social movements is significant to this discussion.

I consider the pervasive characteristics of social organization that influence urban governance. Two relevant problems with urban institutions are that they generally do not promote ecological sustainability and that they do not support youth involvement in decision-making. The barriers faced by youth groups promoting sustainable food practices in the urban environment are discussed, using two case studies. Interviews were conducted with members of the Ontario-based Hamilton Organic Mentorship Experience project to identify the barriers they encountered in trying to participate in urban governance. The second case study is of a group called LifeCycles, located in Victoria, British Columbia. Finally, different roles and strategies for youth to use to influence urban decisions are suggested.

Food Policy for the 21st Century: Can It Be Both Radical and Reasonable?

— *Tim Lang*

The modern food economy is highly complex. This paper argues that the food system can only be understood, not as a static system, but as a dynamic and constantly changing one. It outlines a number of key features, including drivers, of the food system.

After decades of the dominance of production interests in food policy, a period of reaction is well under way. The dominant interests within the food system are being challenged by arguments and by people and organizations committed to protecting the environment, public health, consumers, and the socially disadvantaged. Changes in production and distribution, even changes in cooking, have altered the nature of food. This has both alarmed and activated consumer and public-interest groups. The paper characterizes this struggle as one of forces seeking to control and bend nature and the labour process versus those seeking to democratize food. The outcome of this struggle is uncertain. Even powerful corporate interests face uncertain times. Issues such as climate change, population pressures, consumerism, the internal conflicts of market forces and inequalities driven by globalization, and the restructuring of welfare all threaten the controlling tendencies.

The paper concludes with a call to rethink the role of the state. Market economies only work if consumers have confidence in them. Given the relative lack of power individual consumers have, only the state can exert power on their behalf. The challenges ahead are considerable but exciting. They are practical, intellectual, political, and cultural.

Appendix 2
Contributing Authors

Patricia Allen
Associate Director for Sustainable Food
  Systems
Center for Agroecology and Sustainable
  Food Systems
University of California
Santa Cruz, CA, USA

Deborah Barndt
Faculty of Environmental Studies
York University
Toronto, ON, Canada

Monique Baron
Associate Director
New Jersey Urban Ecology Program
Rutgers University
New Brunswick, NJ, USA
  and
Professor
Department of Nutritional Sciences
Rutgers University
New Brunswick, NJ, USA

Anne C. Bellows
Department of Geography
Rutgers University
New Brunswick, NJ, USA
  and
Project Associate
Center for Russian, Central and East European
  Studies
Rutgers University
New Brunswick, NJ, USA

Zita Botelho
Graduate Student
EcoResearch Chair of Environmental Law
  and Policy
University of Victoria
Victoria, BC, Canada

Kenneth A. Dahlberg
Professor
Political Science and Environmental Studies
Western Michigan University
Kalamazoo, MI, USA

Laura Davis
Elm Farm Research Centre
Berkshire, UK

A.W. Drescher
Applied Physiogeography of the Tropics
  and Subtropics
Universität Freiburg
Freiburg, Germany

Christine Furedy
Urban Studies Program
York University
Toronto, ON, Canada

Elizabeth Graham
Associate Professor
Department of Anthropology
York University
Toronto, ON, Canada
  and
Research Associate
Anthropology
Royal Ontario Museum
Toronto, ON, Canada

Miriam Grant
Department of Geography
University of Calgary
Calgary, AB, Canada

Michael W. Hamm
Associate Professor
Department of Nutritional Sciences
Rutgers University
New Brunswick, NJ, USA
  and
Director
New Jersey Urban Ecology Program
Rutgers University
New Brunswick, NJ, USA

Winston Husbands
Research Director
Daily Bread Food Bank
Toronto, ON, Canada

Desmond Jolly
Small Farm Center
University of California
Davis, CA, USA

Hulya Koc
Associate Professor
Department of Urban and Regional Planning
Faculty of Architecture
Dokuz Eylül University
Izmir, Turkey

Mustafa Koc
Associate Professor
Department of Sociology
Ryerson Polytechnic University
Toronto, ON, Canada

Karen L. Krug
Assistant Professor
Environmental Policy Institute
Brock University
St Catharines, ON, Canada

Tim Lang
Professor
Centre for Food Policy
Thames Valley University
London, UK

Stephen Leckie
Publications Director
Toronto Vegetarian Association
Toronto, ON, Canada

Shona L. Leybourne
Department of Geography
Carleton University
Ottawa, ON, Canada

Virginia Maclaren
Department of Geography
University of Toronto
Toronto, ON, Canada

Rod MacRae
Toronto Food Policy Council
Toronto, ON, Canada

Daniel Maxwell
Food Consumption and Nutrition Division
International Food Policy Research Institute
Washington, DC, USA
and
Nutrition Unit
Noguchi Memorial Institute for Medical Research
University of Ghana
Legon, Ghana

Alison Meares
Chicago Field Representative
Heifer Project International
Chicago Field Office
Chicago, IL, USA

John Middleton
Director of Public Health
Sandwell Health Authority
Sandwell, UK

Angela Moskow
Postgraduate Researcher
Small Farm Center
University of California
Davis, CA, USA

Luc J.A. Mougeot
Senior Program Specialist
Cities Feeding People Program
International Development Research Centre
Ottawa, ON, Canada

Rachel A. Nugent
Associate Professor
Department of Economics
Pacific Lutheran University
Tacoma, WA, USA
and
Staff Economist
Food and Agriculture Organization of the
    United Nations
Rome, Italy

Ellie Perkins
Associate Professor
Faculty of Environmental Studies
York University
Toronto, ON, Canada

Elaine M. Power
Doctoral Candidate
Department of Public Health Sciences
University of Toronto
Toronto, ON, Canada

Graham Riches
Professor and Chair
Social Work Program
Faculty of Health and Human Sciences
University of Northern British Columbia
Prince George, BC, Canada

Harahi Gamez Rodriquez
Metropolitan Park of Havana
Havana, Cuba

Kathryn Scharf
FoodShare
Toronto, ON, Canada

Sue Simpson
Food Policy Advisor
Sandwell Health Authority
Sandwell, UK

Penny Van Esterik
Professor
Department of Anthropology
York University
Toronto, ON, Canada

Joseph Whitney
Professor Emeritus
Department of Geography
University of Toronto
Toronto, ON, Canada

..⁣.⁣.⁣.⁣.⁣.

Appendix 3
Acronyms and Abbreviations

AAFC   Agriculture and Agri-Food Canada

BCE   before the common era
BSE   bovine spongiform encephalopathy

CAFB   Canadian Association of Food Banks
CARE   Cooperative for American Relief Everywhere
CGEEP   Children's Gardening and Environmental Education Program [New Jersey,
              United States]
CIDA   Canadian International Development Agency [Canada]
CIRAD   Centre de coopération internationale en recherche agronomique pour le
              développement (centre for international cooperation on agronomic
              research for development) [France]
COMSA   community-shared agriculture
COO   commuter-omnibus operator [Harare, Zimbabwe]
CPA   Agriculture/Livestock Productive Cooperative [Cuba]
CSA   community-supported agriculture
CSOF   Cook Student Organic Farm [New Jersey, United States]

DBFB   Daily Bread Food Bank [Toronto, Canada]
DFL   direct food link

FAO   Food and Agriculture Organization of the United Nations
FPC   food-policy council

GATT   General Agreement on Tariffs and Trade
GFB   Good Food Box [Toronto, Canada]
GTZ   Gesellschaft für Technische Zusammenarbeit (agency for technical cooperation)
              [Germany]

HDRA   high-density residential area
HOME   Hamilton Organic Mentorship Experience [Canada]
HPI   Heifer Project International

IDRC   International Development Research Centre [Canada]
IPM   integrated pest management
ISGFP   Interdepartmental Steering Group on Food Policy [Canada]

LDC   least-developed country
LFSP   Local Food Systems Project [Minneapolis, MN, United States]

MOA   Ministry of Agriculture [Cuba]

238

NAFTA	North American Free Trade Agreement
NGO	nongovernmental organization
NJUEP	New Jersey Urban Ecology Program
NRI	Natural Resources International [United Kingdom]
NSF	National Schizophrenia Fellowship [United kingdom]
PEC–Gliwice	Gliwice chapter of the Polish Ecological Club [Poland]
PMH	Metropolitan Park of Havana [Cuba]
RSD	Regulation Sales Directory [Izmir, Turkey]
SAP	structural-adjustment program
SGUA	Support Group on Urban Agriculture [UNDP]
SMBC	Sandwell Metropolitan Borough Council [United Kingdom]
SRP	Sandwell Regeneration Partnership [United Kingdom]
SYEP	School Yard Ecology Program [New Jersey, United States]
TFPC	Toronto Food Policy Council [Canada]
UBPC	Basic Unit of Cooperative Production [Cuba]
UNDP	United Nations Development Programme
UNICEF	United Nations Children's Fund
USDA	United States Department of Agriculture
WHO	World Health Organization
WIC	Special Supplemental Food Program for Women, Infants, and Children [United States]
WRUA	waste reuse in urban agriculture

About the Institution

The International Development Research Centre (IDRC) is committed to building a sustainable and equitable world. IDRC funds developing-world researchers, thus enabling the people of the South to find their own solutions to their own problems. IDRC also maintains information networks and forges linkages that allow Canadians and their developing-world partners to benefit equally from a global sharing of knowledge. Through its actions, IDRC is helping others to help themselves.

About the Publisher

IDRC Books publishes research results and scholarly studies on global and regional issues related to sustainable and equitable development. As a specialist in development literature, IDRC Books contributes to the body of knowledge on these issues to further the cause of global understanding and equity. IDRC publications are sold through its head office in Ottawa, Canada, as well as by IDRC's agents and distributors around the world. The full catalogue is available at http://www.idrc.ca/books/index.html.